WILLIAM E. DONOGHUE'S

MUTUAL FUND
SuperStars

Invest in the Best,
Forget About the Rest

Elliott & James
PUBLISHERS, INC.

2212 15th Avenue West
Seattle, Washington 98119

Neither the author nor the publisher is engaged in rendering financial, legal, or accounting services to the reader through the sale of
this book. Since individual situations do vary, the reader should consult a competent professional on questions specific to the individual.

The author and the publisher disclaim any liability for any loss
incurred, directly or indirectly, as a consequence of the use or application of any information contained in this book.

Copyright © 1994 by William E. Donoghue.

No part of this book may be reproduced or transmitted in any form or by any
means, electronic or mechanical, including photocopying, recording, or by
any information storage and retrieval system, without permission in writing
from the publisher. For information address: Elliott & James Publishers, Inc.,
2212 Fifteenth Avenue, West, Seattle, Washington 98119.

Library of Congress Cataloging-in-Publication Data Applied For.

Donoghue, William E.
      Includes index.
      1. Investments.   2. Finance, Personal.
ISBN 0-9637899-0-2

Printed in the United States of America

0 9 8 7 6 5 4 3 2 1

To my mother,
Elizabeth Brumbaugh Donoghue (1912–1992)
whose example of stewardship and moral leadership inspired me
and whose encouragement and love empowered me

and

my grandmother,
Margaret Valentine Brumbaugh (1892–1993)
who accepted us all just as we were and inspired us all
to be more than we dreamed possible.

Preface

Publication of a book is a very special event in an author's life. It comes down to a moment in time when you must say to yourself, "This is a statement I can live with for all time—it is how I understood the world at a point in time." Life is a continuous process, but a book must be finished on a given day after which you can say no more about that subject.

I have been fortunate in my life to have seen publication days come and go on many occasions. It always amazes me that I can conceive of a booklength concept and hold it in focus for the months it takes to translate it into print. This is the ninth time I have performed that miracle.

This book is very special to me. It needed to be written. Many of the subjects addressed in this book sorely needed to be expressed. The end of a long interest rate decline changes forever the entire investment world. Black becomes white, good becomes bad, and safe becomes risky.

More importantly, it comes at a time when millions of intelligent people are making horrendous choices about their financial future. The coming years could easily see a retirement savings crisis of major proportions as people realize that their "too little, too timid, too late," "play it safe" retirement savings practices will come home to roost. The risk of outliving your savings is a frightening one.

It was a major mutual fund industry conference in the Spring of 1993 that the need for this book became clear. After delivering my keynote address, I settled back to listen to a man I have come to respect immensely; J. Carter Beese, Jr., Commissioner of the Securities & Exchange Commission. His passion for campaigning for consumer education to avert the rapidly approaching retirement savings crisis both shocked and challenged me.

This book, along with Donoghue Mutual Fund SuperStars investment conferences and *Donoghue'$ MONEYLETTER*, represents my answer to that challenge.

America simply does not have time to play it safe with retirement savings, and with the changes in the investment markets; "playing it safe" may be the riskiest strategy of all. The risk of not only having insufficient savings but of losing those savings to the "safety" of the fixed-income markets is dramatic.

Aggressive investing is taking more risks, while *assertive* investing is earning higher, safer returns by learning how to manage risk to your advantage. I welcome a new world of well-educated assertive investors using the convenient new no-load mutual fund services to achieve their investment goals.

This book is your first step to joining that elite corps. I am honored to be one man among many chosen to carry the message and "wake the town and tell the people."

WILLIAM E. DONOGHUE

Seattle, WA
March 1994

Acknowledgments

No book is the work of a single person. It takes a team to make it all happen. This book is no exception. While we all had a part in the process, the ultimate responsibility for any errors is, of course, mine.

First, I would like to thank J. Carter Beese, Jr., Commissioner, U.S. Securities & Exchange Commission (SEC), whose inspiration and insights were the seed from which this book grew.

His passionate vision of the impending retirement savings crisis (unwisely chosen investment choices resulting in grossly underfunded retirement savings) and the need for consumer investment education to empower savers to avoid coming up short created the need for the book. I hope my investment strategies can provide readers of this book the tools to retire with dignity, individually avoiding their personal involvement in the retirement saving crisis.

Assisting me in the research and editorial process were Tony Sagami, Amy Smith, Joyce Ochs, Ken Parkinson, Connie Bugbee, Cyndi Andrade, Nancy Marcus Land, Paul Merriman, Brian McCulloch, and Tracy Torgerson. I would also like to thank Allen Grieve, President of Elliott & James, Publishers, for shepherding this book through administratively, Mark Ouimet of Publishers Group West for his patience and encouragement, and Deborah Englander of FORTUNE Book Club for having the vision to select this book as their May 1994 main selection.

I would like to acknowledge the inspiration, support, and insights shared by the literally dozens of SuperStar mutual fund portfolio managers who have participated in my Mutual Fund SuperStar Investment Conferences, with special appreciation to Bruce Johnstone of Fidelity Investments, Frank Cappiello of *Wall $treet Week* and Cappiello-Rushmore Funds, Paul Merriman of the Merriman Family of timed mutual funds, Frank Holmes of United Services Funds, Michael Freedman of Blanchard Funds, Jack White of Jack White & Co., and others who have made our conferences the successes they are.

Finally, I would like to thank Don Phillips and his staff at Morningstar, Inc. for developing the database that allowed me to organize the data on thousands of mutual funds and screen it down to Donoghue's Mutual Fund SuperStars.

If you have corrections to make about this book or suggestions to make which could improve future editions of this book, I invite you to write to me at:

William E. Donoghue
Donoghue's Mutual Fund SuperStars
2212 Fifteenth Avenue West
Seattle, WA 98119

Contents

CHAPTER 1

Are You Ready for SuperStar Investment Returns?

SuperStar Strategies Make Successful Investing Easier

You are in for a treat! I started out with 30 years of investment experience telling me that the search for consistently top-performing, lower-risk mutual funds would be a difficult one. By the time I was finished with my research, I was convinced that even if I set my standards so high it seemed no fund could meet them, my search would be rewarded with a wide variety of excellent choices.

Come along with me and become a SuperStar investor, the kind of investor you always wanted to be. Allow me to show you the way.

THIS IS THE BOOK YOU HAVE BEEN LOOKING FOR!

Novice Investors

If you have just discovered mutual funds and want to get off on the right foot, this is the book you have been looking for! Why? Never in the history of investing have mutual funds been so convenient, so attractive, and so powerful for the informed investor. Equally important, never have so many underinformed investors taken so much risk with seemingly "safe" but highly vulnerable investments, ignored such dramatic, safe profit opportunities, or paid so much to brokers, financial consultants, and other commission-hungry investment "experts" for such bad advice. Let me show you the new mutual fund world's path to SuperStar investment success.

Experienced Investors

You are going to love this book! If you thought you understood mutual fund investing, never in the recent history of the financial markets have your long honored, basic assumptions and ideas of "common sense" investing set you up for such unnecessary risks.

You probably already know that you have undersaved for your retirement and overestimated your ability to work long enough to meet your goals. So, funding your retirement with powerful growth vehicles should be your top priority. Today's very real threats of permanent unemployment, involuntary early retirement, and underfunded pensions cry for investors to wake up and supercharge their investments while they still have time.

Millions of Americans simply do not have time to "play it safe" with their retirement. Time is no longer on your side, nor are those "safe" investments safe. Read on. My SuperStar investment strategies can still allow you to accomplish your goals.

The evolution of mutual fund investing strategies over the past two years has been moving so fast you may well want to sit back and rethink the "tried and true" investment advice you have followed for so long. Many of the basic investment assumptions have changed dramatically.

HIGH INTEREST RATES MADE US FORGET LONG-TERM INVESTING

In the 1980s it seemed so easy to invest. You could go down to your local bank and buy a double-digit CD. You could invest in a virtually riskless money fund and earn 14, 15, or 16 percent.

Unfortunately, we became accustomed to the double-digit interest rates of the 1980s. Now interest rates are at a 30-year low. Can you believe it? Treasury bills pay less than 3 percent and long-term Treasury bond rates hover around 6 percent. You are lucky if you can get a five-year bank CD at 5 percent.

ATTENTION, RETIREMENT SAVERS! IS YOURS A STORY OF "TOO LITTLE, TOO TIMID, TOO LATE"?

The greatest tragedy of our times is that too many retirement savers have saved too little, invested much too timidly and been forced (by company "restructurings" and layoffs) to retire too soon. The sad reality is that most Americans don't have the luxury of enough time to play it safe with their retirement savings and still afford to retire with dignity. If you ever expect to see that financial security, *now* is the time to find the confidence and investment savvy to invest assertively.

This book represents my humble contribution to help you discover the strength and confidence within you to meet your financial challenges. It's a whole new world out there, and information is power.

THE INVESTMENT RULES OF THE ROAD HAVE CHANGED DRAMATICALLY

It's time to rethink your investment strategies:

1. The End of the Great Interest Rate Decline. We are at 25- to 30-year lows in interest rates. How long do you think "declining interest rates are the tide that raises all boats" strategies will work? Not long, in a rising interest rate market.

2. The Growth of Tax-Sheltered Retirement Plans. "Don't trade your portfolio too much, the tax consequences will kill you," used to be good and sound investment advice. Now, with a greater and greater percentage of investors' money in tax-sheltered IRA (individuals), 401(k) (corporate employees), 457 (state employees), and 403(b)7 (nonprofit organization and government employees) accounts, where upgrading your investment portfolio has *no* tax consequences, you need to rethink your investment strategies.

3. The Renaissance in International Funds. Countries and regions that were written off as investment markets—China,

Southeast Asia, Mexico, and Latin America—are emerging as strong, high growth economies. The high interest rates that stifled growth in Europe are declining, setting off a strong, sustainable stock market boom in Europe.

All this is occurring at a time when massive layoffs and the very real threat of permanent unemployment in the United States have undermined consumer confidence in the economy and have flattened growth. Domestic stock and bond markets are especially vulnerable when consumer spending is suppressed. All these markets need is rising interest rates to destroy billions of dollars of American wealth.

This time around international investing has two very exciting themes:

a)   The decline of the developed countries (with the exception of Europe) and the rise of the underdeveloped countries as investment opportunities.

b)   The exciting opportunities in Asia and Latin America, where the currencies are often tied to the U.S. dollar, thus reducing the risk of currency fluctuations that affect investments in Japan and Europe.

4.   The Growth in Mutual Fund Acceptance. After waiting over a decade for the banks to provide the growth in investment services that banking deregulation promised, investors have given up in frustration and shifted their savings to mutual funds. While the banking industry seemed totally absorbed in its own profitability, often at the expense of customers, no-load mutual funds continued to innovate new, low-cost tax shelters and powerful investment services that have served their customers well.

5.   The Discovery of Investing Convenience. Savvy investors are just discovering the innovative, efficient and low- or no-cost, no-load mutual fund investment services being offered, surprisingly, from the discount brokerage industry. After consumers learned how to invest directly with no-load (no sales charge) mutual fund families, along came a few discount brokerage firms with an even better choice: no-annual-fee accounts and no-transaction-fee, no-load mutual fund investments.

Now investors can truly and efficiently "invest with the best and forget about the rest" in a single account and with greatly simplified tax accounting (a value well worth any cost). Ah, but is this a good time to invest?

THERE IS A RIGHT TIME TO INVEST—NOW!!

Now is the best time in history to invest in mutual funds. After following the dramatic progress of mutual funds for over 30 years as a CPA/auditor, educator, writer, best-selling author, columnist, consultant, award-winning newsletter writer, and successful money manager, I am still thrilled and excited about writing this book for you!

Mutual Funds Have Arrived!

Never in history have mutual funds been more convenient, more powerful, more essential, and more misunderstood investment tools. If you have an investment goal—retirement, education, second home, a new car, or a new boat—the most powerful tool you can have is a working knowledge of mutual funds.

Retirement Savings Have Boomed!

Take your retirement savings as an example. Millions of people have been taking advantage of Individual Retirement Accounts (IRAs) for years and have reached the point where a significant amount, maybe most of their savings, is in these powerful, tax-sheltered investments. Since 1981, IRA accounts have increased by more than 48 times! In 1981, there were 500,000 IRA accounts. Now, according to the Investment Company Institute, the mutual fund industry trade organization, there are 24 million accounts with assets totaling $211 billion.

Mutual Funds Have Redefined "Safety"

Our parents' or grandparents' generation lived through the Great Depression—banks failed, insurance companies failed, and corporations failed. They needed FDIC protection. People with painful memories of the 1929 Crash and the Great Depression prize safety highly. They demanded the protection of federal deposit insurance. For that reason, they saw a federally insured bank account as the only "safe" place for their savings.

Think about that. Why would you invest in an institution (a bank or S&L) so risky that the federal government has to provide deposit insurance to make it safe for you to invest with the institution? It used to make sense since banks and thrift institutions (S&Ls and savings banks) seldom failed. Does that make sense to you today? Why not invest in a safe alternative like a money fund?

World War II pulled us out of the Great Depression. After the war, the economy boomed and investment times were much more certain. Interest rates were low most of the time (well under 6 percent), and they didn't change much.

In the 1940s, 1950s, and 1960s, corporations kept their promises and repaid their bonds when due, and guaranteed their employees' pensions. Bank failures were rare after federal deposit insurance was introduced. Insurance companies were bastions of prudent investment management, and the stock market was a good long-term resilient investment, although it had its ups and downs.

Beginning in the 1970s, however, the weaknesses in our financial services industry began to show. The rising interest rates from 1970 to 1982 caused thousands of banks and S&Ls to fail. The stage was set for the excesses of the 1980s.

A NEW STANDARD FOR SAFETY

An old friend of mine always said, "I have been poor three times in my life, and let me tell you that being poor is tolerable unless you have been rich first!" Face it! After bailing out the savings and loan industry and facing huge federal budget deficits that will take generations to repay, the government won't be able to bail you out again. Don't count on it! In fact, the FDIC is barely solvent.

It's time we started investing our money in financial institutions that not only operate in an ethical, responsible, and economically justifiable manner but provide very real investment opportunities to grow our savings into accounts on which we can depend for a secure retirement. That is what mutual funds *do* and banks *don't*.

WHILE *YOU* WERE LOOKING ELSEWHERE, RETIREMENT SAVING BECAME *OUR* RESPONSIBILITY

In "the good old days" of just a few years ago, retirement saving was our employer's job and defined benefit (pension) plans were its responsibility. The company guaranteed a pension to workers and had to find the money to pay for it.

In "the good new days" today, more and more of our retirement savings are falling on our shoulders. Defined contribution 401(k) and 403(b)7 plans are becoming the norm for workers.

Now, the employer can make a fixed "defined contribution" (a percentage of your salary), provide you with the investment choices, and be finished with its responsibility.

The success or failure of your retirement savings investments is on your shoulders, not your employer's. Now it's up to you to invest wisely.

The sad story is that many of you are investing unwisely and that employers are not offering the right investment choices. Read on and I will lay out the best and worst choices and a plan to get your employer to offer a wider and better choice of investment options.

MAJOR BANKS FAIL—AND SO DO MAJOR INSURANCE COMPANIES

We no longer can assume that a major bank or insurance company is a safe harbor for our savings. We have seen, and continue to see, hundreds of bank failures, even in the 1990s. Depositors with less than $100,000 were 100 percent insured, but uninsured depositors with larger amounts have increasingly lost money—especially in smaller banks. The larger banks, some effectively bankrupt, are kept alive because neither the FDIC nor the Treasury is willing or able to bail out the depositors.

No One Has Told You about the Life Insurance Bailout Coming

Several large life insurance companies also have gone belly up. In fact, the traditional life insurance industry is not unlike a Ponzi scheme. The simple facts are that when life insurance policies were sold, the actuaries made certain assumptions about what return would have to be earned on the money to keep their promises. Then they *lost* money.

Instead of making money in the 1980s, many insurance companies lost big time, investing in what are now seen as "see-through" (unoccupied) office buildings, empty shopping centers, tear-down condos (which went unsold and were occasionally condemned before they were occupied), risky junk bonds, defaulted commercial mortgages, and other equally bad investments. The fact is that they simply did not have the investment assets to make the money to keep their promises.

It is becoming increasingly essential to get a credible safety rating on your insurance company before investing. (Weiss Research is a good choice; A. M. Best is a bad choice.) There are strong life insurance companies, but big is no longer a guarantee of strong. Wise investors must be sure they are doing business with a life insurer that will likely outlive them.

Who will bail out the policyholders of failed insurance companies? In most states, it is YOU, the taxpayers, who will foot that bill.

In most states, the life insurance companies collect a state premium tax when you pay your premium notice, which they turn over to the state. In some states, those hidden taxes can amount to a significant percent of the state's budget.

There is also a state guaranty association in every state that exists to bail out the policyholders of failed insurance companies. Again in most states, the surviving insurance companies contribute to this bailout. Then, they turn around and deduct their contributions from their state premium collections.

The states don't get the premium money and have to make it up somewhere. There are only two choices: cut state services or raise taxes. Any way you look at it, that is a state income taxpayer bailout.

Variable Insurance Is a Safe, Tax-Sheltered Investment

If we learned the lesson of the 1980s, it is that many insurance companies are not institutions to which you can safely entrust your money **without making sure that the company has a high safety rating.** They simply cannot be trusted to invest your money safely without proper supervision, and you do not want to add new money to the already depreciated pot from which your benefits must be paid. You don't need that kind of risk!

With variable insurance, the investment of your cash value, which determines your ultimate payout, is under *your* control and protected from the insurance company's creditors. Instead of your investment being placed in the general checkbook of the insurance company, your money goes into the SEC-regulated mutual fund-like separate accounts of your choice.

If the insurance company fails, you still have full access to your separate account balances, and while the insurance company may not keep all its promises, your assets are safe. The Securities & Exchange Commission (SEC) sees to that. Variable insurance has many more attractive attributes as we will see in a later chapter.

THE 1980S ARE A STORY OF FAILED PROMISES

Ironically, if the lessons of the eighties have taught us anything, it is that banks and S&Ls as well as insurance companies *need* to be insured. When "the great communicator," President Ronald Reagan, decided to become "the great deregulator," we all paid.

He allowed these appropriately heavily regulated financial institutions (i.e., banks, S&Ls, and insurance companies) to take on greater risks to compete with more efficient financial institutions. Thousands of banks and S&Ls, freed of the kind of responsible regulation that safeguarded our savings and protected them from competitive pressures, simply were unprepared to enter the competitive world of finance.

Yes, our individual savings accounts were insured to $100,000 per bank after 1981. Yes, as these banks and S&Ls failed, we were required collectively to pay the bill for this unfortunate miscalculation to the tune of $500,000,000,000.00. Yes, that's $500 billion dollars (500,000 million dollars)!

A Devastating Bill to Pay

The sad story is that the bill for the banking bailout was a price we were ill-prepared to pay. As a nation, we had not saved properly to afford such extravagances, and, in the nineties, we face a monumental deficit that has bankrupted the government's ability to "guarantee" our financial security.

The FDIC no longer has the reserves to allow huge, yet weak, banks to fail and therefore delays their collapse at a time when we as a nation cannot afford it. It was in this environment that investors like you and me discovered a financial institution both powerful and safe enough for an entire nation to rely upon—mutual funds.

MUTUAL FUNDS HAVE GAINED AMERICA'S RESPECT

Over the past ten years, investors have turned to mutual funds as a safe and efficient way to invest for asset growth in stocks and bonds. Today there are more than 4,500 funds with over $2 trillion in assets. In 1980, there were 564 funds with $135 billion in assets. From 1980 through 1992, the average diversified U.S. stock fund grew at an annual rate of nearly 10 percent.

That's what I call explosive growth. Investors poured money into equity funds once the bull market surged. And over the past ten years, the average stock fund grew at an attractive annual rate of 12 percent.

THE INSIDE STORY ON MUTUAL FUND INVESTING

It may come as a surprise to many investors (and a relief to all) to discover that mutual funds are one of the most effectively

TABLE 1.1
The Decade-Long Mutual Fund "Boom"

Year	Asset Increase	Year	Asset Increase
1980	42.6%	1987	7.5% (b)
1981	79.1	1988	5.2
1982	22.9	1989	21.2
1983	−1.3 (a)	1990	8.6
1984	26.6	1991	22.4
1985	33.7	1992	18.3
1986	44.6	1993	26.1

(a) The year following Banking Deregulation
(b) The year of The Stock Market Crash
Source: Investment Company Institute

regulated financial institutions on the face of the earth. The Investment Company Act of 1940, the basic road map for mutual fund regulation, was enacted over a half a century ago and still stands as one of the most effective financial services regulatory laws ever passed.

Mutual fund regulation is based on a very simple concept: The investor is an owner of the mutual fund and all those connected with the fund's operations are the investor's employees. By law, mutual funds must fully disclose in a prospectus all relevant facts about the fund, including the types of investments, the fund's investment objectives, the terms of the contracts with the fund's investment advisors, the custodian responsible for safeguarding the assets, the transfer agent that keeps track of who owns the fund's shares, and other key relationship and operating policies.

Mutual funds are "regulated investment companies." By law they must distribute at least 98 percent of all earnings and realized capital gains in order to be tax-exempt. This allows them to pass profits on to the investors in the same taxable form as if the investor had earned them directly.

ARE YOU READY TO INVEST IN MUTUAL FUNDS?

Investing is like learning to drive a car. A car can be a lethal weapon. However, if you master driving your car, you can transform your life. You can have friends across town, across the state or across the country; you can go shopping, get to cultural events, or go to church. Owning a car can facilitate a much more satisfying life for you and your family.

Investing can be a disconcerting experience, but like driving, it can transform your life. It can seem complex at first, but it is a skill well worth learning. Learning to save systematically and to invest successfully will allow you to buy that car, buy a new or second home for your family, pay for an education for a family member, build a nest egg against the risk of disability or permanent unemployment, and, most importantly, allow for a financially secure retirement.

YOUR ROAD MAP TO SUCCESS

Read on and you will learn how to become a confident investor. You can learn the hard way—from mistakes—but everyone learns from their mistakes. You can learn the easy way, which is by understanding the investment choices, the risks, and the opportunities. That's what investing is all about.

As you learn from mistakes and (hopefully) successes, you will become a savvy and confident investor. Some folks get addicted to the thrill and confidence of success; others feel a strong sense of empowerment; and still others find their skills and confidence inspires others. Now you know why I enjoy teaching about investment strategies.

A long time ago, I decided that what I should do is teach buyers how to purchase financial services. I am always on the side of the buyer, and the sellers respect that. Deep down, I am "a do-gooder trying to do well." The more good I do, the better I do financially, and the more stable my finances are, so the more I can continue to afford to do good.

THE ULTIMATE NO-LOAD MUTUAL FUND INVESTING STRATEGY

Forget everything you have ever heard about mutual funds—all the old wife's tales, all the "common sense" guidelines, all the "my friend told me this is always true" fallacies you have heard over the years. **Invest with the best and forget about the rest**. It's just that simple. The trick is finding *the best*.

There are more than 4,500 mutual funds on the market today, and there will probably be 6,000 a year from now. I am going to show you the SuperStar way to sort out the best from all the rest.

The sad part is that most funds are mediocre performers, and many are losers. Many cannot even beat the averages. The

S&P 500 has outperformed the majority of all equity mutual funds over the past couple of decades.

For most investors, it may seem difficult to manage a winning portfolio, but for you, it will seem easy as you learn my very simple strategies. The "trick" is simple: You don't have to know how to pick stocks; you simply have to know who *does* know how to pick stocks well. The best part of my approach is that mutual fund track records are public information, and, because mutual funds are well regulated, the information is reliable and accurate.

EVEN THE PROS STAND IN AWE BEFORE A SUPERSTAR MANAGER

A recent *USA Today* article reported on the success of a portfolio the paper had constructed using the top stock picks of about 50 of the nation's best "stock pickers." It lost money.

I host a series of seminars under the banner of *Donoghue's MUTUAL FUNDS SUPERSTARS Conferences.* (This year we will be presenting two-day seminars (Advance registration $99 per person) in Orlando, Dallas, Boston, San Francisco, Chicago, and Las Vegas.

TABLE 1.2
Donoghue's Mutual Fund SuperStars Conferences
1994–1995 National Tour

May 19–21, 1994   LAS VEGAS, NV*
    Bally's Hotel & Resort

August 15–17, 1994   SAN FRANCISCO, CA*
    ANA Hotel (formerly Le Meridien)

September 23–25, 1994   CHICAGO, IL
    Palmer House Hilton

November 15–17, 1994   BOSTON, MA*
    Boston Park Plaza Hotel

January 30–February 1, 1995   ORLANDO, FL*
    Disney Contemporary Resort, Lake Buena Vista

May 18–20, 1995   LAS VEGAS, NV*
    Bally's Hotel & Resort

For a schedule call 800-226-0323. Those educational conferences with an * are scheduled to be the two days prior to the Investment Seminars Inc. MONEY SHOWS, which are a major broad-based investment exposition with hundreds of exhibitors attended by thousands of people. As a Donoghue's Mutual Fund SuperStars attendee, you can stay a day or so after our conference and attend the ISI MONEY SHOW **free**— as my guest. Call 1-800-226-0323 to register or for further information.

These seminars are an excellent opportunity to meet as many as two dozen of my SuperStar portfolio managers, plus recognized investment experts like Frank Cappiello from *Wall Street Week*, Terry Savage, author of *Terry Savage's New Money Strategies for the 90s* (Harper Business, 1993), and Bruce Johnstone, legendary portfolio manager from Fidelity Investments.

SUPERSTAR INVESTING IS NOT EASY—EVEN FOR THE PROS

We have conducted panels of the nation's top portfolio managers describing their favorite stocks. These well-considered portfolios of individual stocks often failed to make money, although the SuperStar portfolio managers *funds* certainly do make money.

The discouraging part of this story is that if we held a conference with the *worst* portfolio managers in America, their stories would be equally plausible! However, if you knew their performance track records, they would not be so credible.

LET ME INTRODUCE YOU TO THE VERY BEST PORTFOLIO MANAGERS

Over the years, I have developed a healthy respect for the skills it takes to build a successful portfolio. I have learned from the pros, and I have learned how to select the professionals whose funds I want in my portfolios. Sadly, I have also made a lot of friends whose funds I can no longer recommend.

Allow me to introduce you to some of the best portfolio managers in the world and their funds. That's why I wrote this book.

If you invest in the best—top-performing, low-risk, high-return mutual funds—build an asset allocation portfolio with investments of leading funds in each of several bull markets (with **growing** market values), and are willing to upgrade your portfolio periodically, you can make a lot of money. It's actually a lot easier and less stressful than you might imagine. Read on and I will show you my SuperStar Strategies.

This book is all about how to invest your hard-earned money in low-cost, no-load mutual funds (including a select few low-load Fidelity funds as well), while reducing your risk and maximizing your return at the same time. I can hardly hold myself back!

I have been waiting to write this book for so long and fill you in on the secret to successful investing. Actually, it's no secret: You invest in well-managed, no-load mutual funds for the long term, diversify, avoid unnecessary taxes on your investment earnings, and make handsome profits.

THE SUPERSTAR FUND SELECTION PROCESS

The best way to sort out the wheat from the chaff is to use a screen or sieve. The same is true when you are panning for gold. I have developed a special series of fund screens for sorting out the best mutual funds for you.

Through my screening process—which I will guide you through in the upcoming chapters—you will see how to sort out the funds that you needn't consider as investment choices. We will sort out the attractive, direct-marketed, no-salesperson-will-call, no-load mutual funds from the sales force-marketed, load (sales commission) funds, so you can avoid paying unnecessary sales commissions.

We will consider large and small funds. We will sort out the funds that are out of your price range. Did you know that some funds require $1,000,000 or more to open an account? We keep our initial screen to funds that have minimum initial investments of $25,000 or less. (Don't worry, most have minimums of $2500 or less.)

Our final cut will reduce the number of funds so we can compare apples with apples. By sorting the funds into a series of sub-universes, we can find the funds with the right styles, separate the ones most likely to provide SuperStar returns from those who "made a bundle" because they were in the right securities at the right time rather than because they were managed well.

THE BEST TIME TO INVEST

Never in modern history has it been more convenient to invest in mutual funds. No matter what your reason for saving, mutual funds are a powerful investment vehicle.

Mutual funds are the best way for the average person to invest. I predict that one of every two American households will have an investment portfolio with at least one mutual fund in it in just a few years. That's about double the current rate.

The major reasons are obvious:

1. **Competitive Performance.** Very simply, if you are serious about reaching your investment goals and have limited

money to invest, your only chance for success is to incorporate domestic and international stock and bond mutual funds into your portfolio. Bank CDs and bonds will just not do the job.

2. **Diversification.** It is practically impossible for the average investor to build a portfolio that can match the professional diversification of a mutual fund and still be as liquid and convenient. When you want to upgrade your portfolio, you can do so with one phone call. You can't do that if you hold a variety of individual stocks and bonds. It is equally impossible for that portfolio to be acquired as economically as a mutual fund can buy the same securities due to its inherent economies of scale. Furthermore, the caliber of investment vehicles available to mutual fund portfolio managers is far superior to those available through retail brokers.

3. **Professional Management.** The quality of professional management available from the SuperStar mutual funds is out of the reach of all but the most affluent individuals. The ability to upgrade your portfolio by changing managers and funds removes the emotional ties these affluent individuals must face. You are better off with SuperStar mutual fund investing.

4. **Low Cost.** There are more than 1,300 no-load mutual funds from dozens of mutual fund families to pick from. There is no need to pay a stock broker a commission of any kind. All you need is to make a toll-free phone call to invest with the best-managed funds in the nation.

BUYING NO-LOAD FUNDS THROUGH DISCOUNT BROKERS CAN BE CHEAPER THAN FREE

Discount brokerage firms now offer no-transaction-fee, no-load mutual fund trading under one roof. You can invest in a wide variety of mutual funds from a huge selection of mutual fund families.

You get one statement and can buy and switch funds without paying transactions fees. The ability to upgrade your mutual fund portfolio with a simple phone call gives the fund investor yet another advantage over the direct investor because there is no reason to feel allegiance to a broker.

You also can buy other no-load mutual funds through these brokerage programs. However, you may have to pay a transaction fee based on the size of the trade. The minimum charge is about $25 for a typical $2,000 IRA purchase. This is well worth the price of admission for your one statement. If you invest directly with the fund groups, you might have a suitcase full of statements. And that is one big pain in the neck!

Five "Nos" Make a Resounding "Yes"

Want a teaser? If you open a $10,000 minimum IRA in Schwab's OneSource plan, you can:

1. Open a Schwab One Account for NO fee.

2. Choose from over 200 NO-load mutual funds.

3. Invest in those funds with NO transaction fees.

4. Pay NO annual IRA fees.

5. Have NO tax consequences when you upgrade your portfolio.

There's More

You can buy 230 no-load funds without paying transaction costs, through Charles Schwab's OneSource program. If you have Fidelity Brokerage's FundsNetwork, you can trade 200 funds with no fee. Jack White & Co. has 240 funds in its no-transaction-fee program, while Waterhouse Securities has a program with 75 funds.

The best news is that there are currently over 500 different funds in 64 mutual fund families participating in one or more of the three major no-transaction-fee programs. It is my bet that in the next year or so most no-load mutual funds will sign up with several of the major no-transaction-fee systems. For now, only Schwab OneSource and Fidelity FundsNetwork have enough of the top performing and most popular fund families to be worth the time of the serious investor.

PREVIEWS OF COMING ATTRACTIONS

Are you ready to embark on your journey to becoming a Super-Star Mutual Fund Investor? I'll bet you are.

Here's a preview of the journey on which I plan to take you—knowing where you are going is half of a journey's success.

Chapter 2: How Well Do You Understand Mutual Funds? No-Load Mutual Funds Work for You, the Shareholder

In Chapter 2 we are going to introduce you to the added value that no-load mutual fund services can deliver. When you begin to appreciate what mutual funds can do for you, you will be delighted to know all those things you wanted to do were possible—and often available at no extra charge.

You see, in the 1980s mutual funds delivered the full-service banking that banks promised in the 1970s. At your bank, you are a customer; at your mutual fund, you are an OWNER. That encourages a whole different attitude, doesn't it?

Chapter 3: How Much Do You Trust Mutual Fund Managers? Surprise! This Time the Government Is Watching Them for You

Surprise, surprise, we found good news in Washington, DC. During my 30 years of experience in the financial services world, I have had a chance to watch banking and mutual fund regulation from the front row and the back stage.

Folks, you are going to be relieved to know that if there ever was a financial institution that works well for you, keeps its promises (the ones it *makes*, not the ones you *want* them to make), and is as safe as an investment can be, it's mutual funds. Mutual funds are often misunderstood, but they hold more of America's savings—more of America's sophisticated dreams—than any other financial institution. One in four American families already use mutual funds to save for their dreams.

Chapter 4: Can You Match the Strategy with the Investment Goal? Knowing How Means More for You, Less for the Tax Man

You have to know where you are going to get on the right investment track and arrive on time and fully prepared. In Chapter 4 we are going to sort out your investment goals and carefully define the investment environments (taxable and tax-sheltered) in which they will thrive.

Each environment has its own investment strategies to maximize your long-term goals, meet your short-term needs, and increase the odds of building your investment capital with real SuperStar style. Once you have a clear idea where you want to go, we can develop some investment strategies to get you on the *fast* track to financial success.

The Donoghue Signal Strategy has been my best long-term strategy for investing in the U.S. stock markets. However, in today's markets, the combination of my powerful SuperStar dynamic global asset allocation strategies and my Mutual Fund SuperStar fund selection process are what you need to shift your investment portfolios into high gear.

Chapter 5: Do You Know How to Find SuperStar Mutual Funds? Lower-Risk, Consistently Top Performers Abound

Now that you have a good understanding of the nature of mutual funds and their regulation, the dramatic changes in the financial markets, and matching your investment goals with the type of investment portfolio that will get you there, you still need the fuel to turbocharge your investment returns. You need to find the right mutual funds for the job.

Designing the criteria for zeroing in on the right mutual funds for you was the most satisfying and demanding part of the research for this book. I set my standards high:

► The funds had to be in the right asset classes, among the top-performing types of funds of the day.

► They had to be outstanding and consistent leaders among their peers (other funds with similar objectives).

► They had to be capable of being persistent top performers at lower risk than their peers.

The search was surprisingly successful and encouraging. SuperStar mutual funds—consistent, lower-risk top performers—do exist and there are many of them. In Chapter 5 we will screen the entire universe to uncover the SuperStar funds for your portfolio.

Chapter 6: Why Should You Use a Discount Broker to Buy No-Loads? Because It Can Be Cheaper Than Buying Direct

Life *is* getting simple—and just a bit confusing. Just when I convinced you to avoid stockbrokers and invest in no-load mutual funds, I am recommending you pay a discount broker to assist you in facilitating the management of your portfolio of no-load mutual funds. Then I tell you that you can get that same discount broker to work with you for FREE with no transaction fees. In fact, investing with a discount broker can be cheaper than buying direct. (You guessed it—no annual IRA fees.)

It is just that simple. In Chapter 7 I will let you in on exactly how the right discount broker can work to your benefit.

Chapter 7: Which Discount Broker Is Right for You? Making the Right Choice(s) Can Add Extra Investment Power

Okay, just when I told you how easy it was to buy mutual funds from a discount broker, here I am letting you in on the details. I know you all have faced those terrifying words, "some assembly required," and survived nearly every Christmas of your life. You understand that a little inside knowledge of the shortcuts is what you need to make just about anything fit together smoothly.

Read on. We will let you in on some money-saving and time-saving hints about what to ask these brokers to do for you.

Chapter 8: Which Stock Investment Style Is Right for You? Make Your Choice: Value, Growth, Blend, or Sector Funds

Now we are getting to the **Big Payoff**. With literally 4,458 mutual funds to choose from, finding the right ones can be a bit daunting. This should be some of the most fascinating reading in the book.

I am going to walk you through the wilderness of mutual funds and get you focused on the few hundred funds that are ideally suited to meet your needs. In Chapter 8 we will start with organizing how you think about the diversified domestic stock funds.

Chapter 9: Can the Overseas Mutual Funds Continue to Soar? The International Investment Boom Is Just Beginning

In Chapter 9 we are going to expand your horizons and take a critical look at the international stock and bond funds. The wonderful surprises awaiting us are:

▶   That, with few exceptions, carefully selected domestic junk bond funds turn out to be higher-yielding and more reliable investments than confusing and risk-filled international bond funds.

►   That we may want to leave most (but not all) domestic stock funds behind when we discover the hidden secrets of international stock fund selection.

Chapter 10: Should You Trust the Indices or the Managers? Your Choice: Index, Total Return, or "Safe Harbor" Funds?

For those of you who suspect that there is an easier way to invest, we now introduce you to the legendary, highly popular, oft-touted, and overrated *index funds,* the do-it-for-me *total return funds* and some surprisingly attractive *safe harbor funds* for lazy, but savvy, investors. The last category is where we separate the funds with very plausible and exciting "stories" from those that can deliver the goods, year after year.

Chapter 11: Are You Ready to Put Your Money Where Your Mouth Is? The Right Funds at the Right Time Equals SuperStar Profits

In Chapter 12 we get down to brass tacks, take one last look at the entire scope of mutual funds to see if we have missed any attractive choices, and after assembling out SuperStars Team candidates, put together our Mutual Fund SuperStars investment portfolio.

Chapter 12: Can You Do Well and Do Good Too? Make a Covenant with Your Society and Prosper

We all wish that we could live in a world where we allocate our investment resources to socially conscious companies and away from the many polluters and dehumanizers. It seems to make good sense that a socially conscious company should be financially successful as well. However, our good sense tells us that, in today's "dog-eat-dog" world, we see too many examples of irresponsible companies hiding their socially reprehensible practices behind corporate image advertising campaigns and predatory legal staffs.

Guess what, folks? The Covenant Socially Conscious rating system allows you to combine your social goals with your investment goals. Don't skip this chapter! It will make you money and allow you to sleep at night, as well, knowing you are doing the right thing.

Chapter 13: Is the Government Taking Too Much of Your Profits? 18 Legal Tax-Avoidance Strategies to Keep Clinton at Bay

Learning how to keep your investment earnings is as important as learning how to make money. With the new "Clinton Tax Bill" in place, the CPA in me needed to advise you on my most powerful after-tax investment strategies.

I am especially proud of this chapter, since it pulls together into a single chapter my best investment tax-planning advice. "This chapter alone is worth the price of the book many times over," he said in his most humble voice.

Chapter 14: What Are You Going to Do When Interest Rates Rise? Get Out of Their Way, I Hope. Doing Nothing Can Be Frightening

The greatest challenges mutual fund investors will face in the coming years is the challenge of rising interest rates. Even if rates do not rise for a year or so, they WILL rise, bond fund values WILL decline, and naive investors WILL lose money in the "safest" investments.

Even if the interest rate news were positive and interest rates fell a bit further, the big profits (capital gains) are behind us and low dividend distribution rates are upon us. Even if the bond markets had a very successful year (which is unlikely), they could not earn before or after taxes anywhere near what my SuperStar investing strategies can do for you, arguably with much less risk.

Read this chapter with interest (excuse the pun), although I must tell you if you have already gotten this far in the book, I will have already convinced you to shift your money out of interest-rate-sensitive investments and into situations where you will make more money without having to worry about whether rates stay anemic, rise and destroy, or decline and tempt.

Chapter 15: How Should You Invest after You Retire? So You Don't Run Out of Money Before You Run Out of Life

The amazing thing to me is that, with so many retirees 65 and over naively investing for "income" in fully loaded bond funds, few writers have addressed this national disgrace—a waste of retirement assets. How can your investment advisor recommend that you pay him or her 4 to 5 percent to invest in a government bond fund which is likely to lose you more money than it earns, as interest rates rise.

Retirement is "the investment opportunity of a lifetime." You deserve to rise above the investment ignorance of others and have the reassurance of fending for yourself to gain the greatest rewards from your life's savings.

Which do you want to do—follow the investment advice of your uninformed friends to play it safe and end up curtailing your retirement lifestyle, or learn how to manage risks to your benefit and turn that skill into a lifetime of financial security? I thought you would choose to adopt my strategies!

Chapter 16: When Would You Like to Stop Paying Taxes on Your Investment Profits? You Could Double Your Retirement Income and Retire with Dignity

Finally, what do you do if you want to shelter from taxes a large lump sum of money to use in your retirement? Two thousand dollars a year in an IRA is a drop in the bucket for many investors.

There is a very simple, flexible and attractive plan that can finally shelter your money for your use. (I will bet your stock broker is about ready to pitch you yet another exotic, complex plan for a "pie in the sky" tax shelter—just as they did with the limited partnerships in the 1980s. These were great tax shelters—you got to write off all your losses and you have to wait to see if you will get anything back.

My plan is not that. You will, however, have to read this chapter to fully understand it.

INVESTMENT SUCCESS IN WITHIN YOUR GRASP

"Wealth without risk," with apologies to Charles Givens, is a pipe dream. Building a safe and sound asset allocation portfolio with dramatically high-return, surprisingly low-risk, and comfortingly reliable no-load SuperStar mutual funds is available to those willing to make an informed and confident choice. It's a whole lot better than "playing it safe" and losing your shirt.

ALL ABOARD!

Are you ready to embark on your journey to becoming a Super-Star Mutual Fund Investor? I'll bet you are!

I'll start with some basics and then show you how to get on the right investment track. From there, we'll shift gears to the fast track to financial success. We'll stop along the way to consider such key topics as international investing, how to handle rising interest rates, how to plan for your retirement, and how to invest in a socially conscious manner and make a better return!

Join me as I take you through the world of mutual funds.

CHAPTER 2

How Well Do You
Understand Mutual Funds?

No-Load Mutual Funds
Work for You, the Shareholder

Remember, the most sophisticated investor had to start with mastering the basics of investing. Even after 30 years of studying mutual fund investing, I still revisit the basics to refocus my strategies. In today's rapidly changing world, the basic assumptions are in constant flux so you must go back to square one occasionally to understand why you are using a specific investment strategy to make the necessary midcourse corrections.

So, to become a true SuperStar investor you must learn the ABCs of mutual fund investing. Even if you see yourself already a successful investor, a review of the basics will likely reveal new and valuable insights into your strategies. Don't be bashful even if you are an experienced and successful investor. Sometimes "common sense" is not so common.

HERE WE GO . . .

Allow me to guide you to a fuller understanding of this very important and often misunderstood financial instrument, the *mutual fund*. So much has been written about mutual funds in recent years that is based on out-of-date assumptions and full of misunderstandings that you might find some very profitable new insights.

MUTUAL FUNDS ARE ALL THE RAGE—FOR GOOD REASON

As of year end 1993, mutual funds had over $2 trillion under management—that's more of America's savings than has been entrusted to all the commercial banks and thrift institutions (S&Ls, credit unions, and mutual savings banks) combined. One of every four American families (actually 28 percent) invests in mutual funds, according to the Investment Company Institute (ICI), the Washington, DC-based mutual fund trade association. That means that 72 percent of the American public is missing out on a great opportunity.

Most households own at least two funds: a stock or equity fund and a fixed-income fund (a bond or money market fund). There are more than 70 million shareholder accounts with total assets of more than $2 trillion and, even as you read this book, assets are growing rapidly due to both rising market values and the tide of new money from investors. Last year alone, net sales of mutual funds totaled over $200 billion.

DOES THIS INVESTOR PROFILE SOUND A BIT LIKE YOU?

Savvy investors are building their retirement reserves and their family's financial security by taking advantage of mutual funds. According to ICI data, the average seasoned mutual fund investor is 46 years old, has a household income of $50,000, assets of $120,000, and maintains relationships with two mutual fund families. (This "older" generation has only in the past decade rediscovered mutual funds.)

New investors are typically younger (37 years old), slightly less affluent ($40,000 household income with $60,000 in assets) and currently maintain a relationship with only one mutual fund family. (IRAs and 401(k) programs have introduced a whole new generation to mutual funds and popular magazines like *Money* have encouraged and empowered investors to invest in mutual funds.)

About half of both groups are college graduates. They invest in an average of two mutual funds, and about 57 percent of the investors are men. The average mutual fund-investing household has $43,000 invested in mutual funds—that's 38 percent of its $113,000 average total financial assets. (I wonder how much of that money will find its way to mutual funds when those folks wake up and smell the profits!)

NO QUESTION! GO NO-LOAD FOR RETIREMENT SAVINGS!

Mutual funds come in two basic flavors: load mutual funds, which are sold by stock and insurance brokers who charge a sales commission (called a *load*) to investors, and no-load mutual funds, which investors buy directly from the fund families at no commission. The only reason for a commission is to pay the salesperson.

If you learn how to buy directly you can avoid the salesperson and save money. (All funds have the same kind of operating expenses that are charged directly to the fund. If a broker tells you he is selling no-load funds, he is probably not telling the truth about funds with hidden loads. Tell him "No!")

No-load mutual funds are the best choice for most investors, unless they are incapable of learning about mutual funds. (Then turning them over to a commissioned salesperson sounds like a dubious choice, doesn't it?) No-loads are very efficient investment choices, especially for small payments, since without the load, 100 percent of your money goes to work for you immediately. No-loads have the investment power that virtually assures long-term growth, especially in your tax-sheltered retirement account.

MONEY FUNDS FIRST INTRODUCED INVESTORS TO MUTUAL FUNDS

Money market funds are cited by millions as their first introduction to mutual funds. In much of the 1980s, they provided double-digit investment returns at virtually no risk. Today, they are still very safe but do not offer sufficiently high rewards to warrant any significant part of your attention.

I know that comes as a shock coming from the man who popularized money funds and authored *William E. Donoghue's COMPLETE MONEY MARKET GUIDE,* but that's reality. My company has over $200 million dollars of client money under management, and we have virtually none of it invested in money funds (except to facilitate systematic payment programs).

Money funds are certainly safe, but discussion of them as IRA investment vehicles stopped long ago when their yields dropped below 10 percent. While some super-cautious advisors may themselves choose to invest their IRA money in a CD or a money fund, they know better!

Retirement assets account for 21 percent of all mutual fund assets and about 40 percent of no-load mutual fund assets. (Doesn't that sound absurd when you think of how little money in loaded funds is invested in IRAs? What are these brokers selling—high commission high-risk investments? Hmmmm . . .) In total, mutual funds account for 29 percent of all IRA assets, a proportion that is growing rapidly as today's low interest rate environment drives money out of CDs and into stock and bond mutual funds.

Money Magazine reports that 35 percent of its readers own at least one long-term equity fund as part of their company's 401(k) plan. Add in the savings of employees of nonprofit organizations in their 403(b) plans, state employees in 457 plans, and small business employees and self-employed individuals in SEP-IRAs, Keogh, and profit-sharing plans, and it's clear that America is increasingly counting on mutual funds for its retirement security.

MOST MUTUAL FUND INVESTORS PAY TOO MUCH

Unfortunately, the majority of mutual fund investors pay dearly for their investments. Sixty percent of all mutual fund investors pay commissions or sales charges to brokers, financial planners, or other commission-based salespeople. This is simply for the privilege of investing in mutual funds. Only 40 percent of all fund investors (and *all* of my followers) realize they can buy no-load (no sales charge) mutual funds.

Paying a sales charge to buy a fund costs you dearly. The average load fund hits you with a 5 percent sales charge. In 1992, net mutual fund sales totaled $200 billion. That means brokers, financial planners, and others collected a hefty $10 billion in commissions. And they still didn't recommend mutual funds for IRAs! What an expensive disservice to their customers!

I Don't Need, nor Do I Want, a Broker Holding My Hand

Personal hand-holding by a stockbroker isn't worth the fat commissions you pay for it. (The only justification most brokers have for their commissions is, "We helped a lot of little old ladies who just can't invest themselves!" They love to say that.) Super-Star investors maximize their returns by investing in the best performing no-load funds as well as selected low-load Fidelity Investments funds.

Just because there is no load on no-load mutual funds, it does not follow that they are free, only that these funds attach no extra sales charge to pay for intermediary salespersons. All funds (both load and no-load) have expenses that must be paid for fund operations. These expenses are for investment advisors, lawyers, distributors and/or administrators, lawyers, transfer agents, lawyers, custodians, lawyers, accountants, and lawyers. (Did I mention lawyers?) The expenses are deducted from fund assets each day.

A Load Only Buys Problems

My major reason for recommending no-load funds is their greatest single advantage: "No salesman will call." The problem with buying even the best front-end or back-end loaded mutual funds is that you must establish a relationship with a commission-driven broker.

It is not that the brokers' funds are better or worse (they can be either), it is that they will try to sell you many other investments that sound plausible but are simply not the kind of investments you should be choosing. A rule of thumb for dealing with brokers is that the higher the commission, the higher the risk.

Especially vulnerable to brokers' pitches are those who look solely for yield (monthly income dividends or interest). There is allegedly a long-rumored broker sales manual with only three pages. Page 1 says, "Sell what you understand." The broker quickly turns to find something easier. Page 2 says, "Sell yield." Page 3 says, "Read page 2 one more time."

What they really mean is, "Tell the client about the yield but not the risk." With the very real current threat of rising interest rates, the risk of fixed-income investments (bonds, CDs, and other income-paying investments) is great. With low interest rates, the opportunity to make money is low and the risk is very high.

When interest rates are as low as they are today, the yields do not warrant your attention. To get higher monthly yields, you have to go farther out on the limb (longer maturities or higher credit or market risks). To do so means that if rates stay low you get lousy returns, and if interest rates rise you get lousy returns and capital losses (nondeductible for tax purposes unless you sell the security and take the loss). Buy and hold and you pay taxes and lose money at the same time (unless you sell, you get no tax relief for your losses). It is unlikely to get better any time soon.

The Load Is Not the Last Bill

Ironically, load funds are often more likely to charge higher expenses than many no-load funds. To those patient enough to read the prospectus, all costs are disclosed. Fortunately, all fund performance is reported, after all costs except the loads, so you can make your decision on the net benefits to you.

What Brokers Sell Is Not What People Who Buy Choose

Load funds are most often sold on superficial "yield" quotes to brokerage customers who are described as "decision-dependent," that is, they prefer not to make their own decisions. These investors are most often sold bond or other fixed-income funds.

Most of the funds at the top of Table 2.1—those sold by brokers—are fixed-income funds, except for the global equity (diluted international stock) funds, which were a disaster in 1992 when they were sold to investors but a good deal in 1993 after most load fund investors had already sold their international stock positions in disgust, only to miss their meteoric rise.

On the other hand, no-load funds are bought by independent investors of their own volition. These "decision makers" most often buy aggressive growth and precious metals stock funds, the better choices.

A good example of this phenomenon is that about 40 percent of all no-load fund assets represent IRA or similar accounts while 21 percent of all fund assets are in IRAs. Few brokers will settle for selling their clients mutual funds for their IRAs because the amount is too small. They would rather sell them the latest and most highly commissionable investment choice and churn it with the other assets in the customer's account.

There is no conclusive evidence that says paying a commission to a salesman causes the fund's portfolio manager to buy better investments. This is not to say that there are not excellent load funds in every category; there are. However, the evidence is that few investors actually encounter these funds. Most of them are steered to fixed-income funds. Quite simply put, brokers

TABLE 2.1
Comparison of Load and No-Load Fund Sales

	Load	*No-Load*
Funds Load Fund Investors Are Sold		
Global equity	83.0%	17.0%
Ginnie Mae	81.1	18.9
US Government income	79.3	20.7
High yield bond	78.5	21.5
State municipal bond (L-term)	72.2	27.8
Global bond	68.1	31.9
Growth & income	61.6	38.4
Long-term municipal bond	61.5	38.5
Income-mixed	57.7	42.3
Funds Both Load and No-Load Fund Investors Buy		
Growth	56.9	43.1
Income-equity	54.1	45.9
Income-bond	52.7	47.3
Corporate bond	47.8	52.2
Balanced	49.4	50.6
Flexible income	45.7	54.3
International	45.0	55.0
Funds No-Load Fund Investors Buy		
Aggressive growth	30.2	69.8
Precious metals	18.7	81.3

Source: Investment Company Institute, *Mutual Fund Fact Book*, 1992

tend to be lazy. Rather than sell clients what they should want (equity funds), they sell them what they can easily understand (fixed-income funds with "high yields").

Bad Advice at a High Price

"Full Service" (or is it "Fool Service") brokers' clients are sold bond funds, mostly government and municipal bond funds. How many governments do you think the broker researched to recommend a government fund? There is only one federal government and, quite frankly, I don't see that one standing up well to close scrutiny. What do you think these brokers did to justify a 3 to 5 percent commission? If interest rates are rising and people are losing money in government bond funds, why pay them for misleading you, especially at the bottom of the interest rate cycle?

WHY BOND FUNDS MAY BE RISKY

If interest rates rise, you are better off investing in short-term bonds than bond funds. Short-term bonds will mature (return their principal at a certain date); bond funds make no such guarantee.

Bond funds guarantee that if interest rates rise, their total return will be less than they promised (due to losses in resale or market value). It is likely that your total return will be negative (a loss of principal) and that you will pay taxes on the dividends you insist on earning as you are losing money—unless you sell and take the loss!

SLYC INVESTING FOR ALL

As I've said a thousand times before, no-load mutual funds are SLYC (slick) investments. No-load mutual funds are:

▶ **S**afe because they are highly regulated by federal and state governments. While highly regulated is not the same as insured, if our government had regulated banks and S&Ls as closely as they have mutual funds, their CDs would not need federal insurance to be safe.

▶ **L**iquid because your money is never more than a toll-free telephone call away from your checking account. More importantly, your money is never subject to substantial interest penalties (as bank CDs are).

▶ **Y**ields, or total returns, can be very attractive for the savvy investor. Double digit total returns (dividends plus market value increases) are not uncommon and are never far from the reach of savvy investors.

▶ **C**atastrophe-proofed to protect you from failures that have plagued weak banks, S&Ls, credit unions, life insurance companies, and other less effectively regulated financial institutions.

Mutual funds simply cannot fail. For a mutual fund to lose all of its value, all of the companies (plus the federal government) that stand behind all of the securities would have to fail and lose all of their value (such a highly unlikely event that we can say it will **NEVER** happen). A mutual fund share can be worth less than you paid for it but it will never be worth nothing.

So, how much could you lose? Short-term losses of more than 10 to 20 percent are rare. They often are recovered in a few weeks and are widely covered in the press. There is less risk than you might have expected and, with the asset allocation strategies you will be learning in this book, you can minimize your risks.

WHY I LIKE MUTUAL FUNDS

People ask me every day why I recommend mutual funds as the single best way to build your wealth and protect your assets from inflation. The reasons are simple:

Professional Management.   Mutual fund managers are just a cut above other financial professionals. First, they are experienced, federally tested, and licensed professionals. Second, their performance is constantly reviewed by the funds' independent directors, who authorize their lucrative contracts. Mutual funds are the most economical way to get the best to work for you. Remember, "Invest in the best, forget about the rest." I am very serious about that.

Diversification.   Each mutual fund is carefully managed to meet the exacting diversification standards prescribed by the Securities and Exchange Commission (SEC). It is also professionally diversified to improve the odds of attaining the fund's investment goals within its risk parameters.

Investing in one fund allows you to diversify away the risk of a single security's market or event risk. Diversifying among a few funds allows you still more protection, and diversifying among several different types of assets (asset allocation) adds still more protection and potential return to your portfolio.

Fractional Investments.   This is a fancy term to say that, once you have met the fund's minimum initial or subsequent investments, you can invest any amount of money in the fund. If the minimum investment was, say, $1000 and you wanted to invest $12,864.93, you could do so. You would end up with shares, purchased at the next daily share pricing, rounded to three digits down to the penny you invested. There are no units of investment prices less than a penny.

I love it when some investors pull me aside and tell me that they invest in funds with low prices since they feel the funds' prices can go up more. Sorry, it doesn't work that way. The price is simply the market value of the fund's portfolio divided by the number of shares outstanding.

All holdings are proportional, so small price or big price simply depends on the number of shares outstanding. Similarly, the popularity of a fund has no effect on the price per share since that price is derived from the market values of the portfolio securities. Got it?

Low Minimum Investments. In addition, some funds have very low minimum initial investment requirements, which open up mutual funds to nearly any investor with a checking or savings account. For example, Twentieth Century Investors in Kansas City, MO (800-345-2021), will allow you to open an account with any amount, provided you agree to make automatic electronic monthly investments of at least $25 per month. United Services Funds (800-US-FUNDS) and Janus Funds (800-525-3713) offer similar programs with slightly higher minimums.

All funds listed in this book offer minimums of $25,000 or less, and most have minimums as low as $2500 or $1000. In addition, most funds offer lower minimum investments on initial investments in IRA accounts and subsequent investments for either IRA or taxable accounts.

Convenient Liquidity. In many cases, you can switch or exchange your shares of one fund for those of another fund in the same family. Switching, or use of the telephone exchange privilege, is a very popular mutual fund service. In addition, funds offer checking and telephone redemption services (the ability to call the fund and have a prescribed number of shares redeemed and the cash wired to your checking account).

You are wise to apply for the telephone exchange or redemption and/or checking privileges when you first open your account. After that, you will have to get a guaranteed signature from a bank or broker to make changes, which is a bit of a nuisance.

With these privileges, you can switch some or all of your stock shares into the fund family's money fund and simply write a check to pay a bill. Remember the stock fund sale is a taxable event (you realize a taxable gain or loss on your shares), and you only want to use telephone redemption on taxable accounts—not your IRA where you could trigger unnecessary tax penalties and withholding.

Think about it! Mutual funds offer greater liquidity than your bank CD!

Low Cost Services. Mutual funds offer high value, low-cost professional management and accounting services because they can process millions of transactions at very low cost. Where else can you get a professional to manage as little as $1,000 or $10,000 for a fee as little as 1 to 2 percent a year? Few professional investment advisors will touch an account less than $250,000. (Even my money management firm, WEDCO [1-800-642-4276], requires a $70,000 minimum relationship.)

Setting Up Check-a-Month Plans. If you choose to set up a convenient automatic check-a-month investment plan or a check-a-month redemption plan (to provide retirement cash flow, for example), you are only a phone call away. It's more convenient than you could ever imagine, and it's usually free.

LET'S TALK DIVERSIFICATION

When you invest in a mutual fund, you invest in a professionally managed portfolio of stocks, bonds, and/or money market instruments. You can rest comfortably because that pool of securities is managed by a professional money manager who has a staff of trained research analysts working for him or her.

Mutual fund portfolios own at least 20 and, more likely, hundreds of different securities in their portfolios. To be a diversified mutual fund, federal law requires that a minimum of 75 percent of a fund's assets be invested so that no more than 5 percent of a diversified fund's assets are invested in the obligations of any single issue or 20 percent are invested in any one industry. The exception would be a select number of non-diversified mutual funds and sector funds that choose to concentrate their investments into a single specific sector of the economy.

That's the basic law, but most mutual funds' internal investment policies are even more restrictive than their prospectuses. It is not uncommon for a fund to be restricted from investing more than 1 to 5 percent of their portfolios in the obligations of any single issuer.

Diversification reduces the risk that you'll lose money if one or two large holdings in the portfolio plunge in price. That way you are not as vulnerable to an individual stock's fortunes. Although diversification is no assurance that you will never lose money, it simply means that you are not vulnerable to a single security's market risk.

Three Ways to Diversify Your Investments with Mutual Funds

Diversification among Securities.   You can diversify your investment within a given market by investing in a single mutual fund, which will be, in turn, invested in dozens, if not hundreds of securities. For example, a growth stock fund would be diversified in many individual stocks in a portfolio designed to achieve an investment objective, i.e., growth.

Diversification among Funds in an Asset Class.   When you know which class of funds you want to invest in (e.g., international emerging markets funds), it is often wise to invest in two or three funds in that asset class. Investing in two or three funds in each class adds diversification among securities, among investment managers' styles and strategies, and among different portfolios, each of which has its individual quirks.

If you are trying to cash in on a new investment trend, such as investing in stocks in dozens of underdeveloped countries, you might pick two or three of the top-performing funds in that category, e.g., Lexington, Montgomery, and Fidelity emerging markets funds.

Inevitably, one of the funds will provide less than stellar results compared to the others, and by having your money invested in three, if you wanted to upgrade the lackluster fund and move that money into the stronger funds, you would only have to realize currently taxable profits on one fund while most of your profits (the **un**realized gains) could continue to be tax deferred in the other two. It simply makes better tax sense to have that choice. If all three do well, more power to you.

With tax-deferred portfolios these tax consequences do not exist. You can go with a single fund choice and/or upgrade to the new leaders with impunity—and no tax consequences until you withdraw your assets from the plan.

Diversification among Asset Classes or Asset Allocation.   It is always wise to spread your risks by participating in several rising bull markets. For example, today you may want to include emerging market, diversified international and selected domestic stock funds, junk bond funds, total return funds, gold mining share funds, and maybe real estate funds in your portfolio. This is called *asset allocation.* The asset classes are selected first for their investment opportunity and second for their ability to reduce the volatility of the total portfolio while increasing the risk-adjusted return. They are the most stable road to low risks and high returns.

WHAT'LL IT BE, WHOLE EGGS IN A SAFE BASKET OR AN OMELET?

Here's how diversification saves the day. Let's say, for example, you are a shareholder in the "Go For It" growth stock fund. The fund, with assets of $10 million, has a 2 percent stake in a hypothetical stock, Front Page Inc. The fund also invests in 100 other issuers because the portfolio manager prefers to be well diversified.

A fire breaks out a Front Page's production facility. Losses are estimated in the millions, and the stock's price drops from $10 per share to $8 per share. That day, the fund's position in Front Page Inc. drops 20 percent. What was worth $200,000 yesterday is worth $160,000 today. An investor who owned only Front Page would be pretty upset with such a loss. I wouldn't want to lose 20 percent of my money in one day. Who would?

The Go For It Growth Fund, however, owns 99 other stocks in a wide variety of industries. The day Front Page's stock fell, the overall stock market rallied. The Dow Jones Industrial Average and the Standard & Poor's (S&P) 500 gained 1 percent in value that day.

Our stock fund's holdings rose with the performance of the overall market because our portfolio manager is a pretty good stock picker. The value of the fund gained a total of 1.2 percent the same day Front Page's stock nosedived.

The value of the rest of the fund increased to $10,120,000, less a $40,000 decline on one stock—Front Page—and resulted in a net gain of $80,000, bringing the portfolio's value to $10,080,000. Even though we took a big hit on one stock, our fund gained 0.8 percent for the day. We didn't outperform the market averages, but diversification saved the day!

IT'S ALL IN THE—EXTENDED—FAMILY!

Most mutual funds are also part of a mutual fund family, a group of funds that are marketed by a single organization. The actual management of the funds may be by a single investment management firm or subcontracted to others depending on the management style of the family.

Today, it makes little sense to limit yourself to the funds in a single family. No one mutual fund family has an exclusive hold on the SuperStar performers in every category you will want in your portfolio. For example, you may want to invest in the Montgomery Emerging Markets, the Fidelity Capital & Income Fund (a junk bond fund), Oakmark International Fund, and Evergreen Global Real Estate Fund. To invest in them all means dealing with four different fund families, easy for now, but difficult when you want to reallocate your portfolio as the market shifts.

The easier choice is to open an account at a discount broker (Charles Schwab and Co., for example) where you can combine all of these funds into a single account. Some funds, like Oakmark International are currently available with no transaction fee (the fee to purchase a no-load fund from a discount broker, which is much less than a full load), and others like T. Rowe Price New Asia Fund are available for a small fee. This enables you to have all your fund positions in a single account.

Also, with an account at a discount broker, all your dividend and capital gains distributions for the year will come on a single Form 1099-DIV (the form used by the funds to report your distributions to the IRS). Your accountant will love you for that alone.

Several "extended family" discount broker/fund programs exist: Charles Schwab & Co., Fidelity Brokerage, Jack White & Co., Waterhouse Securities, and Muriel Siebert & Co., to name the more prominent. Not all, however, offer a no-transaction-fee program or have a broad range of choices. (If you want to learn more about using discount brokers right now and can't wait, you can go ahead and read Chapters 6 and 7 now.)

NO-LOAD, NO-FEE, MULTI-FAMILY INVESTING

With a no-transaction-fee (NTF) program, for example, you can buy most Dreyfus funds from Fidelity Brokerage's FUNDS Network program as cheaply as you can buy them directly from Dreyfus. For those of you who are skeptics, allow me to inform you that mutual fund "no transaction fee" (NTF) discount broker programs have kicked out funds that offered "A" and "B" shares where the cost is passed on to the customer by restricting the NTF purchases to the more expensive "B" shares.

These programs are paid for by first charging the fund the cost of services being done by the broker and then charging the fund's managers the rest of the cost. The net additional cost to the investors of investing NTF or direct is zero. (Trust me.)

You can also trade funds (even if the fund family has not agreed to subsidize the brokers' distribution costs) by paying the discount broker a small transaction fee. (Vanguard, the low-cost provider of fund management services, simply does not have room in their tight budget to pay the discount brokers for NTF programs.) These fees are not inconsequential, but they are reasonable, especially considering how convenient it makes maintaining a multi-fund family mutual fund portfolio.

MULTINATIONAL INVESTING

You can invest conveniently and economically in the U.S. and in international stock or bond markets via mutual funds. International investing offers yet another layer of diversification. Split up the old investment pie among U.S. and international stock funds, U.S. and international bond funds and money funds, and you also reduce your risks and increase your investment opportunity.

My mother used to say, "You can't put all your eggs in one basket, Bill." If that's not enough, an old neighbor of mine, who liked to play cards, backed Mom up by saying, "You can't bet the ranch on a single hand." Mom was right. If your U.S. stock fund is down, there's a good chance your international fund will be up. I'm high on international stock funds this year. I'll go into more detail about creative investment diversification later in this book when I introduce you to my Mutual Fund SuperStars investing strategy.

KEEPING YOUR PORTFOLIO LIQUID

Liquidity, the ability to access your investment money, is a very important reason for investing in mutual funds. Many conventional advisors recommend that you keep at least the equivalent of three months' salary in a bank account as a reserve for bad times. I think that's crazy! Why tie your money up in a low- or no-profit account that, after taxes, will not keep up with inflation?

All mutual funds are liquid. If you want to build up your reserves, you have to be a serious investor right now! Reserves are a very important part of any serious '90s investors' portfolio due to the very real threat of forced early retirements and permanent layoffs that even white collar workers, executives, and lawyers are facing today.

Liquidity Comes in Two Flavors

When people talk about liquidity, they are talking about two very different concepts:

Can You Get Your Money Back?   Will Rogers used to say, "I'm not as much concerned about the return **on** my money as the return **of** my money." You need to be aware of both. All open-end mutual funds are liquid and stand ready to buy back your shares at the current market value. All mutual funds will settle promptly, usually the next day. That's one kind of liquidity.

However, if you buy a bond fund and interest rates rise cause the fund's value to drop, you will not be able to get all of your money back, just the full current value of your account. This is different from saying you can get back what you invested. Some of what you invested has been "given up to the market" as reflected in the decrease in the value of your account.

That other kind of liquidity is called *liquidity at par.* It refers to bonds issued at par value and redeemed at par value plus accrued interest at maturity. Liquidity at par means you can get back what you invested.

Can You Get Your Money Back Intact?   The possibility of not getting your money back intact normally disappears the longer you invest your money. It is a risk worth taking. However, the value of having meager reserves in a crisis and having no time to wait for maturity is a greater risk than the investment risk. As you read this book, you will learn how to manage risks. I lost a lot money avoiding risk before I learned how to manage risk.

Suppose you had two choices—a safe money fund earning 4 percent and a risky equity fund that carried the risk of losing 10 percent of its value in a very short time, but over time you stood a good chance to earn 20 percent a year.

After the first quarter you are up 5 percent in the risky fund, versus 1 percent in the safe fund. But if 1 of those 10 percent dips occurred, you would end up with a loss of 5 percent for the quarter.

After nine months, however, you have earned 15 percent, and if you lose 10 percent now, you will still be ahead of the safe fund with a total return on the riskier fund of 5 percent versus 3 percent (5 percent for three quarters versus 1 percent for three quarters).

As you can see, the longer you invest, the more likely—even in the worst-case scenario—you will be well ahead of the return of the alternative investment. Of course, those 10 percent dips will still take your breath away.

Now you are beginning to understand why people are willing to take the risks of the stock market over CDs for long-term investing and why I say, "Avoiding risk will get you nowhere. Learning to manage risk will get you anywhere."

REDEMPTIONS ARE CONVENIENT

You can always request to redeem shares simply by calling the fund's toll-free number. You should request telephone redemption privileges when you open your account, so you can get money wired to your bank account on short notice. If you forget, your fund can advise you how to add that flexibility to your account in short order.

Telephone Redemption

The telephone exchange privilege enables investors to switch and exchange shares of one fund (a redemption) for shares of another (a purchase or investment) within the fund family or extended family simply with a phone call. For example, you may want to get a stock fund out of the way of a raging bear market or upgrade your disappointing adjustable rate mortgage (ARM) fund to a more impressive short-term, high-yield (junk) bond fund.

There are a few funds that require written notice rather than a telephone call. With the convenience of FAX messages, that is a much simpler process than ever before. However, the fund may require an authenticated signature to do so. Any broker, bank, or mutual savings bank can help you, often for free or for a small fee.

Automated Investment and Redemption

One of the greatest features for many novice investors is the ability to invest systematically by payroll deduction or direct charge to your bank account. The automated investment feature is excellent for systematic investment programs where dollar cost averaging strategies are part of your overall strategy. Automatic redemption services, usually free, are an excellent way to add some supplemental cash flow to your bank account or to provide retirement cash flow.

WHEN TO DOLLAR COST AVERAGE

Dollar cost averaging assumes that by investing a fixed amount each period (usually each payroll period or each month), over the long term, you can buy shares at an average price that is less than the average price per share during the period. This works simply because when the share price falls, you can buy more shares with the same amount of money. Mathematically, this is a lower cost way to invest. It does not guarantee profits.

I highly recommend "paying yourself first" by investing something each pay period. The regularity of an automatic investment program is a great way to build up your investment portfolio, and dollar cost averaging is an attractive attribute of such a practice.

WHEN NOT TO DOLLAR COST AVERAGE

Unless you are saving systematically (paying yourself first and investing a little every payday), I seldom recommend dollar cost averaging to investors as an investment strategy for the following reasons.

Asset Allocation Reduces the Risk and Increases the Odds of Success

When you have a lump sum to invest, you don't want to have to place a significant part of it aside in a money fund until you can gradually invest the money on a dollar cost averaging basis. You want to get the money invested and working for you as quickly as possible.

Dollar cost averaging is designed to help you reduce the cost of your investments and reduce the risk of investing at the wrong time. Asset allocation strategies spread those risks by suggesting that you diversify risk among several investment classes, all of which are operating on different timetables and cycles.

By building an effective asset allocation portfolio, you can "hit the ground running" with a safer investment program. This permits people to invest a lump sum immediately, without an unproductive waiting period where much of the money is idle as the dollar cost averaging is played out over time. Dollar cost averaging is for naive investors who feel that no other strategy can improve their odds.

Study This Book and You Won't Be Naive!

Dollar cost averaging is an effective way to systematically invest for the long-term if you know *nothing* about investing (not your situation if you are reading this book!) or if you are investing in a difficult-to-forecast market, such as gold mutual funds. (That is why I suggest dollar cost averaging for most savvy investors working their way into a 5 to 10 percent long-term position in gold funds.)

MUTUAL FUNDS' "PERFORMANCE IS THE ONLY ANSWER" CLUB

The reason you want to invest in mutual funds in the first place is not to "play it safe" and stay poor but to manage risk to your benefit and build your wealth. The beauty of mutual fund investing is that past performance data are readily available in many forms (e.g., *The Wall Street Journal, New York Times, USA Today,* and various magazines and newsletters). While I would feel comfortable with the accuracy of mutual fund tables prepared by Morningstar, Inc. or Lipper Analytical Services or money fund tables from *Donoghue's MONEY FUND REPORT,* I would not rely on the NASD newspaper tables that list hastily collected data without careful reliability checking.

It's time for the skeptics and the SEC regulators to pop up and give their perennial and appropriate warning "past performance is no guarantee of future performance." I agree, but it is an excellent guide for assessing probability of investment success in our strategies.

THUMBING YOUR NOSE AT THE SKEPTICS

Investment performance has few absolute rules of thumb, but a few I have discovered and find useful include:

► Falling interest rates tend to stimulate profitable opportunities and decrease risk in both the stock and bond markets.

► Rising interest rates tend to stimulate poor performance and increase risk in both the stock and bond markets.

► The stock and bond markets have little to do with today's economy and more to do with anticipation of future profits and inflationary trends, respectively.

► Shorter-term bond investments are less vulnerable to rising interest rates than longer-term bond investments.

► Money funds are excellent capital preservation vehicles when they pay a return higher than inflation but, in today's markets, are poor investments.

► When interest rates rise, fixed-income investments with the lowest credit risk are often the investments that lose the most principal value. The following investments are ranked from the riskiest to the safest in a rising interest rate environment: collateralized mortgage obligations (CMOs) (riskiest), zero-coupon bonds, tax-free municipal bonds, government bonds, Ginnie Maes, corporate bonds, and junk bonds (safest).

▶ Over the long term, stocks outperform bonds, which outperform money market investments.

▶ Paying a load to a broker to invest in a fund guarantees an immediate loss and places an investor at a significant disadvantage. There is absolutely no connection between paying a broker a commission and the performance of the investment.

▶ High expenses have little to do with the performance of stock funds and a lot to do with the performance of bond funds.

▶ Tax-sheltered investments compound performance faster than taxable investments.

▶ Stock funds have a significant amount of natural tax-deferral for long-term investors and some stock funds defer taxes better than others (due to tax-efficient management strategies).

▶ Index funds produce average performance. Stock index funds outperform about 70 percent of stock funds but seldom outperform the SuperStar mutual funds. In addition, stock index funds lose money in bear markets while Super-Star investors diversify their risk elsewhere and either make money or lose less.

▶ Informed investors make better choices, manage risk, and make more money.

Making you an informed investor is my goal and the reason I wrote this book.

CHAPTER 3

How Much Do You Trust Mutual Fund Managers?

Surprise! This Time the Government Is Watching Them for You

It is comforting to know that Washington takes firm steps to make sure mutual funds are the safest financial organizations in America. No mutual fund has ever failed. They can't because every mutual fund consists of hundreds of securities and all of them would have to become worthless before a mutual fund would fail—and that is not going to happen!

MUTUAL FUNDS ARE ORGANIZED FOR YOUR PROTECTION

I first encountered mutual funds over 30 years ago, when I was assigned by Price Waterhouse & Co. to audit two mutual funds, a major public accounting firm and my employer at the time. What struck me was that the regulation of mutual funds was designed to protect all investors. It was, in effect, financial democracy. All investors were treated equally regardless of how many shares they owned or how much money they had invested.

According to accounting theory, the most secure organization has a clear division of duties so as to make it highly improbable that any individual can control enough of the transactions to steal assets from the company. This is called *internal control*.

The regulation and operation of mutual funds is a model in effective internal control. These internal controls are what protect you, the mutual fund shareholder.

MUTUAL FUND REGULATION NEEDED NO REFORM—IT WORKS!

Over the years, I have had the opportunity to attend and to keynote or chair conferences in many financial services industries (variable insurance, mutual fund operations and marketing, commercial banking, savings & loan operations, investment management, financial planning, stock brokerage, etc.). I can assure you that it is a rare conference where the subject of fiduciary responsibility for customers' assets ever comes up!

On the other hand, the subject of responsibility for customers' assets *always* comes up at a mutual fund industry conference because that concept is central to the industry's regulation. Indeed, it is the central subject of conversation in many ways. (Oh, don't expect to hear it discussed at a stockbroker or load fund conference. That would be too much to expect. But at a no-load conference, count on it!)

HOW DO THESE INTERNAL CONTROLS WORK?

Writers, directors, actors, and producers all work together to create a movie. Similarly, the carefully crafted production known as a mutual fund consists of several key components that, woven together, form a tightly structured organization. Key people in a fund organization include the following.

The Investment Advisor

For shareholders, the investment advisor is the most visible and important member of a mutual fund organization. The investment advisor hires the *portfolio manager* who selects the specific portfolio investments in which the fund will invest. Each must fit the fund's established policies, guidelines, and objectives, an excruciatingly detailed and challenging effort.

The investment advisor is also responsible for seeing that the purchase and sale is conducted to assure the fund receives "best execution," or the most appropriate purchasing method at a fair market price. Investment advisors cannot participate unfairly in the commissions generated from their trading activity, meaning that all their transactions are conducted at "arm's length." Thus they cannot execute trades to their own benefit.

Unlike stockbrokers who are paid on a commission basis, investment advisers are paid an annual fee (accrued daily) based on a percentage of the fund's average daily assets. If they perform well, the fund's assets grow and so does their compensation.

The Distributor/Administrator

All funds have a distributor/administrator who is responsible for making the fund conveniently available to investors. As the name implies, the distributor is in charge of marketing and distribution. Typically, the distributors/administrators are the original organizers of the fund.

The distributor/administrator also provides accounting and legal services, oversees internal procedures and controls, and coordinates the fund's operations with its directors. The distributor/administrator also prepares and files Securities and Exchange Commission (SEC), tax, shareholder, and other required reports.

The Board of Directors

Under the Investment Company Act of 1940, each fund is required to have a board of directors composed of five or more individuals, the majority of whom, in most cases, must be disinterested parties, independent of any of the other parties contracted to work with or for the fund. (They are referred to as the independent directors.) The balance of the board (the "inside" directors), are interested parties who are often executives of the fund administrator, distributor, investment advisor or other parties involved in the fund's operations.

Fund directors, particularly the independent ("outside") directors, are required to swear loyalty to the fund and its shareholders and to serve as watchdogs for shareholder protection. They exercise ultimate control over how and by whom the fund is managed. They are charged with the responsibility to oversee and approve or disapprove contracts with, and set policies and procedures for, all the subcontractors (investment advisors, sponsor/distributors, transfer agents, custodians, and legal and accounting counsel) that serve the fund.

The outside or independent directors have the power to fire any of the parties serving the fund and, on occasion, even to fire the administrators who founded the fund. In the early eighties, one institutional money fund's directors replaced Salomon Brothers and First National Bank of Chicago as administrator and investment advisor, respectively, overnight with Goldman Sachs (which won both contracts). That was quite a blow to the prestige of both organizations, which had allegedly become lax in their supervision of management.

Directors are charged with overseeing the operation of the fund and ultimately answering to the shareholders. Although even an incompetent or unresponsive board of directors can be hard to unseat due to the apathy of most investors, investors dissatisfied with performance or service often "vote with their feet." They redeem their shares of the fund and invest elsewhere, a very effective control feature.

The Transfer Agent

The transfer agent is charged with shareholder communications. It is the transfer agent's responsibility to maintain accurate records of shareholder accounts, to send out statements and proxies, if necessary, and to communicate daily the number of shares outstanding to the custodian.

Transfer agents also calculate dividends and authorize payment by the fund's custodian. In addition, they prepare and mail periodic account statements, provide federal income tax information, shareholder notices and confirmation statements, and maintain a customer service department to respond to account inquiries.

The millions of mutual fund transactions executed each year require gargantuan behind-the-scenes record keeping and data processing efforts. Transfer agents who do not keep shareholders happy ultimately lose clients. To avoid this, some fund families maintain the responsibilities of transfer agencies in-house to improve and assure quality control.

The Custodian

The custodian, which physically holds the portfolio securities of a fund, is either a trust department of a commercial bank or a trust company. The custodian's job is to safeguard those securities in a vault, or in the case of Treasury bills that are kept on a computer "book entry" system, to deliver them only in exchange for immediate cash payment when they are sold and to pay for them in full when they are received.

When the custodian receives the daily number of shares outstanding from the transfer agent, it then values the portfolio of the fund. The net asset value per share is calculated and used to price that day's shareholder investments (purchases) and redemptions (sales).

Sufficient controls are maintained to safeguard the securities. An inordinate amount of continuous legal effort keeps the custodian abreast of the finest points of commercial law and securities regulation to protect the funds' full and clear ownership of the portfolio securities. The custodian, however, does not protect the value of those securities, that is the role of the investment advisor.

The Owners of the Fund: You, the Shareholders

The most important part of fund management is—*you!* You, as the shareholder, are an owner of the fund and the center of all its activities. The fund is legally required to send shareholders relevant literature, including proxy materials and annual reports.

The rights of mutual fund shareholders are similar to shareholders of any corporation, and in this case, an investment company. All mutual fund shares are voting stock. Shareholders may elect individuals to the board of directors, ratify the board's choice of an independent public accountant at an annual meeting, and have a role in approving investment advisory contracts.

THE MUTUAL FUND MARKETPLACE: HOW SHARES ARE TRADED

Open-end mutual funds stand ready to sell or redeem shares of the fund at all times. It is a busy, smooth-functioning, and well-controlled process. Most people are familiar with frenetic scenes on the floors of the Chicago Mercantile Exchange, the New York Stock Exchange, and other major trading arenas. Although mutual funds do not have the equivalent of a fast-paced, centralized trading floor, the process of buying and selling shares can be equally exciting.

Funds typically distribute shares through a principal administrator/underwriter, which is the same as the administrator/sponsor. Some underwriters (broker-affiliated load funds like Merrill Lynch) employ their own sales forces, while others (vendors of independent load funds) distribute shares through a network of broker-dealers. In either case, a sales charge, typically ranging from 3.0 percent to 8.5 percent, usually is included in the offering price.

A mutual fund salesperson can be paid via a front-end sales charge or an annual charge levied by the fund (referred to as a 12(b)1 fee), which can be as much as 0.75 percent a year. These 12(b)1 fees are usually accompanied by a back-end load or exit fee that kicks in if an investor sells shares before a specified period of time, generally five or six years. I call these last back-end loaded fund, go-loads, because you pay when you go.

Investors also may purchase fund shares directly from the underwriter with little or no sales charge. Since these direct marketed *no-load* (or in the case of Fidelity Investments, low-load) funds are purchased directly from the fund underwriter, you can avoid the middlepersons (is that politically correct or what?), otherwise known as commissioned salespeople.

Despite being direct marketed, most no-load funds incur heavy advertising expenses that they hope to make up through annual management fees. On the other hand, some fund families, like Evergreen, spend little on advertising but instead market by word-of-mouth and public relations.

ADVERTISING IS CAREFULLY REGULATED

Mutual fund advertising is closely regulated by the SEC, with the assistance of the NASD (National Association of Securities Dealers, the funds' self-regulatory organization). Advertisements that you see in newspapers and magazines are called *tombstone ads.* They contain limited and general information about the fund. Currently, shareholders cannot buy a mutual fund directly through an advertisement. They must be sent the prospectus first.

Fund marketers point out that they may mail as many as 100 prospectuses to get one new investor. That is a cost that is borne by all the shareholders. They argue that if curious investors were permitted either to request a prospectus before investing or have the prospectus sent with the confirmation after they have invested (as already happens with broker-sold funds), it would be easier and cheaper for all concerned.

It is argued that few investors actually read the prospectus, anyway—a claim few will dispute. Even the marketers' worst critics will concede that the hard-to-read, detailed technical disclosure in a prospectus satisfies the funds' legal disclosure requirements but provides investors with precious little useful information. "Disclosure is not the same as information," quipped one industry executive.

Regulatory approval of *off-the-page advertising,* which would allow investors to send money when responding to fund advertising without first receiving a full prospectus, is currently being considered by the SEC. Even if this change is approved by the SEC, the ad will still contain all the important information in the prospectus. (Such an ad is referred to as a *summary prospectus,* a legal document not taken lightly by fund marketers. This means that their liability to disclose all relevant information to potential investors is the same as if they sent a full prospectus.)

SEC approval of off-the-page advertising will be a great convenience to mutual fund investors, both in costs and time. I, for one, strongly support this change. When you consider that both full-service and discount brokers send the prospectus after the sale with the confirmation and that investors will be able to get a prospectus up front as always if they desire, this is a logical and responsible procedure for the SEC to approve.

THE BASIS OF REGULATION: SOME VERY EFFECTIVE LAWS

Companies establishing a mutual fund are required to comply with a myriad of regulations geared to protecting shareholder interests. Starting a mutual fund can be a costly, complex process. That process is designed to discourage con artists looking for a quick buck.

First, mutual fund organizers must contend with the United States Securities and Exchange Commission (SEC). The bible of mutual fund regulation is the Investment Company Act of 1940. Mutual funds that offer shares to the public are required to register them in accordance with federal law and state *blue sky* regulations. Finally, anyone selling shares to the public must be a licensed stock broker or a registered representative of a no-load fund.

The Investment Company Act of 1940

In my mind, this is the finest piece of financial regulation ever passed. It was designed by visionaries from the mutual fund industry itself. These industry insiders reportedly wrote the regulations more tightly than Congress would have done on its own. This strong self-discipline has characterized mutual fund industry leadership ever since.

The Investment Company Act goes well beyond most state and federal anti-fraud and disclosure rules and encompasses protective restrictions on mutual funds, investment advisers, directors, officers, employees, and principal underwriters. The Act prohibits self-dealing and conflicts of interest between affiliated individuals, such as investment advisors, and the fund. These individuals may not knowingly sell to, or purchase from, a fund securities or other property, nor may they borrow money from it. The Act also limits commissions that brokers receive for selling a mutual fund.

Mutual funds must also maintain detailed records of securities they own. They must file detailed reports with the SEC, including financial statements that contain an opinion from an outside certified public accounting firm. Because they continuously offer new shares to the public, mutual funds are subject to special SEC registration rules that allow them to register an indefinite number of shares.

The Securities Act of 1933

This Act requires that all potential shareholders receive the latest prospectus before they invest and places significant restrictions on advertising content. The 1933 Act provides for registration of all public securities, including those offered by mutual funds.

The Securities Exchange Act of 1934

This Act regulates practices by broker-dealers, including principal underwriters who sell mutual funds. It provides that all broker-dealers must register with the SEC and become members of a national securities exchange or the National Association of Securities Dealers (NASD). Registered broker-dealers must maintain detailed records on their financial positions and customer transactions, segregate customer securities in custodial accounts, and file reports on an annual basis with the SEC.

The Investment Advisors Act of 1940

Under the Investment Advisors Act, all investment advisors to mutual funds must be registered. Registration gives regulators the ability to evaluate applicants before they enter the business. (Sort of mutual fund "gun control.") The most effective protection registration provides is the threat of license revocation. Break the rules and you lose your license. The funds must also meet record keeping, reporting, and other requirements.

The Internal Revenue Code of 1954

The 1954 Internal Revenue Code helps ensure that the tax burden placed on mutual fund shareholders remains similar to those who invest in individual stocks. It accomplishes this by essentially treating the fund as an investment conduit, or *regulated investment company*.

Because the mutual fund qualifies as a regulated investment company (by distributing at least 98 percent of its realized income and capital gains in the current year), the fund is allowed to deduct those distributions from its taxable income and gains for federal and state tax purposes. the funds currently distribute profits and net income to shareholders, who in turn report these distributions on their tax returns. To qualify as a regulated investment company a fund must meet a number of requirements, including prescribed diversification standards.

Blue Sky Laws

In addition to federal law, most states have regulations regarding securities offerings to their residents and requirements for broker-dealers doing business in their jurisdictions. These blue sky laws outline the procedures for registration of shares, which is often accomplished automatically when the mutual fund files with the SEC. State statutes may also impose limits on mutual fund expenses or restrict speculative investment activity. Blue sky laws provide an additional layer of protection on top of federal laws.

READ THE PROSPECTUS BEFORE YOU INVEST

Later on in this book I'll show you how to invest in the best managed mutual funds. One of the most important things you should do before you invest is make sure you know what you are investing in. You do so by *carefully* reading a prospectus. If you don't read this important document, you could run into trouble. While often difficult to read, you should make an effort to do so before investing or soon after investing, even if you think you already know enough about the fund.

There Are No Government Guarantees of Principal Safety

I was speaking in the Midwest in the late 1980s, and a retired couple came up to me afterward to have a chat.

"Bill, we put $10,000 in a U.S. government securities fund," said the husband. "Our broker said it was 100 percent safe and backed by Uncle Sam. The fund yielded 10 percent. We thought that was great—better than the bank. But the value of our account dropped when interest rates went up."

Many people get confused by the U.S. government guarantee. In the mid-1980s there was much concern about securities firms that sold government funds to investors who didn't understand that a U.S. government guarantee was a guarantee against the default of individual portfolio securities, not a guarantee against market value losses due to rising interest rates.

Mutual funds are not government guaranteed, but they can invest in securities that are government guaranteed against every risk except the only real risk you have—market risk. If you want that guarantee, buy a government bond and hold it to maturity, and you will get paid.

You've got to read the prospectus carefully. That document spells out the risks.

Here's what you will find in a prospectus:

▶   A statement about the investment objectives and investment policy of the fund.

▶   Fund expenses. You usually see a fee table. In addition, there is information that shows how the fund performed, less fees, versus an index or benchmark. There are no hidden fees.

▶   Investment restrictions—in what and how the fund will invest your money.

▶   Portfolio turnover—an indication of how frequently the portfolio is traded.

▶   Information that identifies the fund manager, directors, trustees, and members of the advisory board.

▶   The name of the custodian bank that holds the assets in a separate account.

▶   Allocation of brokerage. If the fund has an organizational link with a brokerage firm, this section reveals the percentage of brokerage commissions being paid to the broker affiliate.

▶   The fund's policy on voluntary accumulation or automatic investment plans. That's were money is automatically withdrawn from your checking account each month and deposited into the fund.

▶   Litigation. This section tells you if there are any current or pending legal actions against the fund.

► Determination of net asset value. This section explains how the fund calculates the net asset value of the fund.

► How to buy shares. The fund's initial and subsequent investments are listed. This section also provides directions for investing electronically or by mail. For load funds, there is information on how the sales charge is reduced if you invest large sums of money.

► How to redeem shares. This section tells you whether you need an authorized signature and how to use the telephone redemption privileges (see Chapter 2).

► A special service section describes dividend and capital gain reinvestment privileges, accumulation and withdrawal plans, as well as retirement savings plans.

► Tax information. The fund must describe its policy and tax status concerning dividends and capital gains. Keep in mind that funds must distribute at least 98 percent of their net income and realized capital gains to qualify as a regulated investment company under the Internal Revenue Code.

► Withdrawal plans. Information on how to withdraw money regularly from the fund.

► Statement of additional information. You have to request this document from the fund group. It may cover details that are not included in the prospectus.

HOW SHOULD YOU REGISTER YOUR SHARES?

When you receive your mutual fund application, be sure to talk to your accountant, lawyer, or financial advisor about how to register your fund shares. If you have a complex financial situation, make sure you set up the account the right way. The way you hold title to your property will affect how your loved ones will inherit your assets.

If you want to own all the shares in your name, you register your account as *fee simple*. Then you will designate who will inherit your investments.

If you own the fund in *joint tenancy with right of survivorship*, you own the property with someone else. You can give your interest away or sell it. But you can't leave your interest to someone else when you die. When you own property with your spouse, you both share in the ownership and control of the asset. Upon the death of one spouse, ownership of the mutual fund is automatically passed on to the surviving spouse.

With *tenancy in common,* you own part of it and can give your share away, sell or leave your part of the property to others when you die. Under this arrangement, you can own property with your spouse or others.

Tenants-in-common may own unequal interests in a mutual fund. For example, you may own 50 percent of the fund assets, while your spouse and your brother own 25 percent each. When the first spouse dies, however, his or her percentage passes on to his or her designated beneficiary based on a will, trust agreement, or *intestate succession.* It does not automatically go to the surviving spouse.

ARE YOU READY?

Now that you know more about the unique consumer protection aspects and effective safety nets built into mutual fund regulations, let's get on with the business of investing creatively in mutual funds. The next two chapters will help you decide on the investment strategies most appropriate for meeting your realistic investment goals and how to identify the best funds to Super-Charge your investment results.

CHAPTER 4

Can You Match the Strategy With the Investment Goal?

Knowing How Means More for You, Less for the Tax Man

Peter Drucker, the management philosopher, loved to get his students' work back into focus by reminding them that, "Efficiency is getting things **done** right, effectiveness is getting the **right** things done." Wise words. Read on, and I will teach you how to be an effective investor.

WHAT TYPES OF INVESTING DO *YOU* WANT DONE *RIGHT?*

You can arrange your investment strategies in as many ways as the investment goals you want to achieve: retirement, college education for a family member, your first home, a new and better home, a vacation home, emergency medical expense, a boat or van, vacation travel, or whatever "blows up your skirt," as a dear friend of mine says so colorfully.

However, for the purposes of this book, I am going to assume that just three basic types of portfolios will address almost all of your investment goals:

▶ *Portfolio A: Your Tax-Sheltered Retirement Savings*

▶ *Portfolio B: Your Taxable Long-Term Savings*

▶ *Portfolio C: Portfolio A or B with Cash Flow Generation*

A MINIMUM THREE- TO FIVE-YEAR TIME HORIZON

Each of these portfolios assumes that your investment goals (the primary use for the portfolio's assets) will not require a major withdrawal from principal for at least three to five years, and many even provide for added capital. In reality, most savings programs involve multiple investment goals and a series of withdrawals over a longer period than originally planned, especially if you are a successful investor and your results exceed your goals.

This certainly describes retirement savings, the bulk of which are normally not used for ten to twenty years after retirement. Even if you have just retired, you need to think of yourself as a long-term investor, especially with the mixed blessings of longevity, for which few of us are ever prepared.

INVESTING FOR INCOME IS UNWISE
AND COUNTERPRODUCTIVE

It seems conservative and wise to pick investments that demonstrate their success in traditional terms (traditional to bank-bound investors, at least) by paying you regular income. Yet investing for income was a big mistake for most investors in the past and almost certainly will be so in the coming years.

1. *Your Income Is Taxed Currently.* Under our income tax system, income is a punishable offense. In today's low-rate markets, after you deduct taxes and inflation, income investors are getting poorer not richer.

2. *Today's Rates Are Abysmally Low.* When you force an investment to throw off current income (as with a bank CD or a bond funds), you are forcing yourself to accept, in today's markets, a very low return.

3. *Your Principal Is Unnecessarily at Risk.* In addition, if you invest in most fixed-income investments, you are taking the risk that the impact of rising rates will shrink the value of your principal dramatically.

For that reason, when interest rates are rising, always invest in (short-term) bonds rather than bond funds. Bonds mature (pay back their full principal at a given time) and bond funds don't. (In a rising interest rate market, you will never get your principal back intact from a bond fund.)

4. *You Are Better Off Getting Tax-Deferred Capital Gains.* Investing in bonds or CDs for growth is foolish. Why would you want to earn low yields, risk the loss of principal, and pay premature taxes every year? You are only forcing yourself to pay out in taxes money that is better off invested in tax-deferred capital gains for your benefit, not the government's.

Many investors overlook the fact that a stock mutual fund often earns you appreciation (increases in the value of your shares) on unrealized capital gains (capital gains on investments not yet sold) that is tax-deferred until the fund sells or realizes its gains. A stock fund distributes only the realized capital gains (realized by actually selling the appreciated stock). Unrealized capital gains (from long-term stock holdings) are tax-deferred, even for taxable investors.

I know there are those among you who would rather pay the taxes up front than pay them later simply because you don't like to have accrued debts. Your concern is probably that you fear not having enough money to pay those taxes later. That is a valid concern, except in this case. With mutual funds you will certainly have the money to pay the taxes since your taxes come due *only if you sell.*

Defer the taxes, invest the government's share to your benefit, and pocket the profits. Even after taxes, the majority of a profit is better than no profit at all. Trust me on this one.

5. *You Risk Paying Taxes on Your Losses.* If interest rates rise and your bond fund values decline a greater amount than your interest (e.g., a small rise in interest rates can wipe out an entire year's interest), you end up paying taxes on the interest, and you cannot deduct your losses without selling your investments. The bottom line? You end up losing money and paying taxes on your losses.

6. *For Growth, Invest in Stock Funds, Not Bond Funds.* If you are investing for growth, invest in assets that can grow in value. You then defer the taxes on that growth until future years when it is distributed to you as a taxable capital gain, or you sell and realize your gains. These are good descriptions of stock funds and bad descriptions of CDs, bonds, or bond funds.

HEY, BILL! WHERE IS THE RISK TOLERANCE DISCUSSION?

About this time, most books would ask you to measure your risk tolerance and decide if you are a conservative, active, or aggressive investor. I have a simple philosophy: Let's deal with your lack of investment education before we try to measure your risk tolerance.

Most fear of risk is simply an expression of fear of the unknown. Let's educate you about investments so there is less of the unknown to deal with, and you will find that you can tolerate a lot more risk. In fact, you will learn that the secret of investment success is *managing* risk, not avoiding it!

I refuse to write a book that simply regurgitates the old clichés that have kept investors from investment success for so long. **American investors don't have enough time to save for retirement to afford the luxury of "playing it safe." Timidity today is a guaranty of a humble retirement lifestyle tomorrow.**

Read that last paragraph again. I am not advocating reckless investing or speculation. I am advocating cautiously and objectively identifying consistent, high-return, lower risk investments and building a portfolio allocated among them.

All investors are conservative. We *all* want to conserve our principal. However, *assertive* investors take known, prudent risks that they can manage and understand to earn high returns.

So, let's get serious and assume that all of you will be assertive investors willing to knowledgeably manage risk rather than live to avoid it. OK? OK!

(If that makes you a bit apprehensive, keep reading. You are going to discover a whole new investment personality as we open your mind and expand your horizons. You're a winner on your way to what investors refer to as "a good experience." Be patient.)

Now, let's get back to the big three portfolios.

PORTFOLIO A: YOUR TAX-SHELTERED RETIREMENT SAVINGS

This portfolio could be an IRA, SEP-IRA, 401(k), 403(b)7, 457, or any tax-deferred retirement savings program. The same strategies could also be applied to variable annuities or variable life insurance policies.

What distinguishes these portfolios from taxable portfolios are two very simple characteristics:

1. *No-Tax-Consequence Upgrading Opportunities.* In the absence of transaction costs, and I have already explained to you the joys of no-or low-transaction-fee investing at discount brokers, at least for your IRA (more details in Chapters 6 and 7), *there are no tax consequences for trading or upgrading your portfolio.*

This means that if you do not upgrade your investments occasionally to stay in tune with the investment times, you are simply stealing from your retirement plan's future payoff. Being lazy or timid now is setting a lower-than-necessary living standard for your retirement lifestyle. It's your choice.

2. *Unnecessarily Limited Investment Choices.* In most retirement plans you are limited to the choices offered by the plan's sponsor. However, it is *your* retirement that we are talking about, not your employer's.

Converting a pension plan from a *defined benefit* plan (a pension plan where **your employer is responsible** if there is not enough money in the plan to meet the pension obligation) to a *defined contribution* plan (where your employer's responsibility—in the absence of a questionable future class action suit—is finished when it provides its matching contribution), makes **you** responsible for there being enough money at retirement. Such a change should make employers highly motivated to respond to your requests for more and better investment choices. Plan participants should be sitting down in groups with their plan administrator and requesting a fuller range of better investment choices.

What requests should you make? Right now, the desirable investments missing from most retirement plans are an assertive international (not watered-down global) stock fund, a global real estate fund, a precious metals fund, and a high-yield junk bond fund or a flexible bond fund to take advantage of European bond opportunities.

(You may want to consider requesting information on a Donoghue's Mutual Fund SuperStars portfolio from W. E. Donoghue & Co., Inc. (my money management firm 800-642-4276) or something equally attractive from another investment advisor. Using an advisor-managed account is one way you can have the "best" of all the fund choices available in a single account. The "best" of those choices is at discretion of the advisor and with no up-front guarantees, of course—we are talking securities.)

Playing it safe with your retirement investments can be a huge mistake for investors planning to retire with a certain lifestyle in mind. First of all, few of us have saved enough for retirement. Second, few of us will be allowed to work as long as we had planned. Third, this generation has costs other generations never faced: college expenses for children of older parents, parents outliving their retirement savings, delayed retirement savings programs, discouraging tax increases, and multiple families (the "me" generation generated a lot of "us" bills for failed marriages). You can see why I emphasize that retirement savings is not a subject to be taken lightly.

Tax-sheltered retirement programs need to be invested a lot more assertively than they have been. There is simply not enough money available or time remaining for the luxury of "playing it safe" with your retirement savings plan. Traditional retirement investments will not provide enough money for a decent retirement.

PORTFOLIO B: YOUR LONG-TERM TAXABLE LONG-TERM SAVINGS

This kind of portfolio is similar to a tax-sheltered savings or wealth building program except that it has no tax-deferral advantages, and taxes must be paid on current dividends and long-term capital gains distributions.

They say, "If you like sausage and taxes, you don't want to see either of them being made." With taxes being "made" on cable TV's C-Span right in my living room, I can only hope that sausage makers restrain themselves a bit longer. "Making taxes" seems to be a never-ending process, and this Clinton administration seems determined to bring "tax and spend" technology to all-time heights under the guise of *deficit reduction.* Ouch!

The challenge taxable investors must face is compounded by the wide range of investment choices and the temptation to switch investments too often to keep up with the winners. You must balance the temptation to be invested in the latest "hot" fund against the wisdom to avoid taking profits too soon, paying taxes too soon, and losing compounding momentum. The longer you can stay with a top performing fund, the longer you can defer your gains and allow the money you would have paid in taxes to earn new profits for you.

The ideal investment for a taxable investor is a fund that is well-managed and stays with the leaders. It trades its portfolio very gradually, pays no capital gains distributions, invests in growth stocks that pay little in dividends and "lets your profits run," as they say.

Reality seldom allows that to happen. Stock markets soar, correct and/or crash (or, even worse, threaten to do so, tempting you to "lock in your profits"), costing you your hard-earned profits. Well-respected funds have years when they cannot keep up with the new leaders. Other investments outperform stock funds for a time (as CDs did for many years in the late 1970s and early 1980s), and you are sorely tempted to take your profits and run.

But what do you do when the tides flow against the stock market as in the case of a bear market (always difficult to see except in retrospect) or a sideways market? Index funds are one answer. They seldom trade their portfolio securities, allowing for maximum compounding (in theory). In spite of being, by definition, "average," they beat hundreds of inferior funds. But what good are these funds when a bear market is eating away at your gains or when international markets are booming and you have chosen an S&P 500 domestic index fund?

The best answers, as it always seems to be in life, are never perfectly clear. However, I have developed two strategies about investing taxable portfolios that have served me and my clients well over the years. The first is The Donoghue Signal Strategy, which I discussed in my last book (see Appendix C for a short explanation). The the second is my dynamic global asset allocation strategy—the subject of most of this book—which, in my mind, is most likely to make the most money in the coming years.

A BETTER CHOICE FOR TODAY: GLOBAL ASSET ALLOCATION

The Global Asset Allocation Strategy is designed for the more experienced and savvy mutual fund investor who has learned that international stock and bond funds have a major role to play in a powerful long-term investment strategy. For the successful 1990s investor, learning the ropes of global asset allocation is clearly the name of the game.

Especially for your tax-sheltered retirement money (no tax consequences for upgrading), such a strategy will be essential if you have any real hope of reaching your investment goals. Remember that the choices you make today will determine the quality of your retirement lifestyle, and you will likely live a lot longer than you planned.

Incorporating global and international funds into your portfolio is actually quite simple using The Donoghue's Mutual Fund SuperStars investment strategies. All you have to do is look at the current Donoghue SuperStars listings, review the types of funds having the greatest success, identify the most consistent, lowest risk performers, assess their *Achilles' Heels* (what can go wrong), and invest in the best and forget about the rest. As to investing overseas, if you see many international and/or global funds at the top of the lists, it is time to include them in your portfolio.

You may not get "in" first or get "out" first, but you can enjoy the often surprisingly long swings in these markets while reducing your exposure to the aging domestic bull market. As a matter of fact, you are likely to sell a fund not because it is about to perform poorly but because another fund is performing superbly.

PORTFOLIO C: PORTFOLIO A OR B WITH CASH FLOW GENERATION

This final portfolio could be either of the first two portfolios except that investors will, from time to time (or regularly), draw upon it to supplement their income with additional cash flow for whatever purpose they may choose (after all, it *is* the investor's money). If you think you are looking for "income," start thinking "cash flow" and you will have more spendable cash, pay less in current taxes, and build your assets while you use them.

Cash Flow Stimulation

Repeat after me, "I pay my bills with cash, not income. Cash is money I can spend, income is a term the IRS uses to describe money I have to pay taxes on." This is a very important concept for you to understand.

The concept is simple, but millions misunderstand it. Any mutual fund can arrange to send you a check-a-month in one of two ways: (1) it can send you a dividend check, or (2) it can reinvest your dividends and then redeem enough shares to pay you a fixed amount (your choice of how much) each month. This latter choice is the better one.

The Risk of Investing for Income Today

If you invest for income, you are forced to invest in mutual funds that pay current income. Those funds are interest-rate sensitive. With interest rates rising, they will lose value as they pay your income.

Tax Benefits of Investing for Portfolio Growth

If you invest for growth, much of your profits are in the form of rising market values of securities in the fund's portfolio and in your portfolio. If neither you nor the fund sells those securities, your profits are tax-deferred and can earn new profits on a before-tax basis.

Priming the Cash Flow Pump

To prime your cash flow pump, you simply reinvest all of your dividends and capital gains distributions (on which you must, of course, pay taxes) in the same funds that produced them. To get at your cash flow, you then select one fund in your portfolio (usually the safest and lowest-yielding one) and request that the fund send you a check each month in the amount you need. (Drawing down up to 8 percent of your portfolio is usually a good estimate.)

You must replace the money you withdraw periodically, as you rebalance your portfolio, so there is always enough in the fund that sends you your monthly check. Many funds require a $10,000 minimum balance to do a regular check a month. However, you can simply redeem the shares each month yourself and have the proceeds transferred by a telephone redemption to your checking account.

Make Sure You Don't Run Out of Money Too Soon

Since your cash flow needs are likely to be smaller than your total return (dividends + capital gains + or − the change in the market value of your portfolio) is likely to be, you can get the cash flow you need, and your portfolio will grow as well. In my mother's words, you will never "run out of money before you run out of life."

More Spendable Cash = Better Lifestyle

You will likely earn *more* spendable cash because instead of withdrawing from each of the funds in your portfolio, you will withdraw from one, usually the least productive one in your portfolio. Your withdrawals represent cash inflow to your checkbook and taxes on the dividends and capital gains represent outflow from your checkbook; the net of the two represents cash flow.

Because you are drawing your cash flow out of only one fund in your portfolio, you are likely to invade the principal of that position. That "return of principal" is tax-free, since you already paid taxes on it.

By allowing part of your profits to continue to earn undisturbed in other parts of your portfolio, you are allowing those profits to be tax-deferred. Your portfolio is growing, you are getting the cash flow you need and, since part of your cash flow is "return of principal," you are paying less taxes, which means more spendable cash.

Summary

That's the long explanation. To implement this strategy you only need do a few things:

▶ Arrange to automatically reinvest your dividends and capital gains distributions in each fund.

▶ Arrange for one fund in the portfolio to have an automatic redemption of enough shares to send you a check-a-month in a fixed amount (as much as 8 percent of your total portfolio is a fairly safe choice).

▶ Remember to add enough cash to the fund periodically with automatic redemption to make sure there is enough to keep the redemption checks coming. (This would be a good time to sell off shares that have capital losses, so you can deduct the losses and reduce your tax liabilities.)

▶ Remember to pay taxes on your dividends and capital gains distributions as well as capital gains and losses on any redemptions you may make.

Do that and you will have: (1) a regular cash flow, (2) more spendable cash, and if your investment choices are good, (3) your money will outlive you. As a result you can enjoy life more fully, rely on a regular cash flow supplement, legally defer taxes on a portion of your profits, and, I hope, remember where you got this great advice.

What if Your Money Shrinks?

As with any investment strategy that seeks higher returns by managing risks, from time to time you will lose some market value in your portfolio. If you stick with my strategies, you will increase the odds of earning that loss back and more. Be patient and enjoy your life.

Mom's CD-Beater Cash Flow Strategy

Allow me to illustrate how I did this for my sainted mother. (The full story of how I developed this unique strategy for my mother is in Chapter 15.) For now, I will tell you a shortened version to make my point.

If you invest your taxable or tax-sheltered portfolio for growth—using either my Donoghue Signal Strategy or my Global Asset Allocation strategies—you significantly reduce the risk of ever running out of money. Certainly 10 to 15 percent double-digit average annual returns are possible over any five-year period. You will never see that kind of opportunity in fixed-income investments in the next few years.

If you have constructed a strong global asset allocation portfolio, updated it periodically (a minimum quarterly review is wise), and spread your risk among a few types of funds, you can safely withdraw 8 to 10 percent profits annually and *still* see your portfolio grow. Mom got her check each month, and her portfolio was designed to grow faster than she withdrew.

LET'S LOOK AT THIS FROM A DIFFERENT PERSPECTIVE

The rule of thumb that many advisors love to quote is that "the percentage of your portfolio exposed to the stock market should be 100 minus your age." If you are 30, then you should have 70 percent of your portfolio in the stock market. If you are 70, only 30 percent.

That sounds like good advice. After all, the stock market does include some significant short-term risks for naive investors. There are stock market crashes, such as in 1987, and there are long-term bear markets such as in the mid-1970s.

However, that advice assumes that you know nothing about investing and that you are a buy-and-hold investor, considerations that are probably *not* true for YOU, my reader, because you have that extra edge—relevant and available statistical information, an understanding of the financial markets, and the strategies I am teaching you in this book.

Now what about Mom? Well, Mom or Pop, as it may be, needs cash flow now and a growing portfolio that assures that the assets necessary to generate the cash flow they need later will be there, regardless of how long they live.

Since, the bulk of today's retirees can reasonably expect to be alive five years from now, it is reasonable to invest as if you did not need a large part of your money for five years or more. If you do that, you do not have to worry about short-term market fluctuations. When you can do that, accept some short-term fluctuation in market value of individual investments, you can invest in investment choices that have significantly greater investment potential.

What strategy should you use to manage Mom's, Pop's, or your own post-retirement savings? Strategy C—*Mom's CD-Beater Cashflow Portfolio,* which is actually Strategy A or B with one very simple variation—it provides for systematic redemptions to provide a check-a-month to income-oriented investors.

Why should you reinvest all of your dividends and capital gains distributions (on which you have to pay taxes) and then set up a systematic redemption program to get a check-a-month? For one of several simple reasons:

1. ***To Create Order from Chaos.*** You need the check-a-month to be a reliable event and in a fixed amount (which can be changed at any time you wish, of course) because unlike your bills, dividends and capital gains distributions do not come every month; a redemption check can.

2. ***To Maximize Tax-Deferral of Unrealized Gains.*** If you follow Strategy C and choose investments that are likely to increase in value over time, a large portion of the growth of your portfolio will be unrealized capital gains on which the taxes are deferred until you sell or "realize" your profits. Of course, you will want to reinvest in the strongest growth generation investments in your portfolio.

3. ***For More Spendable Cash.*** If you follow this strategy, over time you will be able to withdraw, for example, at a reasonable rate of, say, 8 percent or higher, from a portfolio that is earning an average return higher than that. By taking your cash flow partially from the principal in part of your portfolio, you are getting tax-free return of principal. By allowing your capital gains to run in other parts of your portfolio, you get tax-deferred capital gains. You win both ways: partially tax-free cash flow and greater tax-deferred gains.

NOW THAT YOU HAVE CHOSEN YOUR PORTFOLIO TYPE, LET'S GET ON WITH INVESTING

As you become better informed and more confident, you will take a much more assertive and well-focused investment stance. Given that most investors have a long way to go in their savings strategies and a uncomfortably short time to do it, a firm and determined strategy is appropriate.

Americans do not have time to "play it safe," which, as traditionally defined has its own unique and inherent risk. "Playing it smart" is clearly the way to go for mutual fund investors.

I am convinced that mutual fund services and strategies are understood and understandable and that mutual fund investors are much more capable of managing their money than the press normally acknowledges. I believe that you can take charge of your own finances if you have some degree of success to encourage you. Reading this book is the first step toward your financial independence.

CHAPTER 5

Do You Know How to Find SuperStar Mutual Funds?

Lower-Risk, Consistently Top Performers Abound

"Yesterday's SuperStars are seldom tomorrow's SuperStars," the skeptics will say, God bless 'em. They just don't seem to want you to make money. If a fund loses money, they report a disaster (even if *you* just made a big killing). If a fund makes money, they predict a disaster.

Actually, I must admit, they *are* right, most of the time. It is very tough for any fund to stay at the top of the list year after year. As a matter of fact, if you are only looking for the single best fund at the *very* top of the list to repeat with absolute certainty, the skeptics' discouraging forecast will almost always come true. The history of mutual funds is littered with stories of highly volatile funds that pop up, have their day in the sun, and drop out of sight again for years.

SUPERSTAR FUNDS DO EXIST

There are many well-managed funds, or simply well-positioned funds, in very attractive asset classes that can stay at the top of their game for years, and when it is their game's time in the sun, they produce excellent lower-risk high returns for a surprisingly long period.

NINETY PERCENT OF YOUR INVESTMENT SUCCESS COMES FROM PICKING THE *RIGHT TYPES* OF FUNDS, TEN PERCENT FROM PICKING THE *RIGHT FUNDS*

The most important investment decisions you will make are to be in the right asset classes. As we proceed in our search, the right asset classes almost jump out at us. Currently, for example, the *right* asset classes that demand your attention are precious metals funds, emerging markets and diversified international stock funds, global real estate funds, junk bond funds, and selected asset allocation funds.

Your goal should be to establish for yourself a dynamic global asset allocation portfolio, which is exactly what it says:

Portfolio.   A portfolio is a group of different securities. Your portfolio will consist of several funds.

Asset allocation.   Your portfolio will include several different types of funds to cover several asset classes.

Global.   Your portfolio will be open to both domestic and international assets.

Dynamic.   The composition of your portfolio will change from time to time as new asset classes look more attractive than old ones and you replace old fund choices with new fund choices that appear more profitable.

But that's getting ahead of our story.

CONSISTENT TOP PERFORMERS DO EXIST AND WE WILL FIND THEM FOR YOU

First, to demonstrate to you that there **are** consistent top performers with lowered risks, I will conduct some preliminary research to prove my point. Then, we will systematically review nine important fund types, or fund sub-universes, to make sure we have examined all of the viable choices. The fund types we will explore are value-, growth-, and blend-style diversified domestic stock funds, sector funds, index funds, total return funds and "safe harbor" funds, and international stock and bond funds.

I want to assure you that, with the possible exception of bond funds, we will review the entire spectrum of direct-marketed mutual funds. In today's low-rate environment, bond funds would never be an objective or major choice for a well-informed and confident investor's portfolio.

Once we have "searched the fund encyclopedia" for the most attractive funds, I will guide you to "writing a prescription for your portfolio" yourself. Selecting mutual funds is not rocket science, but you must know where you want to be and with whom you want to work.

PUTTING IT ALL TOGETHER

Later, when we "write your portfolio prescription" for a dynamic global asset allocation portfolio for the 1990s, we will combine our knowledge about selecting the right asset classes, choosing lower-risk, high-return funds in those asset classes, and allocating your investment dollars to build a powerful, lower-risk, higher-return global asset allocation portfolio. Finally, we will look at several convenient, low-cost information sources you can use to keep your portfolio up-to-date.

The success of the strategy I will use to assemble my model portfolio is based largely on common sense, some careful quantitative research, a bit of experience I have gathered over the years, and more than a little bit of good luck. In the process, you will probably be hatching different techniques to add to the mix. After all, it is your money we are talking about investing. Together we will make you a better-informed, more street-savvy, and richer investor. That is our goal.

So, let's address the question of the hour: "Aren't high-performance mutual funds also high risk mutual funds?" The answer is simple: "Sometimes, but not always." Let's see if we can discover some of the exceptions to the rule.

"YES, VIRGINIA, THERE IS A SANTA CLAUS . . ."

. . . And there is a Donoghue's SuperStar portfolio. There are plenty of funds that are consistent, lower-risk, top performers. In fact, I was as surprised to discover that, if I set my standards high and stuck with them, several very attractive funds would

stand up straight and tall and ask to be selected for my Mutual
Fund SuperStar Portfolio.

SETTING UP THE SUPERSTAR SCREENS TO IDENTIFY THE WINNERS

While setting my standards high and sticking to them, I came
up with a series of computerized screens to search through the
Donoghue Direct-Marketed Mutual Fund Universe. The screening process is designed to identify the SuperStar fund candidates three ways.

First, the process finds the funds with the most consistent
performance relative to their peers, that is, a high "Rank in
(Investment) Objective" over several periods. Second, it checks
these funds to see if they exhibit lower risks, as measured by
Morningstar Risk ratings. Then, after they are ranked on recent relevant performance, the screening process identifies
funds that are leaders in the preferred asset classes we will
choose.

To simplify my search for funds with consistent top performance at lower risks, I started first with a:

1. *Long-Term Fund Screen.*   This identifies the funds with
   the best long-term track records (over the past one and
   three years, which is long term in today's rapidly changing
   markets).

2. *Short-Term Fund Screen.*   This screen is broader and
   less demanding in order to identify newer funds and current top-performing funds I would like to add to the mix so
   as not to miss anything. (After all, you do want to build a
   portfolio that is right in tune with the times and in funds
   that are at the top of their game, don't you?)

You can use these screens as examples of a rational process
for establishing your SuperStar portfolio. If you are reading
this book and wish to see what funds would be recommended
right now, call 1-800-982-BILL [1-800-982-2455] to get a FREE
Donoghue's SuperStars update. (If you would like to learn more
about Donoghue's SuperStars On-Line service, the computer
program—a $39.95 value—is FREE by calling 1-800-749-1348.
The program is FREE, and the first update costs $7 each month.
Currently, additional updates during the month are $5, with a

maximum cost of $22 in any one month. You will need an I PC-compatible computer, a modem, and a credit card to use this economical service, which includes sophisticated investment software to gain access to extensive performance data on my recommended SuperStars mutual funds.)

You have probably already guessed that this portfolio is especially attractive to tax-sheltered accounts like IRAs and 401(k)s (if you have enough choices) since it will probably require that you review your portfolio monthly and upgrade your portfolio occasionally. I am sure that, with a little patience, it will certainly be feasible to trade within the rules of no-transaction-fee programs and certainly within the limits of transaction-fee programs at discount brokers. (More on that coming in Chapters 6 and 7.)

SETTING OUR GOALS

Our ideal is to identify mutual funds in many asset classes that are consistently among the top performers in their asset class or investment objective and also have lower risk ratings than their peers. Such SuperStar funds are rare but easily discoverable. As an example, allow me to discuss my favorite SuperStar money fund. It has found its way to the top of my recommended list with the best combination of high yield and low risk.

Example: A Rare True SuperStar Money Fund

A SuperStar money fund does exist, but that won't get us much in the way of profits. For those of you who are curious, that SuperStar money fund is United Services Government Securities Savings Fund (1-800-US-FUNDS).

It has been the *No. 1 top-performing government securities-only money fund* for most of the past three years. It strives to be 100 percent exempt from state and local taxes by limiting its investments to Treasury bills and the select few federal government agencies whose interest qualifies for that tax exemption. The fund charges a very small management fee. In addition, its policy is to manage that fee to keep the fund at or near the top of the list.

Creative, responsible, and professional management makes possible reaching the goal of being the best. Generous management, committed to staying competitive even if it means cutting its fee, makes continued top performance probable. This type of fund is rare.

DESIGNING OUR NET, SETTING OUR STANDARDS, AND FISHING FOR FUNDS

Just like fishing in the Caribbean, we have to throw out our net a few times to identify candidates for our portfolios. Our goal, at this time, is to net a "few good funds" that meet our toughest criteria.

In all cases, we will start with the Donoghue Direct-Marketed Mutual Fund Universe (all no-load funds, plus Fidelity Investments low-load funds up to 3 percent loads, with minimum investments of $25,000 or less, with $50 million or more in assets).

STANDARDS FOR OUR LONG-TERM PRELIMINARY FUND SCREEN

Consistency

We are going to set our standards of consistent performance high. First, we are only going to look at those that have been in the top 25 percent of the funds meeting their objective for both the past 12 and 36 months. This will cut out more than 75 percent of the funds on the list. Our standards are very demanding, and expecting the funds to meet both (12 and 36 months) of those standards is expecting a lot.

For our research database, I have chosen the Morningstar Mutual Funds On-Disc CD-ROM service (the data are stored on a compact disc with read-only memory, hence CD-ROM). It covers 3,434 funds (as of 12/31/93), 840 of which meet the criteria of Donoghue's Direct-Marketed Mutual Fund Universe.

The more consistent a fund's performance has been, the more likely it is that it will continue to provide superior performance in its category. This means fewer portfolio upgrades will be required, hence, the fewer transaction costs (if any) need be incurred.

Lower Risk

Second, we are going to set our risk standards to identify funds with below-average risk as measured by the Morningstar Risk ratings, which measures the downside risks of investing.

The lower the downside risks, the greater the time and the opportunity to get out of the way of a declining market or to withstand occasional corrections. This means that you need face less decline in asset value. Of course, selecting the asset categories carefully can lessen the downside risks as well, especially if we choose assets that are rising in value.

Top Performance

Finally, we are going to set our performance standards high because the returns were high in 1993. Fully 521 funds (out of 3,434) earned more than 20 percent last year.

That's an awfully high standard, so I am setting the minimum performance for inclusion on our list at 15 percent. Last year, 869 funds were able to return 15 percent or more, and 243 of them were in my Donoghue's Direct-Marketed Mutual Fund Universe.

In future years, attractive returns are likely to be lower; however, for now it represents the top 29 percent of funds in my universe. High performance and low risk mean greater profits to protect you from the downside losses you might incur leaving an asset class.

The Preliminary Choices

Of the 840 funds in my universe, only 42 funds (5 percent of the list), could claim that they had earned more than 15 percent, been in the top 25 percent of their category for the last three years and the last year, and did so with below average risk (a Morningstar Risk rating of below 1.0).

That is a lot of carefully screened funds to choose from. Fully 31 of them earned over 20 percent, and 8 were able to earn over 35 percent, quite impressive for such high standards. Take a look at the list in Table 5.1.

Even if you limit your choices only to funds with long-term track records, this still gives you plenty of viable choices. What fascinates me is to see that Fidelity Investments manages half (21) of the 42 funds on the list. I am impressed with that track record of consistent performance (especially if you consider that only four of the funds are Fidelity Select Portfolios, nondiversified sector funds, which normally dominate the top-performers lists).

That kind of quality leadership reminds me very much of Robert Mondavi Napa Valley wines. Many wine connoisseurs start off drinking Mondavi dry wines and then go on to explore the dozens of other intriguing wines among the many boutique wineries. Once they have satisfied themselves that they have not missed any important alternative choices, they come back to the inescapable conclusion that, for consistent excellence, Mondavi Napa Valley wines win hands down.

TABLE 5.1
Donoghue's SuperStar Portfolio Candidates Long-Term Fund Screen

(Funds in Top 25 percent in investment objective for the past 1 and 3 years to 12/31/93, with Morningstar Risk rating of less than 1.0, and 1993 total return of 15.00 percent or greater)

Rank	Fund Name	Investment Objective	1993 Total Return (%)	Mstar Risk (3-Year)
1	*Fidelity Emerging Markets	Foreign	81.76	0.54
2	T. Rowe Price New Asia	Pacific	78.76	0.83
3	*Lexington Worldwide Emerging	Foreign	63.37	0.67
4	*Warburg, Pincus Int'l Eq. Comm.	Foreign	51.26	0.91
5	American Heritage	Aggr. Growth	41.39	0.94
6	Fidelity Sel. Broadcast & Med.	Sp. Unaligned	38.02	0.83
7	Invesco Strat. Leisure	Sp. Unaligned	35.71	0.74
8	Fidelity Sel. Automotive	Sp. Unaligned	35.37	0.54
9	Fidelity Sel. Telecommun.	Sp. Util.	29.65	0.74
10	SteinRoe Capital Opport.	Aggr. Growth	27.52	0.94
11	*Fidelity Sel. Home Finance	Sp. Financ.	27.26	0.94
12	*Bull & Bear Global Income	Worldwide Bond	24.95	0.20
13	Fidelity Magellan	Growth	24.66	0.65
14	Fidelity Blue Chip Growth	Growth	24.50	0.73
15	Fidelity Capital & Income	Corp. Hi Yld.	24.19	0.05
16	First Eagle Fund of America	Growth	23.85	0.69
17	*Berger 101	Growth-Inc.	23.57	0.70
18	*Fidelity Asset Manager	Asset Alloc.	23.29	0.29
19	*Fidelity Value	Growth	22.94	0.58
20	*Mutual Beacon	Growth-Inc.	22.93	0.38
21	Strong Total Return	Growth-Inc.	22.54	0.91
22	*Fidelity Retirement Growth	Growth	22.13	0.72
23	*Founders Balanced	Balanced	21.85	0.57
24	*Fidelity Puritan	Balanced	21.45	0.57
25	Fidelity Contrafund	Growth	21.43	0.65
26	*Fidelity Equity-Income	Equity-Inc.	21.31	0.49
27	*Fidelity Global Bond	Worldwide Bond	21.28	0.43
28	Thomson Equity-Income B	Equity-Inc.	21.23	0.51
29	Invesco Strat. Utilities	Sp. Util.	21.21	0.52
30	Strong Opportunity	Growth	21.19	0.80
31	*SteinRoe Special	Growth	20.42	0.76
32	Fidelity Growth & Income	Growth-Inc.	19.53	0.62
33	Fidelity Balanced	Balanced	19.27	0.40
34	Fidelity Trend	Growth	19.15	0.92
35	*Fidelity Equity-Income II	Equity-Inc.	18.89	0.34
36	Fidelity Convertible Secs	Convert. Bond	17.79	0.61
37	*Strong Income Corp.	General	16.81	0.66
38	*Invesco Industrial Income	Equity-Inc.	16.69	0.63
39	American AAdvantage Equity	Growth-Inc.	16.11	0.66
40	Evergreen Foundation	Balanced	15.71	0.61
41	Fidelity Invest. Grade Bond	Corp. General	15.59	0.71
42	Janus Flexible Income	Income	15.56	0.08

*Also meets Short-Term Fund Screen Criteria.
Source: Morningstar Mutual Funds Inc./The Donoghue Group

Any of the other wineries can produce a better wine in any given year, but not in every given year. To me, Fidelity Investments funds have a lot in common with Robert Mondavi wines.

Coming back to mutual funds, the question you have to ask is, "What about the excellent funds like Oakmark Fund, which have opened in the last three years? Am I overlooking a lot of excellent funds?"

This first, long-term perspective demonstrates that long-term, lower-risk, consistent top performance is readily available. However, when you are deciding on investments that actually go into your portfolio, you want to know which are the right asset classes **now**.

DONOGHUE'S MUTUAL FUND SUPERSTARS FINALISTS

For short-term fund screens I am going to set our standards a bit lower to include many popular funds that are among the top 30 percent of funds in their investment objective. To pare down the list further, I require that they be in the top 30 percent for three recent periods: the past 3, 6, and 12 months.

We cannot use the Morningstar Risk ratings to determine the most currently attractive funds for our short-term screen because they are calculated only for funds with a minimum three-year track record. However, as you will see, most of the funds that show up on our short-term finalists list *have* been around for more than three years and *do* have a Morningstar risk rating to help us in our selection.

Still, my screen identified 64 funds which earned over 15 percent for the year of 1993. Of course, that means we did eliminate funds that were new this year and had less than a one-year track record, but you have to set some minimum standards, don't you?

What happened? Only 14 Fidelity funds make the cut this time. Is Fidelity forgetting how to introduce excellent new funds? Sorry, Fidelity. Just kidding.

THE TOP PERFORMERS ARE NOT NECESSARILY RISKIER INVESTMENTS

The most likely risk on the horizon appears to be a domestic (U.S.) stock market correction that might be triggered by rising domestic interest rates. If that is your sole concern, you should look to invest in international stock and gold or precious metals funds because none of those are highly correlated with the

TABLE 5.2
Donoghue's Mutual Fund SuperStars Finalists Short-Term Fund Screen

(Direct-marketed funds with at least a one-year track record of earnings over 15 percent in 1993, performance in the top 30 percent of their investment objective for the past three, six, and twelve months ended 12/31/93, ranked in the past three months' performance to 12/31/93)

Rank	Fund Name	Investment Objective	3-Month Total Return (%)	1993 Total Return (%)	Mstar Risk (3-Year)
1	Fidelity Emerging Markets	Foreign	39.73	81.76	0.54
2	Lexington Worldwide Emerging	Foreign	31.81	63.37	0.67
3	United Svcs. Gold Shares	Sp. Mtls.	31.67	123.92	4.27
4	Vanguard Spec. Gold & Prec.	Sp. Mtls.	31.20	93.36	2.17
5	Fidelity Sel. Prec. Metals	Sp. Mtls.	30.88	111.64	2.40
6	Montgomery Emerg. Mkts.	Foreign	29.14	58.66	NA
7	Scudder Latin America	Foreign	26.98	74.32	NA
8	Strong International Stock	Foreign	18.70	47.75	NA
9	Sit International Growth	Foreign	18.57	48.37	NA
10	Warburg, Pincus Int'l Eq. Comm.	Foreign	17.28	51.26	0.91
11	Oakmark International	Foreign	15.21	53.58	NA
12	BB&K International Equity	World	15.19	37.84	1.23
13	T. Rowe Price Intl Discovery	Foreign	15.07	49.85	1.12
14	Strong Discovery	Aggr. Growth	10.72	22.21	1.22
15	Evergreen Global Real Estate	Sp. R/E	10.18	51.42	1.12
16	Oakmark	Growth	9.54	30.50	NA
17	Blanchard Global Growth	Asset All.	8.63	24.46	0.70
18	Fidelity Asset Manager: Growth	Asset All.	7.97	26.32	NA
19	SAFECO Growth	Small Co.	7.33	22.19	1.86
20	Fidelity Sel. Indust. Equip.	Sp. Tech	7.25	43.32	0.83
21	Fidelity Asset Manager	Asset All.	7.17	23.29	0.29
22	T. Rowe Price Growth Stock	Growth	6.96	15.56	0.78
23	Fremont Global	Asset All.	6.92	19.60	0.44
24	Fidelity Low-Priced Stock	Small Co.	6.92	20.21	0.60
25	T. Rowe Price Spectrum Growth	Growth	6.53	20.98	0.59
26	Kemper Invmt Diver Inc. Prem.	Corp. HiYld.	6.31	21.11	NA
27	T. Rowe Price Mid-Cap. Growth	Growth	6.24	26.24	NA
28	Berger 101	Growth-Inc.	6.18	23.57	0.70
29	Northeast Investors	Corp. HiYld.	6.09	23.60	0.18
30	Fidelity Retirement Growth	Growth	5.95	22.13	0.72
31	Fidelity Sel. Brokerage& Inv.	Sp. Financ.	5.92	49.30	1.07
32	SAFECO Equity	Growth-Inc.	5.68	30.91	1.02
33	Crabbe Huson Asset Alloc.	Asset All.	5.38	18.21	0.42
34	T. Rowe Price New Horizons	Small Co.	5.33	22.01	1.28
35	Fidelity Global Bond	World Bond	5.24	21.28	0.43
36	Invesco Growth	Growth	5.10	19.02	0.92
37	Neuberger & Berman Sel. Sectors	Growth	5.04	16.33	0.79

Rank	Fund Name	Investment Objective	3-Month Total Return (%)	1993 Total Return (%)	Mstar Risk (3-Year)
38	Olympic Equity-Income	Equity-Inc.	5.04	15.76	0.62
39	Legg Mason Special Invstmt.	Small Co.	4.95	24.13	0.80
40	SteinRoe Capital Opport.	Aggr. Growth	4.93	27.52	0.94
41	Janus Enterprise	Growth	4.90	15.64	NA
42	Fidelity Value	Growth	4.64	22.94	0.58
43	PBHG Growth	Small Co.	4.16	46.57	1.52
44	20th Century Giftrust Inv.	Small Co.	4.15	31.41	1.76
45	Dreyfus Growth & Income	Growth-Inc.	4.09	18.59	NA
46	SteinRoe Special	Growth	4.02	20.42	0.76
47	USAA Investment Cornerstone	Asset All.	3.98	23.73	0.66
48	Vanguard/PRIMECAP	Growth	3.92	18.03	1.08
49	Mutual Beacon	Growth-Inc.	3.86	22.93	0.38
50	Bull & Bear Global Income	World Bond	3.83	24.95	0.20
51	Scudder Capital Growth	Growth	3.67	20.07	1.08
52	Homestead Value	Growth-Inc.	3.65	18.83	0.57
53	Weitz Value	Growth	3.46	19.98	0.43
54	Fidelity Equity-Income	Equity-Inc.	3.37	21.31	0.49
55	Founders Balanced	Balanced	3.33	21.85	0.57
56	Invesco Industrial Income	Equity-Inc.	3.32	16.69	0.63
57	SBSF	Growth-Inc.	3.32	20.41	0.49
58	Fidelity Puritan	Balanced	3.26	21.45	0.57
59	Loomis Sayles Bond	Corp. Bond	3.20	22.22	NA
60	Salomon Brothers Investors	Growth-Inc.	3.14	15.19	0.71
61	Fidelity Equity-Income II	Equity-Inc.	2.60	18.89	0.34
62	Strong Income	Corp. Bond	1.96	16.81	0.66
63	Fidelity Invest. Grade Bond	Corp. Bond	0.59	15.59	0.71
64	Fidelity Sel. Home Finance	Sp. Financ.	−0.73	27.26	0.94

Source: Morningstar Mutual Funds Inc./The Donoghue Group

domestic stock market. This gives your portfolio diversification a big positive boost. While these funds have their own unique risks, their presence does make your portfolio more resistant to a domestic correction.

Another encouraging event occurred in early 1994 in Southeast Asia. In spite of severe corrections and refreshing recoveries, the average Pacific stock fund still made 4.29 percent in January 1994. These markets were incredibly resilient.

Skeptics may still want to think that high return means high risk, but the fund screens disprove that contention and demonstrate that there are lower-risk, high yield, consistently top-performing mutual funds out there. There are more than enough to build a very powerful, well-diversified asset allocation portfolio—especially if you are willing to add a few of the newer non-risk-rated funds to your portfolio when an acceptable alternative is not available.

Well, folks, we have plenty of excellent funds to choose from. Let's save this impressive list and bring it back in Chapter 12 when we assemble our model portfolio. By then we will have reviewed all nine of the fund sub-universes, decided on the asset classes we want in our portfolio, and will be ready to put it all together. At that time we will bring out our SuperStar Portfolio Finalists and see which make the cut and end up in Donoghue's Mutual Fund SuperStar Portfolio.

For now, let's think through the basic philosophy of our investment strategy. If we can agree on the principles or agree to disagree (it's YOUR money, remember!), we can get down to business.

STARTING WITH THE BASICS

The basic principles of Donoghue's Mutual Fund SuperStars philosophy are as follows, all other things being equal:

The Purpose of Investing Is to Produce the Most Attractive Total Returns

When funds are ranked on performance, "The guy who manages the fund at the TOP of the list has the RIGHT strategy—because it worked. The guy at the bottom has the WRONG strategy—because it didn't work." So, recent performance, say within the past year (which says much more about probable future performance than longer-term track records), or in recent years, is an important factor.

Looking at longer-term performance in terms of total returns tells you more about the past years' market opportunities rather than the fund's management skills. Therefore, we look at the funds' rank within their investment objective or peer group for performance potential. Our choice of asset classes will precede our fund selection process, anyway. The asset allocation is always the more important investment decision.

In addition, looking solely at funds with long-term, five- and ten-year track records encourages you to look at funds whose prospectus may well be significantly out of tune with the marketplace. For example, a domestic stock fund not allowed to diversify into foreign stocks has a serious problem with its competitive stance these days. Yet, to change that portfolio restriction would require an awkward and costly shareholder vote.

It was probably true that long ago when the prospectus was written it was logistically imprudent and uncommon to invest in foreign securities. A lot of progress has occurred in the meantime. It certainly is feasible for professionals to invest abroad today.

Looking at long-term track records can be a bit deceptive. A fund that made an excellent track record a decade ago, was ordinary in recent years, and has compounded its old performance over the years since, looks good but could be quite ordinary.

Another trap is a poorly performing fund that has been merged with a better performing fund or, even worse, where a good fund is merged into a bad one. The merger can hide a bad track record or, in the second case, hide a good track record. For these reasons, long-term track records may not be indicative of future SuperStar (top of the line) performance; they may not even be indicative of poor future performance.

Fidelity Magellan, a seasoned fund with an excellent long-term track record, is a good exception to the rule and, more often than not, continues to outpace its younger peers and confound the critics. If you notice, Fidelity Magellan is No. 13 on our long-term screen and nowhere to be seen on our short-term screen. But that old $30 billion elephant sure can dance with the youngsters once in a while!

An Equally Important Part of Investing Is to Produce Attractive Total Returns at *Acceptable Risks*

Investors are well served while striving to attain their investment goals if they can earn top-level performance at acceptable risk levels. Simply said, while it is often true that high total-return investments often tend to come with higher risk, it is the exceptions that make SuperStar funds the most desirable investments for the greatest number of investors.

It is a mark of a true investment genius to design and manage such a fund, and few can hope to achieve such goals. This fact often makes a fund dependent, at least in the short term, on its manager, and that is a factor to watch. Should a fund change managers and try to rest on its laurels, it could drop off the pace.

I would be quite suspicious of the ability of anyone else to manage American Heritage other than Heiko Thieme, the Oakmark Fund other than Robert Sanborn, or Oakmark International other than David Herro. These funds have the unique stamp of their managers.

Watching these managers is important. Watching the managers of Twentieth Century Ultra, a committee-run fund that only buys mid-cap growth stocks and buys them with great skill is not a major issue. Anyone can follow a successful formula, and even if that person were not supremely skilled, it would not affect the fund's performance for years.

Investors are most often *not* speculators. They are simply responsible individuals trying to preserve, build, and increase their wealth and financial security to meet their legitimate lifestyle needs.

Even Superman Achilles Had to Watch His Heels.   So, top-performing SuperStar funds with low risk relative to their "Achilles' heels" are superior candidates for your investment portfolios. What are mutual fund "Achilles' heels"? The greatest sources of investment risk, see Table 5.3.

Watching for Achilles' Heels.   If you are worried about a domestic stock market correction coming, then you have to watch out for funds that are highly correlated with the S&P 500. That means if they have *betas* over 1.0, they are riskier than the stock market. Low betas mean less risk.

Morningstar risk ratings are similar, but they measure only the downside risk. As with betas, the ratings over 1.0 mean greater downside risk than the average for funds in their investment objective. That objective could, however, have a higher or

TABLE 5.3
Mutual Funds and Their "Achilles' Heels"

Type of Fund	"Achilles' Heels" (Examples)	Measures of Risk or Trends
Bond	Rising Int. Rates	Duration Interest rate trends
Domestic Stock	Market correction	Beta Morningstar Risk
	Rising Int. Rates	Interest rate trends
International Stock	Rising U.S. Dollar	Currency tables
	Country risks	Watch News on Japan, Latin America and Southeast Asia
	Market trends	Watch News
Money Funds	High Expenses	Net Yield
Junk Bonds	Default rates	Portfolio Ratings

lower beta than another investment objective group. If you are effective in choosing asset classes, you can reduce risk by avoiding the asset class entirely when the risk/reward ratio is uncomfortably high. For example, rising interest rates would give me discomfort about investing in domestic stocks or bonds.

The fact that gold and international stocks are not highly correlated with the domestic stock market does not mean that they will not decline if we have a domestic correction. It does mean, however, that they are likely to rebound more robustly after the correction as their issues, as opposed to issues affecting domestic stocks, are reinterpreted as positive reasons for recovering prices.

When the value of the dollar in foreign currencies is rising or the dollar is strengthening, it is usually unwise to invest in foreign currencies. That might mean caution for investments in Europe and Japan, where currency risk is a major concern, but less worry when investing in less developed emerging markets like Southeast Asia and Latin America, where currency risks are much lower.

Similarly, it is wise to watch default rates when investing in junk bond funds and avoid money funds where high fund expenses are cutting into already low money fund returns.

Oakmark: Creative (and Very Profitable) Paranoia. "Creative paranoia" is my term for what motivates someone who is always watching for an Achilles' heel in his portfolio. It's meant as a strong compliment to the fund's managers.

In spite of the fact that emerging markets funds' recent performance pushed Oakmark International further down the top-performer lists, it's still one of my favorite funds and has performed exceptionally well. It was the No. 1 top-performing diversified (non-emerging market) international stock fund for 1993, with an outstanding 53.58 percent performance.

The reason for such success is due in part to the portfolio manager's lack of success in finding acceptable low-priced investment in the huge Japanese market. David Herro, the manager, is a value-oriented investor who simply could not find good value in Japanese stocks and thus avoided that volatile market when it had its major correction in 1993.

His brother/sister fund, Oakmark Fund managed by Robert Sanborn (which survived the short-term fund screen), is an excellent U.S. stock fund that has been managed to provide a high performance with a low beta. This fund has purposely built a high-yield portfolio of stocks whose prices on average do not move in concert with the stock market. If we have a market correction in the United States, investors should expect that this fund would lose less than the stock market.

These managers understand the idea of watching their portfolio's Achilles' heels.

Equally Important Is Consistent, Reliable, Lower-Risk, Top Performance Relative to the Fund's Peers

It is one thing to provide attractive returns at acceptable risks. It is yet another to do so consistently and still rank high among the funds with a common investment objective.

Longer-term total-return track records can be deceptive in identifying SuperStar funds (those with all three characteristics: lower risk, high returns, and impressive consistency). As I noted above, I have chosen to include on most of this book's tables the Morningstar *rank within objective* (the lower the number the better) where available and Morningstar Risk rating (where the fund has a three-year track record).

A FINAL COMMENT

In this chapter, we have reviewed both long-term and short-term fund screens to identify funds that are likely to be in the running to be Mutual Fund SuperStar finalists. We came up with a viable list of 64, which are still to be subjected to our final screen.

In the next few chapters, we are going to continue to build our investment tool kit, getting the most out of the convenient new discount brokers' mutual fund marketplace services. Then we will search through the full mutual fund marketplace, introducing ourselves to every asset class and investment objective and finally circling in on building our own investment portfolios.

In the future, when you go to update this whole process, you can go right to the heart of the strategy—analyzing the top-performing asset classes and building your portfolio—with the comforting knowledge that you have not missed or overlooked any fund that might be a bit better or more appropriate as you build your SuperStar Portfolio.

CHAPTER 6

Why Should You Use a Discount Broker to Buy No-Loads?

Because It Can Be Cheaper Than Buying Direct

One of the greatest innovations in no-load mutual fund investing is low- or no-cost, single-statement, multiple-fund-family mutual fund accounts. They are offered by a select group of discount brokers with vision.

In effect, these discount brokers have taken the mutual fund family concept one giant step further and created *extended* mutual fund families so you can conveniently and practically "Invest with the best, and forget about the rest." No longer are you restricted to the funds offered by a single fund family, indeed, hundreds of no-load funds are in your extended fund family.

DISCOUNT BROKERS—THE "GOOD GUYS"

By now, I am sure that I have convinced you to avoid even the sight of a stockbroker. Well, here comes the exception that proves the rule: discount brokers that offer extended fund families.

You see, discount brokers have much in common with direct-marketed mutual funds. Basically, they both supply investment services that are designed to be bought rather than sold.

In this case, discount brokers are offering a service that can greatly simplify your record-keeping needs and also offering you access to hundreds of mutual funds in their "extended" family. It can actually cost you less to buy mutual funds this way than buying them directly.

THREE WAYS TO MANAGE A PORTFOLIO OF NO-LOAD MUTUAL FUNDS

As an investor, you can manage your portfolio in one of three ways:

▶   You can invest in each fund directly.

▶   You can manage your no-load portfolio in a single account and pay a discount broker low transaction fees.

▶   You can manage your no-load portfolio in a single account and pay no transaction costs.

Investing in a single no-load mutual fund is actually fairly simple: Call the fund's toll-free 800 number, request a prospectus by mail, open the envelope, fill out the application (with help from a customer service representative over that same toll-free 800 number, if you desire), write a check, and mail it to the fund family. There will be no sales charges and probably very few fees (for IRAs, wire transfer, checks, etc.). Investing is easy.

To establish a portfolio of mutual funds, you will follow these steps for each fund family you open an account with. The problems you will encounter in managing and trading a portfolio of no-load funds are more complex and surprisingly numerous:

▶   You will have to wait for a prospectus from each new fund you choose before you invest. (This could add three to seven days to your investment process.)

▶ You could encounter difficulty and time delays transferring money from one custodian to another in your tax-sheltered retirement plans such as IRAs. IRA transfers generally will take two to four weeks, and in some cases, as long as three months.

▶ Upon liquidation, even for taxable accounts, you again have a time delay. Your fund will process your redemption request promptly, but then you have to wait for delivery via the postal system—another three to seven days. Your alternative is to have the mutual fund send your cash directly to your bank by a wire transfer, for which your bank could charge you as much as $15 or more.

▶ You will be inundated with mail from each fund: monthly statements, proxy statements, advertising materials, and so on. (Don't worry about the fund selling your name to others. Your privacy is protected by the fact that the list of shareholders is a valuable asset of the fund that is seldom shared with others and certainly not rented to strangers.)

▶ Your dividends and capital gains distributions will probably arrive by mail (if you don't ask to have them reinvested automatically), meaning you will lose interest on your money while it is in the mail.

▶ You will lose additional time between investments and miss out on profitable opportunities while your money is traveling through our postal system.

▶ Perhaps most important, you or your accountant will spend hours sorting through your paperwork preparing your tax return because you will receive a Form 1099-DIV from each fund you own.

I have overdramatized the problems of this choice for a purpose—I have a better idea. Who wants to be limited to a single fund family's mutual funds when you can just as easily have hundreds of excellent choices? Why would you want to receive dozens of monthly statements and dozens of annual Forms 1099-DIV to give to your tax preparer when you could have a single annual statement and a single consolidated Form 1099-DIV regardless of how many different funds you own? The accounting and tax preparer savings alone are worth it.

Several discount brokers offer no-load mutual fund trading services: Charles Schwab & Co.'s Mutual Fund Marketplace® and Fidelity Brokerage's FundsNetwork® are the most attractive and have the broadest choice of top-performing funds. Until about a year ago, these services usually were provided on a transaction-fee basis, but now there are no transaction fees for many mutual funds. In addition, Jack White & Co., Waterhouse Securities, and Muriel Seibert & Co. offer similar programs.

INVESTMENT PLATFORMS—YOUR LAUNCHING PAD TO PROFITS

The development of centralized, multiple-fund-family mutual fund buying and selling, all in one single account, at a discount brokerage firm means you can now consolidate all your mutual fund purchases and sales. I call this revolutionary new service a mutual fund launching pad. Why a launching pad? Because a launching pad is where a rocket takes off, where a vehicle bound for the stars starts its journey, and where a mutual fund investor can turbocharge a portfolio for greater profits.

Developing a portfolio of no-load mutual funds can become complicated. As you learn to "invest in the best, and forget about the rest," you realize that no single fund family offers the best performing funds in every asset category you desire and that moving money between families can be expensive and cumbersome. As you become a more sophisticated investor, you yearn for instantaneous execution of your trades when you are upgrading your portfolio (an especially rewarding effort in your tax-sheltered retirement savings). Equally important, you may want to invest in more than just mutual funds. You may want to invest in stocks and bonds directly, buy federally insured CDs, borrow cheaply on margin (a cheap way to pay down your credit cards), write checks on your investment account, and generally use the services available only through a brokerage account.

ONE-STOP MUTUAL FUND SHOPPING IS THE RIGHT CHANGE FOR YOU

Let's look at what a mutual fund marketplace does for you:

Centralized Buying and Selling.   Imagine walking into a shopping mall with dozens of different stores. As you look down the aisle you see Fidelity, Vanguard, T. Rowe Price, Twentieth Century, Scudder, Janus, and dozens of other mutual fund companies all waiting for your business. Imagine how easy it would be to buy and sell no-load mutual funds in that shopping mall of mutual funds! Well, the shopping mall I just described already exists. You can choose from a long list of hundreds of mutual funds, as many as 900 from dozens of fund families. With one single phone call to your centralized account, you can buy a fund from, Twentieth Century, for example, and sell a fund from Dreyfus. While the list varies slightly from broker to broker, the shopping mall concept is the same.

Consolidated Statements.   Each month, your discount broker will send you one statement, which itemizes all the activity in your account, summarizes all the transactions, and gives you the total value of your entire portfolio. At a glance, you can tell if you made money or lost money in the last month, see all the transactions you made, have all your free credit balances automatically swept into an interest-bearing money market account, and have all fund holdings summarized in one easy-to-read statement.

We are talking *easy* here! You will have no more file folders of dozens of different mutual fund statements to keep track of. All the mountains of paperwork you used to get are now centralized in one common statement. Fidelity even offers an annual cost basis statement that calculates your average gain or loss on any mutual fund redemptions.

Buy and Sell with a Phone Call.   The old pony express system of mailing your investment funds meant that you had no control over the day that your money was invested in a fund. Your money was invested the day it arrived at the fund, this is timing only the postal system controls. With a mutual fund marketplace, you can place a buy or sell order that will be executed at the end of that trading day (each discount broker has different cutoff times for same-day execution). In fact, Fidelity allows you to trade mutual funds via a touch tone telephone through its TouchTone Trader service.

Now you can control the day that your money gets invested or liquidated. You'll quickly know what price you paid as well. All you have to do is look at the next day's paper for the previous day's closing price to know the price you bought or sold at. Of course, a written confirmation is sent with any transaction.

Consolidated 1099-DIV.   At the end of each year, you will get one Form 1099-DIV that summarizes all of your capital gains and dividend income from all of your mutual fund holdings. Either you or your tax preparer can see your entire year's taxable activity at a glance. This by itself should save you a couple of hours of your accountant's billing time.

Automatic Money Fund Sweep.   By sweep, I mean that any free credit balances you acquire, whether from new money you send in, dividends that are declared, or proceeds from sales, are automatically transferred or swept into an interest-bearing money fund account. This insures that your money is always earning interest, regardless of how it is deployed. Should you sell out a fund position without reinvesting it, those dollars will automatically be transferred into your brokerage firm money market account and earn daily dividends up until the time that you either invest in a fund or write a check.

Instant Access to Funds.   The old method required you to wait for a check to be delivered by mail. A mutual fund marketplace allows you to have the sale proceeds immediately transferred into a money fund, from which you can write a check or buy a different mutual fund. You don't get better liquidity than that. This immediate accessibility does two things for you. One, you can have your money if you need it. Schwab will even have a redemption check at your local Schwab branch the very next business day if you need the cash fast! Two, and more important, you can redeploy your money to another profitable fund in a moment's notice. I don't need to tell you how fast the markets can move. How would you have liked your money to be stuck in the postal system jungle during the 1987 stock market crash? The ability to move quickly is becoming a mandate for success in the 1990s.

Extended Trading Hours.   Discount brokers stay open longer than almost all fund families. Schwab and Fidelity stay open 24 hours a day. This gives you extra flexibility to conduct your business when it is convenient for you, not just during the mutual fund family's business hours. In fact, Schwab and Fidelity even give you the opportunity to trade with your personal computer. Mutual fund quotes and trading are now available using your touch tone telephone via Schwab's Telebroker™. The bottom line is that discount brokers are more flexible in their hours of operation than a mutual fund company.

Easier Telephone Access.   I heard hundreds of investors tell me they couldn't get through to their broker the day of the 1987 crash. The telephone volume was so heavy that many investors encountered nothing but busy signals all day and even into the night. Discouraged because they could neither buy nor sell, many investors simply had to sit on the sidelines, stuck with losses they couldn't stem and watching opportunities evaporate because they couldn't act. Discount brokerage firms are designed to handle heavy volume and generally have more telephone lines than a mutual fund ever thought of having. Although not guaranteed, your chances of getting through to a discount broker in times of heavy volume are much higher than with a mutual fund company. Schwab's Telebroker makes it even easier.

Local Branch Offices. Fidelity and Schwab have hundreds of local branches nationally to help you in understanding your statements and to answer other questions in person or pick up a redemption check the next business day.

SOUNDS EXPENSIVE. IS IT?

The quick answer is: No. The more detailed answer is: It depends. First, you have to understand that there are two levels of pricing in the mutual fund marketplace. The first level levies very modest fees for both buying and selling. You pay a small transaction fee, which can be as low as $27 at Jack White, for each buy or sell transaction. The fee varies from each brokerage house and depends upon the size of your investment, but in all cases the fee is reasonable and not a significant hurdle if you are investing $25,000 or more at a time.

These transaction fees are the price you pay for the convenience and efficiencies of a centralized mutual fund marketplace. You know me, I have always been sensitive to expenses—especially when they go to commissioned salespeople—but what I really want for my money is value. As long as I get value for what I pay, I am satisfied and don't mind spending a few bucks. The mutual fund marketplaces certainly provide value for the money you spend. After all, if price were the only thing that mattered, we'd all drive Volkswagens.

SOME FUNDS PAY YOUR TRANSACTION COSTS

The second level of pricing is something you will really like because at this level, there is no charge whatsoever to you! Schwab's Mutual Fund OneSource™ program was the first no-transaction-fee program (with Jack White & Co. nipping at its heels). In July of 1993, they were joined by Fidelity's FundsNetwork program, and the no-transaction-fee program arrived in a big way.

With what Schwab, Fidelity, and I call *no-transaction-fee* or NTF funds, you can buy and sell specific funds at no cost to you. That's right—no charge! "How can there be no charge?" you ask. Simple, instead of you—the consumer—paying a transaction fee for the service, the discount brokers receive a payment from the fund companies for every dollar that is placed through the NTF service. Somebody does pay the discount broker, but with NTF funds it isn't you; it's the mutual fund company.

Fund companies pay the discount broker at least a 25 basis point fee on every dollar that the discount broker places through the NTF program. So, if you invest $25,000 in the Berger 100 fund through a discount broker, Berger Associates will send the discount broker a check for a little over $5 each month ($62.50 annually) that your money remains in the Berger 100 fund. While this may not sound like a lot of money, if you consider 25 basis points on several billions of dollars, it really begins to add up.

TO ANSWER YOU SKEPTICS RIGHT UP FRONT

I know you are saying to yourself, "Okay, I'm not dumb. Where are the hidden charges? This has got to cost me more money somehow, doesn't it?" The answer is: "Not really!" You see, the mutual fund family pays the discount broker at least 25 basis points (0.25 percent) a year on the assets it invested in its funds through the NTF program. Then the fund family charges the fund the same amount it would have charged the fund if you had invested directly. That might amount to 10 to 15 basis points. The fund's managers then pay the rest of the fee themselves, at no additional cost to the investors. Yes, I said *no additional cost to investors*. Don't feel sorry for the fund managers, they are doing fine. In fact, they are grossly profitable. So, now you know that investing in a fund indirectly through a discount broker's NTF program costs no more than investing in a fund directly.

IT'S A GOOD DEAL FOR ALL PARTIES

This is good business for everybody. You, the customer, get to invest in a wide variety of no-load mutual funds at no cost. The fund company makes out because they get a new investor without the hassles and costs of acquiring one, and the discount broker gets a small but very profitable fee for placing the business.

The advantages to the mutual fund company are substantial. When you invest directly with a fund, the company has to accept your 800 phone call, which costs money. They have to send you a prospectus in the mail, which costs money. They have to send you a statement at least quarterly, which costs money. They have to pay a transfer agent and custodian to monitor and track your account, which costs money. All their expenses are borne by the discount broker when you buy a fund through the NTF service. In effect, you transfer the back office expenses of maintaining you as a shareholder from the fund company to the discount broker by using a NTF service.

WHY AREN'T ALL FUNDS NTF?

I wish they were, but two things prevent this. First, the discount brokers are introducing new computer technology that has never been used before. It makes sense for them to go slowly and not make any mistakes. They are adding new funds as they are able to handle the back office requirements of this side of their business. Believe me, lots of funds would love to participate in the NTF programs but can't get in for the time being. I fully expect the number of funds to expand dramatically in the near future as the technology catches up with the demand. Almost all the fund families may soon participate in a discount broker's NTF program.

Two, some fund families don't want to share their lucrative management fees with the discount brokers. They think the minimum 25 to 35 basis point fee charged by the discount brokers is too high, especially for smaller fund families. In my opinion, these fund families are missing the boat. All it will take is some pressure from their shareholders to change their minds. Sooner or later, this group will have no choice but to participate or risk losing market share because of their stubborn greed.

Finally, there will always be some unique funds—like the Vanguard group of funds—that simply cannot afford to pay the NTF fees. Vanguard's *total* management fee is 25 basis points, since it works on a cost-plus basis. There are advantages in being the low-cost provider (that strategy is a good one for bond funds and money funds but not of much value for stock funds) but it does not leave enough room for a partner like a discount broker.

NTF VERSUS NON-NTF FUNDS

Your initial reaction might be to invest only in NTF funds and ignore any funds that have low-loads or charge a transaction fee.

You could do that, but you might be ignoring some great funds by doing so. Not all funds are NTF or will be NTF, although many are.

I'll describe in greater detail the nuances of discount brokers' programs in Chapter 7, but the reality is that there are about three times as many transaction-fee funds as there are NTF funds. Limiting yourself to NTF funds only means that you are ignoring a wide universe of otherwise excellent mutual funds. The transaction fee funds are still a bargain. The ability to make trades over the telephone without the postal delays alone is worth a transaction fee. The next time you want to get out of the way of a market slide ask yourself if the time lost was worth the few dollars saved.

My advice is simply to buy the best funds, regardless of whether or not they are NTF funds. Invest in the best fund using your mutual fund marketplace launching pad, and regard the NTF funds as a bonus when you use them. After all, the absence or presence of a small transaction fee is not going to determine the success of a mutual fund position. You will forget about transaction fees when you profit. The point today is that you need to include both NTF funds and non-NTF funds in your portfolio to be a SuperStar investor.

START YOUR ENGINES, GET READY TO TAKE OFF

Your SuperStar launching pad is ready for takeoff! A new world of flexibility awaits you. Never again will you have to wait for the postal service or have your money sit idle unnecessarily. You have the power to control your financial destiny. Hundreds of the world's best money managers are at your disposal with a single phone call.

Never before has investing in the best and forgetting about the rest been so easy. Never before have there been so few excuses to resist technology and change with the times. Never before has there been such an efficient means to facilitate your financial freedom. In the next chapter, I'll go over the nuts and bolts details of how the major discount brokerage programs work and, even more important, how to maximize the benefits of each mutual fund marketplace.

CHAPTER

7

Which Discount Broker Is Right for You?

Making the Right Choice(s) Can Add Extra Investment Power

In Chapter 6, I discussed the many advantages of using a discount broker's mutual fund marketplace as your launching pad for greater profits. However, each discount broker offers slightly different menus of services, fund choices, and restrictions on the frequency of trading. Your task is to evaluate each discount broker's overall program for compatibility with your investment needs. One discount broker may be well suited for you but a poor choice for someone else.

Currently, 13 discount brokers offer a mutual fund marketplace, but only five of them offer no-transaction-fee (NTF) fund services. Of those five, only three (Schwab, Fidelity, and Jack White) are significant players. By significant players, I mean that they offer a large enough menu of both no-transaction-fee funds (over 200) and transaction-fee funds. I will restrict my reviews to these three firms. The other two NTF players (Waterhouse Securities and Muriel Siebert) have limited programs and may be worth checking out. I am certain that there will be other discount brokers joining them.

Each fund family has slightly different restrictions on trading frequency. The question of which discount broker is the best for you is also a function of how often you trade. For market timers and frequent traders, the Jack White program is the hands down winner. The only rule is that you hold a fund for at least 60 days, and the penalty for not holding 60 days is that you will have to pay the standard commission, which is a maximum of $50. Fidelity and Schwab, however, are much more restrictive.

So, your first screen should be based on your trading frequency. A great menu of no-transaction-fee funds won't do you any good if you end up paying thousands of dollars in commissions because you trade too frequently by the discount broker's standards. Market timers and active traders should use Jack White & Co. Asset allocators and moderate or infrequent traders should review all three and base their decisions on the menu of no-transaction-fee funds.

KEY DIFFERENCES TO LOOK FOR

There are four points that will help you decide on the discount broker that is best for you. These decision factors apply to all 13 discount brokers now offering a mutual funds marketplace.

1. *The Funds Menu.* Each discount brokerage firm has a different menu of mutual funds to choose from, both for NTF funds and funds where there is a transaction fee. In general, most firms offer twice as many transaction fee funds as they do NTF funds. You may first want to screen each discount broker for its menu of NTF funds, as you will want a choice of Super-Star funds and, where possible, you will want to stick with no-cost NTF funds. Having the funds you want available on a no-transaction-fee basis is a big plus, especially if you want to upgrade your portfolio from time to time.

Beyond the NTF funds, there will be an even larger menu of mutual funds available with low transaction fees. The Oakmark Fund, for example, was the best performing diversified domestic stock fund in the country in 1992. It was well worth paying a fee to invest in. The reason it is not NTF is that the fund is reaching a size where the manager may close it to new investments. Overlooking the Oakmark Fund just because you would have had to pay a small transaction fee would have caused you to miss some excellent profits.

Don't be penny-wise and pound foolish. Look at both the NTF and transaction fee menus. Having the funds you need available to meet your investment objectives is the most important consideration of all.

2.   *Trading Restrictions.* Each discount broker has different restrictions on how often you can trade NTF funds and still be allowed to stay in its program. It costs the discount broker money to process your NTF transaction, including mailing you a confirmation and prospectus, so the less you trade, the more money they make. Additionally, the participating funds don't like to see wild fluctuations in their asset base as that makes managing the portfolios more difficult.

Each discount broker has limits on how many short-term trades it will permit. The definition of a short-term trade varies from firm to firm, and the time period over which you are judged varies as well. You should review each discount broker's policies. Your trading frequency will greatly affect which broker is best for you.

Jack White's only trading restriction is that you hold a fund for at least 60 days. Schwab limits your trading to four short-term trades in a 12-month period. Schwab defines short-term trades as a round trip (buy and sell) transaction in less than 6 months. Fidelity is a little more complex. Its restrictions fall into two categories—Fidelity funds and all other funds. With non-Fidelity funds, the trading restrictions are exactly the same as with Charles Schwab, four short-term, round trip trades. With Fidelity funds, however, the restrictions vary from fund to fund.

3.   *Penalties for Trading Too Much.* Just as each discount broker has different rules on how frequently you can trade, the penalty for exceeding those trading rules differs, too. The discount brokers view your access to their NTF programs as a privilege, not a consumer right. Penalties range all the way from transaction fees being levied on future transactions to being banned from the program.

Jack White's, Charles Schwab's and Fidelity's penalty is that you have to start paying transaction fees (commissions) on your future mutual fund trades. Paying transaction fees in and by itself is not a bad deal, but as always, free is better than not free. If you want to participate in the NTF programs, you have to stick with the program.

4. *Transaction Fees.*   As you may also invest in mutual funds that charge transaction fees, you should pay close attention to the commission schedule each discount broker has for non-NTF funds. Remember, there are many more transaction fee funds than there are NTF funds, so fees will be an important consideration. Again, the fees will vary considerably from broker to broker. The specific fee structure for each of the three discount brokers is discussed next.

THE THREE CANDIDATES

There are over 500 funds in 64 no-load fund families currently participating in one or more of the most popular no-transaction-fee programs. I expect in the coming years that there will be several programs with dramatically wider ranges of fund choices. For now, however, your interest should be focused on Schwab and Fidelity.

The biggest advantage Fidelity FundsNetwork has over the other discount brokers is the ability to buy many of the highly popular low-load Fidelity funds (all but Fidelity Magellan, New Millennium, and Select Portfolios) on a no-load basis for retirement accounts. (Non-retirement accounts at Fidelity still pay the low loads.) This fact alone makes the Fidelity FundsNetwork a worthy candidate, especially for dedicated Fidelity fund investors.

Beyond that, each discount broker has different advantages and disadvantages that will be more or less important to you. Is there a clear winner in this mutual fund sweepstakes? No. Each discount broker's mutual fund marketplace is unique and worthy of your consideration. The following is a review of the pros and cons of the three major players in the mutual fund marketplaces.

CHARLES SCHWAB ONESOURCE™ (800-2-NO-LOAD)

Charles Schwab was the first to recognize the potential of a consolidated mutual fund portfolio management system. Charles Schwab, himself, deserves the credit, and we send along our thanks for his vision. His cutting-edge innovation is the reason we are even talking about this revolutionary management system.

The Funds Menu.   Charles Schwab & Co.'s mutual fund marketplace currently offers over 800 funds, 230 of which are in their OneSource™ NTF program. Schwab has no shortage of alliances with well regarded mutual funds. The choices are diverse and worthy candidates in all the Superstar subuniverses. The fund families included in the Schwab NTF program are:

BARON	LEXINGTON
BENHAM	MONTGOMERY
BERGER	NEUBERGER & BERMAN
CAPPIELLO RUSHMORE	OAKMARK
COHEN & STEERS	RUSHMORE
DREYFUS	SCHWAB
EVERGREEN	SKYLINE
FEDERATED	STEINROE
FOUNDERS	STRONG
IAI	TWENTIETH CENTURY
INVESCO	UNITED SERVICES
JANUS	WARBURG, PINCUS
WRIGHT EQUIFUNDS	KAUFMANN
YACKTMAN	

A complete listing of all the specific funds is available directly from Schwab. Current availability for fee and no-transaction-fee funds is indicated on my mutual fund listings in the back of this book.

Trading Restrictions.   Schwab currently allows you four short-term trades within a rolling 12-month period. Schwab defines a short-term trade as a buy and sell (round-trip) of the same fund within 6 months. As long as you hold a fund 6 months and a day, there are no trading restrictions whatsoever. Starting May 1, 1994, the review period will change to a calendar year, which will simplify things a bit. (The rolling 12-month period put the burden on you to keep tabs.) You still don't want to violate the trading restrictions. Don't forget, partial redemptions will also count as short-term trades.

Penalties for Trading Too Much.   If you violate Schwab's trading restrictions, your ability to trade on a no-transaction-fee basis will be revoked. You can still buy and sell NTF funds, but you will have to pay transaction fees. However, you can still trade transaction fee funds to your heart's content. Schwab gets a commission every time you trade, so they couldn't care less how many times you trade transaction-fee funds within reasonable limits.

Schwab does have an appeal process whereby you can appeal to the branch manager of the nearest Schwab office. That local manager has the authority to reinstate you to the NTF program. My research has shown that the local managers are usually very cooperative and for anything other than the most active day traders, reinstatement is fairly easy to get. Even if you don't get reinstated right away, you can very likely expect to be reinstated after a 12-month banishment.

Transaction Charges.   Although there are more than 200 NTF funds, there are also more than 600 transaction-fee funds. You pay a commission to buy and sell these 600 + funds based upon the dollar amount of your transaction. Schwab's commission schedule is:

Transaction Amount	Commission
$0–$15,000	0.6% of principal
$15,001–$100,000	0.6% of first $15,000 plus 0.2% on amounts over $15,000
$100,001 +	0.6% of first $15,000 plus 0.2% of amounts next $85,000 plus 0.02% on amounts over $100,001.

Schwab trades are subject to an overriding $29 transaction fee, so investors with small trades will find the fees prohibitive. Small investors may want to stick exclusively with NTF funds because of the $29 minimum commission.

Summary.   Charles Schwab has many outstanding fund families participating in its NTF program. The trading restrictions throw a kink into the plans of any fairly active trader, and beware of violating the short-term trading rules. Should you trade transaction-fee funds, the transaction fees can add up, especially if you trade frequently.

Donoghue Tips. You may want to open up more than one account at Schwab. The trading restrictions are per account, so it may be wise to set up a couple of different accounts (single, joint, IRA) to multiply your short-term trading opportunities. You also will want to concentrate your holdings into fewer funds than you may be accustomed to. Diversifying into dozens of different funds will increase the odds of violating the short-term trading rules.

All of this is academic if you are a long-term, buy-and-hold investor. Once you are comfortable with the rules, you will probably find that Schwab's Mutual Fund OneSource™ program will fit your needs to a "T."

FIDELITY FUNDS NETWORK (800-544-9697)

Fidelity has one great advantage that no other discount broker can offer—the ability to trade Fidelity funds (except Magellan, New Millennium, and Select funds) at no load in tax-qualified accounts, such as IRAs, 401(k)s, Keoghs, profit-sharing plan, and the like. Fidelity funds are available through the other discount brokers on a transaction fee basis, but you also have to pay Fidelity *entrance fee* loads on their low-load funds on top of that.

With Fidelity funds, you need to know about *fee tracking*, a service that helps you avoid unnecessary costs by giving you credit for the fees you have already paid. Essentially, you pay loads only on additional money you add to the program. For example, if you invest $10,000 in Fidelity Magellan and pay the 3 percent load, earn another $3,000 in profits, sell that position, and then buy another 3 percent load Fidelity fund, you will pay a 3 percent load only if you invest more than $13,000, and only then on the difference between $13,000 and the total amount invested.

Funds Menu. Fidelity currently offers 375 no-load funds from 35 different fund families. Some of the fund families overlap with the Charles Schwab program and include many fine funds with excellent long-term track records. Fidelity also offers a large number of load funds within their FundsNetwork program, but who cares! Why would anyone want to buy load funds from a discount broker in the first place? The following fund families are available NTF through the Fidelity FundsNetwork:

BENHAM	FOUNDERS
BERGER	JANUS
DREYFUS	NEUBERGER & BERMAN
EVERGREEN	STEINROE
FIDELITY	STRONG

This is a relatively new service, so the specific fund families participating is subject to change. Again, not all funds within each of these families is available NTF, most notably the Fidelity funds themselves (at least with your taxable accounts).

Trading Restrictions.   Investors will have to deal with two sets of trading restrictions with Fidelity. First, are the trading restrictions with non-Fidelity funds—four short-term trades. On the fifth short-term trade, Fidelity reserves the right to begin charging you transaction fees on all your trades. Fidelity defines a short-term trade as a round-trip within 6 months, the same as Schwab.

The second group of Fidelity trading restrictions deals with Fidelity funds. You are not allowed to make more than four round-trip trades in an individual Fidelity fund within a rolling 12-month period. After that, Fidelity reserves the right to refuse your exchange request.

In theory, you can buy and sell a Fidelity fund four times within a 6-month period and not violate the FundsNetwork trading restrictions but still violate the Fidelity funds rules. The effect of these double rules is that you can be more certain about your ability to trade non-Fidelity funds more frequently than you can trade Fidelity funds themselves.

Penalties for Trading Too Much.   Fidelity treats frequent traders the same as Schwab does; it revokes their privilege to trade on a no-transaction-fee basis. Fidelity says it reserves the right to initiate transaction fees on too frequent NTF, non-Fidelity fund traders. However, should you violate the trading policies on Fidelity funds themselves, you could be in for a severe penalty. Fidelity might bar you from owning Fidelity funds forever. That's right—Fidelity doesn't want your business if you trade too much.

Transaction Charges. Just like Schwab, Fidelity charges a transaction fee based upon the dollar amount of your investment in non-NTF funds. The fee schedule is:

Transaction Amount Commission

$0–5,000	$17.50 plus 0.8% of principal
$5,001–$10,000	$29.50 plus 0.4% of principal
$10,001–$25,000	$39.50 plus 0.2% of principal
$25,001–$95,000	$67.50 plus 0.1% of principal
$95,001 +	$157.50 plus 0.08% of principal

Fidelity's minimum commission charge is $28.

Summary. Fidelity's biggest advantage is the waiver of the sales charges on Fidelity funds in retirement accounts (except for Fidelity Magellan, New Millennium, and Select Portfolios). That alone may be enough to make Fidelity FundsNetwork your best choice. The absence of Twentieth Century, INVESCO, Montgomery, Lexington, and Oakmark, all very attractive families, is a disappointment. Fidelity gives you a lot of flexibility to trade non-Fidelity funds with their 6 month holding requirement (same as Schwab's). Beware of trading Fidelity funds too frequently, though. The penalty is banishment to the Fidelity prison of too-frequent traders.

Donoghue Tips. Open a second account so you can double the amount of Fidelity trades that you can do. Only four trades per fund in a 12-month period is restrictive should market conditions change, especially if you hold a large number of fund positions. Be aware that Fidelity tracks activity by Social Security number, so multiple accounts may not gain you anything. Finally, Fidelity will always allow you to exchange into cash.

JACK WHITE & COMPANY (800-323-3263)

San Diego-based Jack White may be a little known player in the national mutual fund sweepstakes, but the company has moved aggressively to become a major force. Jack White offers more funds (albeit many that I can't currently recommend) and lower transaction fees than either Schwab or Fidelity. Jack White is also a deep-discount broker, which means that he is cheap! White's fees are among the lowest in the discount brokerage industry, in addition to being the lowest among the three firms profiled in this chapter. Take a look, you might like what you see at Jack White.

Funds Menu. Jack White offers a larger number of funds (317) from over 50 different fund families on an NTF basis, which puts it in first place for the number of funds available NTF. In addition, the firm offers more than 400 funds on a transaction-fee basis. That's the good news; the bad news is that many of them are what I would call less-than-stellar performers. But if you are looking for a wide variety, Jack White is the discount brokerage that offers the most. Fund families include:

ALLIANCE	FEDERATED
ASM	FLEX
BABSON	FREMONT
BARON	FUNDAMENTAL
BARTLETT	GATEWAY
BENHAM	GINTEL
BERGER MANAGERS	IAI
BJB	IDEX
BLANCHARD	KAUFMANN
BOSTON COMPANY	LAUREL
BULL & BEAR	LEEB
CALIF INVESTMENT TRUST	LEXINGTON
CAPPIELLO RUSHMORE	LMH
CRABBE HUSON	LOOMIS SAYLES
DOMINI	MERGER
DREMAN	MERRIMAN
DREYFUS	ORI
ECLIPSE	PERMANENT PORTFOLIO
EQUIFUNDS	PERRITT
EVERGREEEN	PFAMCO
FAIRMONT	PIMCO

REICH & TANG	VALUE LINE
ROBERTSON STEPHENS	VOLUMETRIC
RUSHMORE	WARBURG PINCUS
SELECTED	WASATCH
SEI	WAYNE HUMMER
STEINROE	WILLIAM BLAIR
SOUND SHORE	WRIGHT
TOQUEVILLE	YACKTMAN
UNITED SERVICES	

Trading Restrictions.   You won't find many restrictions at Jack White. In fact, White is the most liberal of all the discount brokers in terms of trading restrictions. White's only requirement is that you hold a fund for at least 60 days to avoid a transaction fee. You do, however, pay a transaction fee on the very first trade that violates the 60-day holding period, but that is all that happens—you pay a transaction fee on that trade. Even after you violate the 60-day holding period, your next NTF trade is still NTF. No penalty, no probation period, no nothing. For very active traders, Jack White is, without question, the best alternative.

Penalties for Trading Too Much.   Virtually none. As I mentioned, the only penalty is Jack White's low maximum commission of $50. The worst case scenario is you pay $50 and then go on your merry way.

Transaction Charges.   Jack White wins hands down again in this category. The minimum commission of $27 and the low maximum commission of $50 make White's program the cheapest in the industry.

Transaction Amount	Commission
$0–$10,000	$27
$10,001–$25,000	$35
$25,001 +	$50

Very frequent traders and market timers might consider doing all their fund business through Jack White because if you pay a transaction fee, you can trade to your heart's content. At a maximum $50 commission per transaction, you might be better off paying Jack White than risking violating the trading rules at Schwab or Fidelity. One catch—Jack White's minimum dollar amount is $5,000 per trade. Small investors apparently aren't welcome at Jack White.

Summary. Jack White's mutual fund marketplace is flexible and cheap. The 60-day holding requirement should be no problem for investors other than extremely short-term market timers. The $50 maximum commission is peanuts for larger investors. If Jack White ever signs up the fund companies currently in the Schwab and Fidelity programs, he will have the most powerful mutual fund portfolio management system in the industry. Keep your eyes on Jack White for future developments.

Donoghue Tips. Jack White tells a compelling story, but the many fund choices are mediocre for the most part, other than some luminaries like Gateway, Berger, Cappiello, Evergreen, and a few others. Most of the best funds are available only on a transaction-fee basis, which is low due to the $50 maximum commission. There is no need to set up separate accounts because the transaction guidelines are so flexible.

CHOOSE YOUR LAUNCHING PAD FOR HIGHER FUND PROFITS

You now know the benefits and advantages of using a mutual fund marketplace portfolio management system and the ins and outs of the different discount brokerage programs. Your challenge is to act on the information you have just learned and prepare your mutual fund rocket ship for takeoff.

The days of the pony express mutual fund buying system are long gone and best left to the uninformed and uninitiated. Sophisticated no-load mutual fund buyers like you are going to invest like professionals by using a modern portfolio management system at Schwab, Fidelity, or Jack White.

HOW TO SET UP AN ACCOUNT

Setting up your discount brokerage account is easy. Call the toll-free number and request an account-opening kit. The discount broker's customer service reps will be happy to walk you through the paperwork if you need assistance. Fill out the blanks, send in your check, and you are in business.

Transferring established fund positions into discount brokerage accounts is relatively easy. You don't even have to liquidate your old positions, just transfer them without tax consequences. When you transfer fund positions that are NTF funds into a discount brokerage account there is no charge to add them. However, regardless of the fact that they are NTF fund positions, they are not counted as assets for which the funds reimburse the discount broker, so when you sell those positions, you will have to pay a transaction cost on the sale. After that, investments in those funds are NTF.

Once your account is established, you are ready to trade mutual funds by phone. Call your discount broker and start trading. You are now ready to invest like a SuperStar investor.

Which Stock Investment Style Is Right for You?

Make Your Choice: Value, Growth, Blend, or Sector Funds

At the end of December 1993, there were 4,558 different SEC-registered open-end mutual funds. That's a lot of funds to choose from, and picking the best one for you could be quite a challenge. In fact, the press always seems delighted to make that choice more daunting by pointing out that there are twice as many mutual funds as there are stocks on the New York Stock Exchange.

Folks, it just ain't that confusing. Stick with me and we can rapidly eliminate more than 80 percent of that list before we even get down to looking for the best funds. When we get that done, we'll pare our list down to a few dozen SuperStars. These are the funds you can use to build a high-powered portfolio featuring just a few carefully selected funds. But let's take it one step at a time.

WHAT THE PRESS FORGOT TO TELL YOU

Actually, the press suggest a bogus comparison. If they did their homework, reporters would discover that only 1,717 of the total 4,558 open-end mutual funds invest in stocks at all, and only 463 of those are direct-marketed, no-salesman-required mutual funds. (When we refer to *direct-marketed* funds in this book, we are talking about no-load mutual funds plus the few low-load— up to 3 percent—Fidelity Investments funds). The rest of the mutual funds are money market funds and bond funds that do not invest in stocks.

For the purpose of this book, we will focus on the 840 direct-marketed stock and bond funds. We will exclude the money funds, which were once attractive but are now too low yielding to earn our attention as investments. (This is an *investment guide,* not a checking account guide.) If we narrow our focus even more, we find only 284 diversified domestic (U.S.) stock funds, 70 international stock funds, 377 bond funds, and 109 miscellaneous types of funds (sector funds, asset allocation funds, balanced funds, and various income funds).

SIMPLIFY YOUR FUND CHOICES: DIVIDE AND CONQUER

Until I started to research this book, I had this nagging feeling that there were some types of funds that I was inadvertently overlooking or that my database was somehow incomplete. I worried that I might be missing some funds that would better suit my clients' and subscribers' needs. For years we have carefully defined the characteristics that would qualify a fund to be included in my investment newsletter, *Donoghue'$ MONEYLETTER* (for a *free* sample issue, call 1-800-982-BILL).

However, with the recent publication of the *Morningstar Mutual Funds on Disc CD-ROM* service, I have been able to refine my mutual fund screening process dramatically. While my *Donoghue's MONEYLETTER* staff maintains its own database, I go a step further to keep them on their toes. Each month, I receive a compact disc (CD) just like the kind that play such wonderful music, slip that into my CD reader, and a comprehensive world of mutual funds opens up to me. I have utilized this expanded ability to analyze the full range of mutual funds in researching this book.

Morningstar, Inc., a Chicago-based research organization, has rapidly become the best single source of mutual fund databases in America. Their analysts produce a wealth of data on all kinds of mutual funds: open-end mutual funds, closed-end funds, and even the variable annuity separate accounts. They provide statistics on each and every mutual fund, publish one- to five-star ratings, provide analysts' comments on many funds, and, in general, provide the database on which investment professionals rely for their analysis.

I want it to be very clear right now, however, that the mutual fund tables in this book are my responsibility and, while derived from the *Morningstar Mutual Funds On Disc* service, are completely of my own design. The advice and strategies in this book represent my opinions, not theirs. Information is data in perspective. The information in this book is derived most often from Morningstar's data (and used with their permission), but it is *my* perspective.

THE DONOGHUE SUPERSTARS INVESTMENT ATTITUDE

They call me "the investment advisor with an attitude" because I have a very clear and, surprisingly, controversial approach to mutual fund investing. I call it *reality-based investing*.

My approach is actually simple common sense. I have taken the entire mutual fund universe and reorganized it into nine carefully constructed sub-universes (like those designed for this book) in which the funds are ranked, based on recent (one year or less) performance. It doesn't take a genius to figure out that the fund at the top of the list—the one with the best consistent performance and lowest risk track record—is the *SuperStar* and the fund at the bottom is the *SupperStar,* the one who is eating your supper at your expense.

Rankings are a good place to start studying the SuperStar funds to place in your portfolio. It takes some additional common sense to sort out the funds that are there because of their portfolio managers' brilliance from those that are there because of a major market trend from those that are there because of an unusual event. When it comes to investment brilliance, most often the fund at the top of the list has the best answer and the fund at the bottom has the worst answer.

The problem for many investors is that the guy at the bottom of the list has a sales pitch that is as *plausible* as the one at the top. But, informed investors—those who know the fund's track record—know that the story is not *credible.* The trick is in constructing The Right List and in studying the most successful portfolio managers. That, in a nutshell, is my approach: Find out who the real SuperStars are and get to know their styles.

LET'S BUILD SOME OF THE LISTS (OR SUB-UNIVERSES)

Let me preface my list-building strategies by saying that after we have constructed my dozen favorite sub-universes (in statistical jargon), we will have given *all* of the direct-marketed mutual funds a chance to shine. We will have done a complete sweep through the mutual funds to find those that work best with the Donoghue Mutual Fund SuperStar investment strategies.

A Preview of Coming Attractions, So You Don't Get Lost

The best-performer lists, or sub-universes are shown in Table 8.1 (each one includes the Top 25 or more funds, if available).

RISING INTEREST RATES WILL WORK AGAINST YOU

When interest rates rise—a very big risk—all of the "safe" fixed-income fund investments will absolutely fail to keep the promises of current yields. (The exceptions are money market funds and possibly junk bond funds—but more on them later.) In fact, anything but the shortest term fixed-income fund investments will lose money.

Rising interest rates are death to the bond market, and the bond funds with the lowest credit risks (government and municipal bonds) will have the greatest market risk and lose the greatest amounts. *Good advice of the past can be disastrous advice for the future.*

TABLE 8.1
The Best-Performing Direct-Marketed Funds

Diversified Domestic (U.S.) Stock Funds
   Table 8.2: Donoghue's **Value** Stock SuperStar Candidates
   Table 8.3: Donoghue's **Growth** Stock SuperStar Candidates
   Table 8.4: Donoghue's **Blend** Stock SuperStar Candidates

Domestic Sector Stock and Bond Funds
   Table 8.5: Donoghue's **Stock and Bond Sector** SuperStar
      Candidates

International Stock and/or Bond Funds
   Table 9.2: Donoghue's **International Stock** SuperStar Candidates
   Table 9.3: Donoghue's **International Bond** SuperStar Candidates

Domestic "Easy Answer" Stock and Bond Funds
   Table 10.2: Donoghue's **Index** SuperStar Candidates
   Table 10.3: Donoghue's **Total Return** SuperStar Candidates
   Table 10.4: Donoghue's **Safe Harbor** SuperStar Candidates

If I have any prejudice from my research, it is against bond funds. Investors who cling to "safe" credit risks and fixed-income investments (bond funds and CDs) will lose the most. At best, bond funds will no longer be viable long-term investments, and at worst those who stay with the traditional "buy bonds for safety" advice will suffer a blood bath. Let's take a look at the mutual fund universe and see what we have to work with.

WHY DO I EMPHASIZE ONE-YEAR PERFORMANCE?

For uniformity, I have chosen to rank the funds on a one-year performance basis as of December 31, 1993—a 12-month performance ranking. There is no magic formula for choosing a performance period on which to rank funds, although I find there is little predictive value in track records of more than one year.

In *Donoghue'$ MONEYLETTER*, I rank funds generally on a weighted average of one-, three-, six-, and twelve-month performance. We have found this track record useful in selecting funds for future SuperStar performance. For the purposes of this book I have chosen to use one-year track records starting at the beginning of 1993, which coincides with the major recent uptrends in domestic and international stock funds as well as in the gold market. A one-year track record is a good starting place.

BUILDING YOUR SUPERSTAR CANDIDATES LIST

As we progress through the sub-universes of the full Donoghue Mutual Fund Universe, we will build a list of the most attractive funds for candidates for the SuperStar list. By the end of this chapter, we will have sorted out many of the best.

Are you ready? Oh, yes, I included one juicy little list in an appendix at the end of the book for you to consider as well—The SupperStars of 1993—dead losers I hope you missed because they missed the market badly.

A Bonus List: The Eight Dozen Lemons to Unload Now!!

I have provided in Appendix A and Appendix B lists of eight dozen funds (48 load funds and 48 no-load funds), all $50 million in assets or larger, that are clearly the worst performers for 1993. They were among the lowest yielding funds for the year and were also (I want to build a list of the real duds for the year) in the bottom 10 percent among funds with similar investment objectives. They not only missed out during a bull market, but did worse than 90 percent of the funds with similar investment objectives.

If you were with them, you lost big time because you missed investing in successful funds in a successful year. For most of these funds, if you were to stick with them for the long term, this **was** the long term, and they missed it!

I do not intend to criticize these funds unfairly. If I teach you anything in this book, it will be that being in the right type of fund—the right place to be—is the most critical investment decision you will ever make.

Mea Culpa, My Favorite Bias—Few Bond Funds

For long-term investors, even the highest interest rates available are not sufficient to keep you far enough ahead of inflation and taxes to build a comfortable retirement reserve. Further, given the current pattern of permanent layoffs and early retirement, few Americans will be able to work long enough to build suffi-cient savings to retire comfortably. Given that shorter time to invest, you will need something more powerful than bonds to reach your investment goals.

So, what's the moral here? *Go for it!* The sooner you get be-yond timidly avoiding risk and learn to manage it and profit from its upside, the more likely it is that you will be able to af-ford to retire.

LET'S BUILD YOUR SUPERSTAR LISTS AND FIND THE GUY AT THE TOP

Starting with the 3,434 stock and bond funds (4,458 funds less the money funds) listed on the *Morningstar Mutual Funds On Disc CD-ROM* service, let's first eliminate from consideration the sales force-marketed mutual funds. After all, if we are going to learn how to select mutual funds ourselves, why should we pay a load or sales charge?

Sort #1—Get Down to the Direct-Marketed (Mostly No-Load) Mutual Funds

Our initial sort is first to eliminate the mutual funds that charge a load or sales charge since these are sales force-marketed (broker) funds. We shouldn't have to pay a fee to be sold to if we know how to buy. The reason for focusing on direct-marketed mutual funds is that these are funds that will be available directly to investors without the intervention of commission-hungry salespeople. In addition, these funds are likely to be found in the discount broker programs that are an important part of the future of a no-load mutual fund investors' world.

Number of no-load mutual funds left: 1,372.

Sort #2—Get Down to the Affordable Funds

Surprisingly, among the funds in our first sort, we find several institutional funds with large investment minimums. These are funds that are inaccessible to the average investor because of the amount of money needed to open an account. So, we set a minimum initial investment of $25,000 or less. Don't worry. Many of these funds have minimums as low as $2,500 or $1,000; a few have no minimums; and most offer lower minimums for IRA accounts.

Number of funds left with minimum investments of $25,000 or less: 1,184 (1,133 with minimums of $10,000 or less).

Sort #3—Get Down to the Funds with Sufficient Size

Experienced investors know that when most funds start up, there are usually a small number of investors and a small number of investment positions. I would prefer that a fund reach a minimum size of at least $50 million in assets before recommending it to investors.

By the time it reaches $50 million in assets (quickly for a well-marketed fund and slower for an undermarketed fund), the mutual fund has reached a minimum level of management maturity and portfolio stability to have developed a well-defined investment style. Therefore, I eliminate all of the funds with less than $50 million in assets.

With just these few sorts, we have eliminated 82 percent all of the mutual funds in existence.

Number of funds left with assets over $50 million: 798.

Sort #4—Add Back the Popular Fidelity Investments Funds

When speaking of direct-marketed funds, you simply have to include the Fidelity Investments funds, the bulk of which are marketed directly to the public. Their no-load and low-load funds account for a significant amount of all direct-marketed mutual funds.

Once upon a time, most of the Fidelity Investments funds were no-load funds but at some point they felt that their performance was strong enough to justify a special fee to invest. Their flagship fund, Fidelity Magellan, and its legendary portfolio manager, Peter Lynch, produced the best performance of the decade of the 1980s.

When Fidelity decided to promote its discount brokerage business, it generously offered all but three of its funds (Fidelity Magellan, Fidelity New Millennium and Fidelity Select Portfolios, their sector funds) on a no-load basis to IRA and other tax-sheltered accounts opened directly with Fidelity. Thus for retirement accounts, most Fidelity funds are no-loads in practice, even if they are low-loads officially. Sorry, though, a Schwab account invested in Fidelity funds does not qualify.

For those who invest directly with Fidelity Investments, the loads are softened by a procedure known as *fee tracking*. With fee tracking, you pay a load only once for new money added to the account. For example, if you invest $100,000 in Fidelity Magellan, you pay $3,000 for the privilege. When it grows and you switch it to Fidelity Contrafund, for example, you pay no load unless you add new money to your Fidelity accounts. If you switch that Magellan investment to a stock, such as IBM, and later want to return to Magellan, you will have to pay the load again.

(In all candor, I feel that I must disclose to you that Fidelity sponsored my TV show, exhibits at my conferences, and has retained me as a consultant and expert witness at times. I must also say, in all candor, that I am sure they never thought they could buy my endorsement in any way. I make my recommendations as objectively as possible—all recommendations require judgment—and I never endorse products or services for a fee.)

There are 104 Fidelity funds that meet our criteria; 62 of them are no-load funds, and 42 carry either a 2 percent or 3 percent sales charge. At this point, we add back in the 42 low-load funds.

Number of funds left: 840.

The Donoghue Direct-Marketed Fund Universe

As we progress in our search for candidates for your Donoghue Mutual Fund SuperStar Portfolio, this is the "Donoghue fund universe" to which I will be referring. We have eliminated over 81 percent of the funds from the thousands we began with. Our task of sorting the funds and narrowing down the list is becoming easier. This is our basic universe of funds for consideration to qualify as Donoghue's Mutual Fund SuperStars.

LET'S TAKE A CLOSER LOOK AT THE DOMESTIC STOCK FUNDS

To pinpoint the best diversified domestic U.S. stock funds, we next need to eliminate some funds from our list. Let's sort out the funds we don't need for now: 369 bond funds, 70 international stock funds, 53 nondiversified stock sector (specialty) funds, 19 asset allocation funds, 26 balanced funds, 30 index funds, and 4 funds of funds.

Number of direct-marketed, diversified, domestic stock funds left with minimum initial investments of $25,000 or less and assets of $50 million or more: 269.

Now that's a lot more manageable! We've narrowed our list to only about 6 percent of the funds we started with. That's a long way from the figure that mutual fund detractors use when they quip that "there are more mutual funds than there are stocks on the New York Stock Exchange." Actually, if you look only at the most attractive direct-marketed diversified domestic stock market mutual funds (that's a lot of adjective/qualifiers but it is a more realistic comparison), there are about *ten times more* attractive stocks on the New York Stock Exchange than there are stock funds!

That's an entirely different story than what we started with. For the purposes of this book, a retail fund is one that is generally viable and available to the independent investor public (people like you who don't need brokers to buy mutual funds for them!) with a reasonable—$25,000 or less—minimum and at least $50 million in assets.

LET'S GET CLEAR WHAT KIND OF FUNDS WE ARE LOOKING FOR

Top Performers.   First of all, we want to focus our attention on SuperStar candidates, those at the top of the list. Since all the managers in any category invest in similar types of stocks with relatively similar investment styles, the fund manager at the top is the best manager, at least on first blush. This is a basic truth, because, unless we learn something unusual about him, that manager has taken his or her talents, used the same materials (securities), and produced the best total return. Once identified, we need to study the style of this SuperStar manager to see if he or she can likely produce the same superior returns in the future, assuming that the fund in question is in an asset class that we favor.

Consistent Top Performance in the Fund's Category. One of the important characteristics I look for in a fund is just how well the fund has performed relative to its peers. After all, if I decide I want an international stock fund, I want the *best* international stock fund. So, I research the fund's ranking within its fund objective (*3-Year Rank in Objectives* in the book's tables) over the past three years. The lower the number, the closer to the top of the performance list the manager has been for the past three years. In the case of excellent performance, I would certainly consider a shorter term rating, although three years of top performance relative to one's peers is a great indication of a Super-Star.

Lowered Risk. Next we have to decide how much volatility we can stand. *Beta* is a good indication of volatility, especially if you are looking at a domestic stock fund and are concerned about its vulnerability to a domestic stock market correction. (Statistically, beta measures the slope of the line that describes the average relation between changes in the S&P 500 and a stock's or a stock fund's historical performance.)

A high beta is great in an up market and bad in a down market. A beta of 1.00 means that if the S&P 500 were to fall 1.00 percent, the fund would likely fall 1.00 percent in value. A beta below 1.00 is a good indicator of safety at this late stage of our domestic bull market.

There are times when you might want a high beta fund. For example, if you are trying to time the market and play on the January effect, which is the tendency of small cap stocks to rise dramatically in January, a fund that moves higher than the average will be good for this strategy.

Beta is normally calculated relative to the S&P 500. So, while it may be comforting to see that international stock funds have betas of 0.50 or so and gold funds tend to have negative betas, as those funds do not invest in S&P 500 stocks, the beta statistic is of little value. However, this does mean that by diversifying into gold or international stock funds you are also diversifying your risk relative to a domestic market correction. Such funds, though, have other risks involved that should be evaluated before investing in them.

The Morningstar Risk Measure is another rating I find helpful. It is usually calculated only for periods of three years or more. According to Morningstar Mutual Funds On Disc, Morningstar Risk is described as a comparison of the fund's risk level relative to other funds in its class. Unlike traditional risk measures, which see both greater-than-expected and less-than-expected returns as added risk, our proprietary measure focuses only on the downside.

Since an investor can earn a certain return from T-bills without earning any risk, we define any monthly return less than the T-bill as negative. Thus to calculate Morningstar Risk, we subtract the 3-month T-bill return from each month's return by the fund. We then sum the months wherein the figure is negative, and divide the total losses (not the number of losing months) by the total number of months in the rating period.

The average monthly loss is then compared to those of all equity or all bond funds, or both (for hybrid funds), depending on the fund's objective. The group average is calculated and set equal to 1.00. The resulting Morningstar Risk expresses in percentage points how risky the fund is relative to the average fund. If Morningstar Risk is 1.35 for an equity fund, that fund has been 35 percent riskier than the average equity fund for the period considered.

As you can see, Morningstar risk of less than 1.00—less than the average fund in the category—would be a valuable criterion for selecting an attractive fund candidate for your portfolio.

THREE KINDS OF RETAIL DOMESTIC DIVERSIFIED STOCK FUNDS

As we sharpen our focus on diversified domestic stock funds, we discover there are three basic styles of stock funds we can invest in:

Value Stock Funds:	70 funds
Growth Stock Funds:	74 funds
Blend Stock Funds:	125 funds

Source: Morningstar Mutual Funds On Disc.

WHAT'S THE COMPANY REALLY WORTH? VALUE INVESTING

Value stock fund portfolio managers are essentially frugal financial shoppers looking for bargains. Call them bottomfishers, bargain hunters, or even cheapskates, but "value" managers like to buy stocks that are selling at valuations substantially less than the overall market.

Value portfolio managers attempt to calculate the market value of the company to a knowledgeable and willing buyer (on a per-share basis) and compare that to the current market price per share. If the current price per share is lower, that stock is considered to be trading below its market value. Ratios such as price/earnings (the P/E ratio), price/book, price/sales, and price/cash flow are traditional valuation measures that are used to determine whether or not a stock is a bargain.

Finding the "Ugly Ducklings"

Occasionally, a stock may own vast real estate holdings whose value is reflected on the books at a grossly depreciated or out-of-date value, and which may not be recognized in the price of the stock. In the 1980s, and still today, corporate raiders have focused on the underlying asset value when evaluating a company's breakup value.

Many stocks are cheap for a good reason—poor earnings, mismanagement, or undesirable business conditions. The key question the value portfolio managers must ask is: Are the company's problems temporary or long-term?

If the problems are viewed as temporary and the company is misunderstood by Wall Street, such company's stock can represent an excellent value. Don Yacktman of the Yacktman Fund loves to describe his portfolio holdings as companies that will recover "like beach balls being held under water."

The ultimate objective of value fund managers is for investors, especially institutional investors whose large purchases can drive up the stock's price, to recognize the worth of the value portfolio's stock holdings. Whether that happens or not depends on the manager's ability to separate the true dogs, which deserve to be cheap, from the ugly ducklings waiting to turn into swans. In many ways, the value stock managers are the scouts for the Wall Street big leagues, looking for the undervalued stocks that can be the big time darlings.

Becoming the Swan's Public Relations Agent

To find these swans-to-be, value investors or portfolio managers must study trends in the stock market. They then assess the possibility that the company or its industry will receive some favorable attention by analysts.

When analysts at the major brokerage firms discover a great value, they recommend the stock, brokers sell the stock's story and encourage investors to buy it. When the stock reaches a certain level, the value investors unload their shares and move on to the next stock.

A value stock fund portfolio manager who develops a good reputation for top performance can legally and morally move the price of the stock toward its fair market value. There are several ways a fund manager can accomplish this:

1. One way is to publish the portfolio holdings (as required by the SEC) and hope institutional investors or their brokers notice the stock (the better your performance, the better your reputation, the better your ability to encourage investors to buy a stock).

2. A second way is to speak favorably in public about the stock, thus calling further attention to it.

3. A third way is to be quoted widely about the stock. This process is called *touting* and may or may not work for a given stock. It can also backfire on the manager if the stock's price does not move and he or she loses credibility and shareholders.

A top value stock portfolio manager will interview representatives of hundreds and, perhaps, thousands of companies in a given year. The companies compete to be chosen and have the mantle of credibility conferred upon them.

The rewards are great. If the price of the stock rises, insider holdings of the stock will enrich those who hold it, and the company can use the inflated value of the stock to reduce the number of shares needed for acquisitions. The company also gains access to a significant amount of cheaper financing to allow it to grow.

When it works, it can be very exciting. Ideally, the value stock portfolio manager sells at the peak of the excitement, takes the profits, and ferrets out another ugly duckling.

For Investment Buffs Only

Technically, Morningstar considers funds with "a combined relative [to the S&P 500's ratio] price/earnings ratio and price/book ratio of less than 1.75 [as] . . . value funds." For example, Mutual Beacon Fund, the No. 1 value fund for the first ten months of 1993 (No. 3 for the year), had a price/earnings ratio of 1.05 relative to the price/earnings ratio of the S&P 500. This equals a price/book ratio of 0.54 relative to that of the S&P 500, for a total of 1.59, which is less than 1.75. Thus, it is considered a value fund by Morningstar. This means that compared to the average S&P 500 stock, the Mutual Beacon Fund is only selling for 105 percent of the average price to earnings ratio and 54 percent of the average price to book ratio.

Value stocks, on average, are not overinflated and are probably undervalued—if the portfolio manager is on the mark and has picked the right ones. His track record on that speaks for itself.

Finding Value in Value Stock Funds

Scanning Table 8.2, the Value SuperStars, the first thing to note is the low betas (under 1.0) of most value funds. If a fund with a low beta has delivered dramatic performance in an up market, that fund gets high marks from me.

One of the ways these funds make the top of the list is to have a high *alpha,* which is the measure of how much better the fund's performance was than its expected performance, given its level of risk, measured by beta. A positive alpha is a good measure of excellent portfolio management. (Beta, you recall, measures the fund's correlation with the S&P 500.)

Capitalization is a measurement of total market value of the fund's outstanding stock. Total capitalization is defined as outstanding shares times current price per share. Funds that invest in any size stocks can make it in this market. In our top ten, for example, are funds that invest in all three categories of stocks:

▶ *Small-Cap.* Mutual Beacon, Fidelity Low-Priced Stock, and Lindner invest in small-cap stocks (companies with total market value of less that $1 billion in outstanding stock).

▶ *Mid-Cap.* Oakmark, First Eagle Fund of America, Gradison-McDonald Established Stock, Pelican, and Fidelity Equity-Income II invest in medium-cap companies (companies with a market capitalization of $1-5 billion).

▶ *Large-Cap.* Fidelity Equity-Income and Thomson Equity-Income B invest in large-cap stocks (over $5 billion in total market value).

The final characteristic is that most successful value managers have been around for at least seven years, a sign that experience counts. In addition, you can see that only four (Gradison-McDonald Established Value, T. Rowe Price OTC

TABLE 8.2
Donoghue's Value SuperStar Candidates
25 Top-Performing Direct-Marketed Value Stock Funds—YTD 12/31/93

Rank	Fund Name	Investment Objective	YTD Total Return (%)	YTD Rank in OBJ	3-Year Rank in OBJ	Beta (3-Year)	Mstar Risk (3-Year)	Minimum Initial Purchase ($)	800 #	Availability + No Fee	Fee	Covenant Rating**
1	Oakmark	Growth	30.50	2	NA	NA	NA	1000	476-9625		S F W	1
2	First Eagle Fund of America	Growth	23.85	8	18	0.79	0.69	5000	451-3623		S W	2
3	Mutual Beacon	Growth-Inc	22.93	2	10	0.47	0.38	5000	553-3014		S W	2
4	Fidelity Equity-Income (2%)*	Equity-Inc	21.31	7	6	0.78	0.49	2500	544-8888	F	S W	3
5	Thomson Equity-Income B	Equity-Inc	21.23	8	14	0.69	0.51	1000	227-7337		F	NA
6	Gradison-McDonald Estab.Val.	Growth	20.77	14	53	0.85	0.68	1000	869-5999		W	NA
7	Fidelity Low-Priced Stock (3%)*	Small Company	20.21	29	15	0.81	0.60	2500	544-8888	F	S W	1
8	Pelican	Growth	20.10	16	41	0.73	0.58	5000	617-330-7500			3.5
9	Lindner	Growth	19.85	17	45	0.56	0.51	2000	314-727-5305			1
10	Fidelity Equity-Income II	Equity-Inc	18.89	13	1	0.68	0.34	2500	544-8888	F	S W	3
11	Homestead Value	Growth-Inc	18.83	8	40	0.63	0.57	1000	258-3030			4
12	PNC Small Cap Val Eqty Instl	Small Company	18.67	39	NA	NA	NA	5000	422-6538			NA
13	T. Rowe Price OTC Securities	Small Company	18.40	41	60	0.80	0.87	2500	638-5660		S F W	NA
14	PNC Value Equity Instl	Growth	17.99	22	NA	NA	NA	5000	441-7762			NA
15	Lexington Corporate Leaders	Growth-Inc	17.57	11	46	0.86	0.73	1000	526-0056	S W	F	2.5
16	Eclipse Finl. Asset Equity	Small Company	17.02	47	67	0.80	0.73	1000	872-2710	W		1.5
17	Invesco Industrial Income	Equity-Inc	16.69	23	18	0.86	0.63	1000	525-8085	S	F W	3.5
18	Neuberger&Berman Sel Sectors	Growth	16.33	27	28	1.08	0.79	1000	877-9700	S F	W	4.5
19	American AAdvantage Equity	Growth-Inc	16.11	16	19	0.90	0.66	None	817-967-3509	W		4
20	Fidelity Asset Manager: Inc	Income	15.39	26	NA	NA	NA	2500	544-8888	F	S W	NA
21	Lindner Dividend	Income	14.92	36	7	0.26	0.10	2000	314-727-5305		S W	NA
22	T. Rowe Price Equity-Income	Equity-Inc	14.84	37	26	0.69	0.41	2500	638-5660		S F W	3
23	Galaxy Equity Value Retail	Growth	14.75	33	69	0.85	0.71	2500	628-0414			3
24	Vanguard Equity-Income	Equity-Inc	14.65	40	50	0.80	0.55	3000	662-7447		S F W	4.5
25	Vanguard/Wellesley Income	Income	14.65	39	48	0.37	0.43	3000	662-7447		S F W	NA

*Waived for IRAs maintained at Fidelity
** One to Five "Thumbs Up" (best rating is 5). *Source:* Covenant Investment Management, Copyright 1994.
+ The Donoghue Group, Copyright 1994

S = Charles Schwab & Co.
F = Fidelity FundsNetwork
W = Jack White & Co.

Copyright Morningstar Inc., 1994

Securities, Ellipse Financial Asset Equity, and Galaxy Equity Value Retail) of the top 25 value funds (out of 70 in total) are below average (three-year rank in OBJ higher than 50 percent), which demonstrates consistency of performance.

Who Are the Value SuperStars?

This year's clear winner is Oakmark Fund, an eclectic, value-oriented fund that invests in stocks of all sizes. Portfolio manager Robert Sanborn's Oakmark Fund ranked No. 1 among all diversified stock mutual funds in 1992, only losing out as the Portfolio Manager of the Year to a sector fund. In 1993, he repeated his No. 1 value fund performance with an outstanding track record earning returns more than 27 percent higher than his closest competitor. The fund ended the year with over $1.1 billion dollars in assets, not bad for a fund only 28 months old!

I can tell you with some pride that I identified this fund as a winner early in 1992 when it was only about nine months old. After meeting with Robert Sanborn, I was sufficiently impressed to add the fund to our portfolios, where it still resides over 18 months later. Oakmark been good to my clients and subscribers.

Sanborn's penchant for companies that are very much shareholder-oriented has paid off once again. While his portfolio has taken some losses on drug stocks, its cable TV picks have been big winners. Oakmark's sister fund, Oakmark International, is another excellent fund. It was introduced in September 1992 and has been on our BUY list for most of its life.

Another fund to watch, one with a low Morningstar risk rating, is Mutual Beacon. Mutual Beacon's performance has beaten all but 10 percent of the funds in its objective, and it has a low beta of 0.47. Top (No. 3) performance with low downside risk is always a winner in my book.

TYING YOUR FUTURE TO A ROCKET—GROWTH INVESTING

Intuitively, you would think that every stock fund has as its objective the *growth* of principal and you would be right. Here, however, we are talking about a *growth investing* style, which is quite different from *value investing* (which also has a growth objective).

Growth style managers invest in companies that are experiencing rapid growth in earnings and/or sales. Growth in the size of the business means a greater long-term franchise, since the value of a company can be measured by the net present value of a stream of future earnings or by what you would pay today to have access to a future cash flow. That growth in economic value is a multiple of sales or earnings.

The growth investor is looking for companies whose economic value is growing rapidly. The business world abounds with examples of growth companies that are considered the darlings of Wall Street. Wal-Mart, MicroSoft, and Intel, among others, have seemingly endless opportunities to expand profits.

This optimism places growth stocks at the opposite end of the spectrum from value stocks. Instead of looking for low P/E ratios and low price/book ratios, growth stocks often sell at very high multiples (price/earnings ratios) of their earnings. These rich valuations are the function of a bright outlook and represent a willingness on the part of investors to pay a premium price for these attractive companies. Growth stock analysts concentrate almost solely on earnings growth (see Table 8.3).

Growth investing can be exceptionally profitable, but it is also very volatile (only 5 of the top 25 growth funds have betas below 1.0). Just as high expectations can easily lead to disappointment in life, earnings disappointments (even temporary) can cause growth stock prices to tumble. Ten or twenty percent losses in a short time period are not uncommon.

Bargain Companies Wanted "Dead and/or Alive"

The biggest risk in value investing is that an investor may have to wait years for the stock's ultimate hidden value to be recognized. While growth investors look to the value of a live company, value investors often look at the value of the company dead or dismembered. Growth investors risk volatility of principal; value investors risk having to wait too long. Both risks can be well worth taking.

Investing for the 21st Century

An example of a classic growth stock manager is Twentieth Century Investors in Kansas City, MO. Twentieth Century has been able to amass over $19 billion of stock in companies with accelerating earnings growth in a recession. It takes a lot experience to perform that kind of feat. Indeed, the average tenure of a Twentieth Century portfolio manager is 16.4 years.

Imagine what those stocks' growth will be in a recovery! Well, that's just what the market has been doing: anticipating future earnings growth and driving the prices of selected growth stocks skyward.

It is not uncommon to find a fund like Twentieth Century roll up some spectacular returns like its 86.45 percent return in 1991. (It ranked No. 20 this year with a still respectable

TABLE 8.3
Donoghue's Growth Stock SuperStar Candidates
25 Top-Performing Direct-Marketed Growth Stock Funds—YTD 12/31/93

Rank	Fund Name	Investment Objective	YTD Total Return (%)	YTD Rank in OBJ	3-Year Rank in OBJ	Beta (3-Year)	Mstar Risk (3-Year)	Minimum Initial Purchase ($)	800 #	Availability + No Fee	Fee	Covenant Rating **
1	PBHG Growth	Small Company	46.57	1	3	1.40	1.52	1000	809-8008		W	NA
2	20th Century Giftrust Inv.	Small Company	31.41	6	2	1.68	1.76	250	345-2021	S	F W	NA
3	SAFECO Equity	Growth-Inc	30.91	1	7	1.07	1.02	1000	426-6730	S W	S W	3
4	SteinRoe Capital Opport.	Aggr. Growth	27.52	10	22	1.10	0.94	1000	338-2550	S F W		3.5
5	T. Rowe Price Mid-Cap Growth	Growth	26.24	5	NA	NA	NA	2500	638-5660		S F W	1
6	Founders Growth	Growth	25.53	6	13	1.17	1.16	1000	525-2440	S	W F	2.5
7	Fidelity New Millennium (3%)	Growth	24.67	6	NA	NA	NA	2500	544-8888	F	S W	3
8	Thomson Target B	Growth	24.52	7	NA	NA	NA	1000	227-7337		F	3
9	Fidelity Blue Chip Growth (3%)*	Growth	24.50	7	8	1.20	0.73	2500	544-8888	F	S W	2.5
10	Baron Asset	Small Company	23.48	16	55	0.99	1.04	2000	992-2766	S W		2
11	Invesco Emerging Growth	Small Company	23.32	16	NA	NA	NA	1000	525-8085	S	F W	NA
12	Galaxy Sm. Co. Equity Retail	Small Company	22.75	20	NA	NA	NA	2500	628-0414			NA
13	Brandywine	Growth	22.59	10	5	1.15	1.30	25000	338-1579	S		3.5
14	Strong Total Return	Growth-Inc	22.54	4	20	1.02	0.91	250	368-1030	S F	W	2.5
15	Strong Discovery	Aggr. Growth	22.21	26	29	1.32	1.22	1000	368-1030	S F	W	3
16	SAFECO Growth	Small Company	22.19	22	52	1.36	1.86	1000	426-6730			NA
17	T. Rowe Price New Horizons	Small Company	22.01	23	37	1.21	1.28	2500	638-5660		S F W	1.5
18	20th Century Ultra Investors	Small Company	21.81	12	2	1.65	1.85	1000	345-2021	S	F W	2
19	Columbia Special	Small Company	21.55	26	30	1.26	1.12	2000	547-1707			2.5
20	Fidelity Contrafund (3%)*	Growth	21.43	12	4	1.08	0.65	2500	544-8888	F	S W	2
21	Berger 100	Growth	21.20	12	1	1.33	1.30	250	333-1001	S F W		2
22	RSI Retire. Tr. Emerg. Grth.	Small Company	20.99	27	23	1.23	1.53	None	772-3615			1
23	Scudder Capital Growth	Growth	20.07	16	20	1.29	1.08	1000	225-2470		S F W	3
24	Boston Co. Spec.Grth. Retail	Growth	20.01	17	12	1.24	1.33	1000	225-5267	W		2.5
25	Weitz Value	Growth	19.98	17	30	0.64	0.43	25000	232-4161			3

*Waived for IRAs maintained at Fidelity
**One to Five "Thumbs Up" (best rating is 5). *Source:* Covenant Investment Management, Copyright 1994.
+ The Donoghue Group, Copyright 1994

S = Charles Schwab & Co.
F = Fidelity FundsNetwork
W = Jack White & Co.

Copyright Morningstar Inc., 1994

21.81 percent return.) However, this year the only Twentieth Century growth fund near the top of the list is Twentieth Century Giftrust Investors, which has a minimum ten-year holding period requirement.

Topping Twentieth Century at Its Own Game

The big winner this past year was PBHG Growth, which earned 41.57 percent for the year, beating its nearest rival with a return almost half again higher! Truly SuperStar performance! PBHG is a lot like Twentieth Century Ultra except that it is not 100 percent fully invested at all times and is smaller ($77.9 million vs. $7.8 billion) and more able to stuff its portfolio with only the best stocks.

Are Growth Funds Your Cup of Tea?

Growth stock investing is not for everyone for the following reasons:

▶ *Low Dividend Income.* To start with, growth stocks tend not to pay much in dividends because growing companies often reinvest capital to expand and increase the price per share rather than pay dividends to investors.

▶ *High Volatility.* Funds like Twentieth Century Ultra are famous for their superior long-term returns and infamous for their sudden shifts in value. Ultra can take a nose-dive on very short notice and is the first to take off when interest rates dip. Sub-par (less than 1.00) betas are rare among growth funds, while high betas of 1.25 or more are more common. In fact, Twentieth Century Giftrust Investors has a beta of 1.68 and Twentieth Century Ultra has a stomach-rumbling beta of 1.85. At this point in the interest rate cycle, growth stock funds can be a bumpy ride in the short term and a dubious choice in the long term, due to the risk of rising interest rates.

▶ *High Interest Rate Sensitivity.* Third, growth stock funds are particularly sensitive to interest rates. With rates at 25-year lows, the ability to make long-term commitments to growth funds is somewhat dubious, but, of course, you need to strike while the iron is hot. If interest rates stay low, these funds will do well.

For Investment Buffs Only

Technically, Morningstar considers funds with "a combined relative [relative to the S&P 500's ratio] price/earnings ratio and price/book ratio of 2.25 or more to be growth funds." For example, PBHG Growth Fund, the No. 1 diversified domestic stock fund for 1993, has a price/earnings ratio of 1.65 relative to the S&P 500 P/E ratio and a price/book ratio of 1.51. This equals a total score of 3.16, which is greater than 2.25, so PBHG is considered a growth fund. Compared to the average S&P 500 stock, this fund is selling for 165 percent of the average price to earnings ratio and 151 percent of the average price to book ratio. The price of the average portfolio stock has been driven up more than the general market and its price is relying on estimates of future earnings, a highly vulnerable position.

WHO ARE THE GROWTH SUPERSTARS?

After all my touting of the Twentieth Century Investors' funds, their top performer (excluding their Giftrust fund, which has a 10-year holding period) for 1993 places only 18th out of 73 funds in this category. The top performer, PBHG Growth Fund, sports a high 1.52 beta but has ranked, on average, in the top 2 percent in its category for the past three years. Following at a distance—31.41 percent vs. PBGH's stellar 46.57 percent—is Twentieth Century Giftrust Investors, the No. 2 fund. It is a unique vehicle designed for trust accounts. The minimum term of investment is ten years—that is, you must wait ten years to redeem your shares. With that kind of asset stability, the fund can invest very aggressively, which accounts for its strong performance. The fund is ideally suited for parents or grandparents to save systematically for a child's college education.

The Berger 100 fund was No. 1 in its category for the past three years but ranks only No. 21 on the current list. This is a good example of just how volatile these funds can be. At the end of May 1993, it was showing a loss for the year, and yet it wound up with a 21.20 percent profit by the end of 1993.

For the nimble, a shot of PBHG Growth's excellent performance might be fun because it could give back short-term profits quickly. For the more conservative, No. 3 SAFECO Equity, with a low 1.07 beta (don't confuse this fund with the roller coaster 1.36 beta of SAFECO Growth), and SteinRoe Capital Opportunity (1.10 beta), both of which have good recent performances, might be safer choices.

SOMETIMES A BLENDED STYLE IS BEST

The history of the past few years has been characterized by a rolling correction between the growth and value funds. Value stocks will lead for a time only to see growth stocks overtake them and regain the lead.

In retrospect, trading the pure growth stock funds and value stock funds and shifting from one investment style to the other would have been most appropriate for tax-sheltered retirement accounts where the absence of tax consequences make the trading activity feasible. The extra profit opportunity may be well worth it.

On the other hand, for taxable accounts where staying with a fund for at least a year (to qualify for the 28 percent maximum federal capital gain tax break) is most advantageous, I might argue in favor of the blend funds.

The Heritage Makes the Difference

The true stunner this year is American Heritage. This unique fund is run by German-born Heiko Thieme, who bought out the previous manager in 1990 and has produced an excellent three-year track record: No. 1 in its category with a beta of 1.20.

Morningstar's assessment of American Heritage is colorful: "This fund is either the greatest turnaround story since Kaufmann or a colossal fluke. Two and one-half years worth of great returns don't provide sufficient evidence for a judgment, but the fund may be worthy of serious consideration." What else can you say about a fund which is beating the No. 2 blend stock fund (the more mainstream Fidelity Capital Appreciation) by over 23 percent—41.39 percent vs. 33.41 percent for 1993?

Long-Term Track Records Can Be Deceiving

As you can see by reviewing the track records of the blend funds, few leaders remain after three years (Table 8.4). Three funds of the top 25 could not make the 50th percentile (SBSF, Fidelity Capital Appreciation, and Blanchard Global Growth), and 10 to 40 percent of the list—could not make the top 25 percent in their category for the past three years.

For this category at least, it is obvious that only the short-term track record is important in selecting a fund and that you need to keep your eyes on the fund at all times. Note also that only nine funds have betas in excess of 1.00. Almost two-thirds of the top 24 funds have low betas, with No. 2 Fidelity Capital Appreciation being as low as 0.55 and No. 13 SBSF close behind with a beta of 0.57.

For Those Pesky Investment Buffs

Morningstar considers funds that have a combined relative [relative to the S&P 500's ratio] price/earnings ratio and price/book

TABLE 8.4
Donoghue's Blend Stock SuperStar Candidates
25 Top-Performing Direct-Marketed Blend Stock Funds—YTD 12/31/93

Rank	Fund Name	Investment Objective	YTD Total Return (%)	YTD Rank in OBJ	3-Year Rank in OBJ	Beta (3-Year)	Mstar Risk (3-Year)	Minimum Initial Purchase ($)	800 #	Availability + No Fee	Fee	Covenant Rating**
1	American Heritage	Aggr. Growth	41.39	1	1	1.20	0.94	5000	828-5050		S W	4
2	Fidelity Capital Apprec (3%)*	Aggr. Growth	33.41	6	64	0.55	0.67	2500	544-8888	F	S W	1
3	Loomis Sayles Small Cap	Small Company	24.68	10	NA	NA	NA	2500	633-3330	W	S	NA
4	Fidelity Magellan (3%)	Growth	24.66	7	16	1.06	0.65	2500	544-8888	F	S W	3
5	Legg Mason Special Invstmt.	Small Company	24.13	13	45	0.77	0.80	1000	822-5544		W	1.5
6	Berger 101	Growth-Inc	23.57	2	1	1.03	0.70	250	333-1001	S F W		3
7	Fidelity Value	Growth	22.94	9	16	0.78	0.58	2500	544-8888	F	S W	2
8	Fidelity Retirement Growth	Growth	22.13	11	11	1.10	0.72	500	544-8888	F	S W	3.5
9	Gabelli Asset	Growth	21.84	11	47	0.63	0.52	1000	422-3554		S W	3.5
10	Strong Opportunity	Growth	21.19	13	17	0.94	0.80	1000	368-1030	S F	W	3
11	20th Century Heritage Inv.	Growth	20.43	15	24	1.13	1.04	1000	345-2021	S	F W	2.5
12	SteinRoe Special	Growth	20.42	15	20	1.00	0.76	1000	338-2550	S F W		2
13	SBSF	Growth-Inc	20.41	6	51	0.57	0.49	5000	422-7273		S W	2.5
14	Fidelity Growth & Income (3%)*	Growth-Inc	19.53	6	4	0.97	0.62	2500	544-8888	F	S W	3
15	Fidelity Trend	Growth	19.15	18	15	1.22	0.92	2500	544-8888	F	S W	2.5
16	Invesco Growth	Growth	19.02	19	29	1.13	0.92	1000	525-8085	S	F W	3.5
17	Dreyfus Growth & Income	Growth-Inc	18.59	9	NA	NA	NA	2500	645-6561	S F		3
18	Fidelity	Growth-Inc	18.36	10	32	0.86	0.67	2500	544-8888	F	S W	3
19	Dodge & Cox Stock	Growth-Inc	18.35	10	32	0.96	0.75	2500	415-434-0311		S W	4.5
20	Vanguard/PRIMECAP	Growth	18.03	22	33	1.06	1.08	10000	662-7447		S F W	5
21	Managers Special Equity	Small Company	17.35	45	38	0.99	0.84	10000	835-3879		W	2
22	Vanguard/Trustees' Eqty. U.S.	Growth-Inc	17.24	13	35	0.91	0.81	10000	662-7447		S F W	3
23	Dreyfus New Leaders	Small Company	17.03	46	62	0.87	0.82	2500	645-6561	S F W		1
24	Salomon Brothers Capital	Growth	16.99	25	50	1.27	1.15	1000	725-6666		W	3
25	Managers Cap. Appreciation	Growth	16.68	26	24	1.00	0.90	10000	835-3879		W	3

*Waived for IRAs maintained at Fidelity
** One to Five "Thumbs Up" (best rating is 5). *Source:* Covenant Investment Management, Copyright 1994.
+ The Donoghue Group, Copyright 1994

S = Charles Schwab & Co.
F = Fidelity FundsNetwork
W = Jack White & Co.

ratio of 1.50 to 2.25 to be blend funds. Blend funds can include both growth and value stocks.

As you can see by reviewing the chart, it is tough to get top performance out of large cap stocks. Only three funds—No. 6 Berger 100, No. 16 INVESCO Growth, and No. 19 Dodge & Cox Stock Fund—are large cap investors. Nineteen funds focused on mid-cap stocks, and only three were among the top 25 small cap stocks (No. 3 Loomis Sayles Small Cap, No. 21 Managers Special Equity, and No. 23 Dreyfus New Leaders).

Who Are the Blend Stock SuperStars?

You simply cannot ignore the excellent and consistent performance of Heiko Thieme's American Heritage. His combination of confident, high portfolio turnover, micro-caps, and contrarian positions are setting a high standard to maintain.

In fairness, I should note that Thieme's performance for the last six months of 1993 dropped him further down the list but the fund is still in the top 25 percent of the blend category. If he can recovery his leadership, Thieme's could be a SuperStar fund. No other blend funds have the right combination of consistent low risk, high return performance to be considered SuperStars.

TAMING THE SCARY SECTOR PORTFOLIOS

Now, for the more aggressive investors, I would like to introduce the Sector SuperStars (Table 8.5). Sector funds, by my definition, are usually undiversified, aggressively managed funds invested in a potentially volatile, concentrated sector of the financial markets.

For my purposes, along with sector funds I include specialty funds, such as Fidelity's Select Portfolios, precious metals funds including gold funds, and high quality, long-term bond funds like the Benham Target Maturity Trust zero-coupon Treasury bond funds, which have been an excellent way to aggressively play declining long-term interest rates. If these sound too rich for your blood, you are in the majority of mutual fund investors and you should move on to the next chapter. If not, enter the sector funds.

Conservative Investors, Go to the Next Chapter

If you find selecting an attractive diversified stock fund threatening, you should understand that most investors find the often

TABLE 8.5
Donoghue's Stock-Bond Sector SuperStar Candidates
25 Top-Performing Direct-Marketed Sector Funds—YTD 12/31/93

Rank	Fund Name	Investment Objective	YTD Total Return (%)	YTD Rank in OBJ	3-Year Rank in OBJ	Beta (3-Year)	Mstar Risk (3-Year)	Minimum Initial Purchase ($)	800 #	Availability + No Fee	Fee	Covenant Rating**
1	United Svcs. Gold Shares	Sp. Metals	123.92	3	93	-0.74	4.27	1000	873-8637		S W	NA
2	Fidelity Sel. Prec. Metals (3%)	Sp. Metals	111.64	9	10	-0.42	2.40	2500	544-8888	F	S W	NA
3	Blanchard Precious Metals	Sp. Metals	100.42	16	24	-0.34	2.50	3000	922-7771		S W	NA
4	Vanguard Spec. Gold & Prec.	Sp. Metals	93.36	22	17	-0.30	2.17	3000	662-7447		S F W	NA
5	United Svcs. World Gold	Sp. Metals	89.78	29	6	-0.44	2.57	1000	873-8637		S W	NA
6	Lexington Goldfund	Sp. Metals	86.96	38	65	-0.41	2.44	1000	526-0056	S W		NA
7	Benham Gold Equities Index	Sp. Metals	81.22	41	51	-0.31	2.76	1000	472-3389	S W		NA
8	Fidelity Sel. American Gold (3%)	Sp. Metals	78.68	51	20	-0.19	2.27	2500	544-8888	F	S W	NA
9	Invesco Strat. Gold	Sp. Metals	72.63	61	48	-0.37	2.64	1000	525-8085	S	W	NA
10	Scudder Gold	Sp. Metals	59.35	77	75	-0.24	2.10	1000	225-2470		S W	NA
11	USAA Investment Gold	Sp. Metals	58.33	80	68	-0.30	2.41	1000	382-8722			NA
12	Evergreen Global Real Estate	Sp. Unaligned	51.42	1	34	0.64	1.12	2000	235-0064	F W		NA
13	Fidelity Sel. Brokerage & Inv (3%)	Sp. Financ	49.30	1	20	1.34	1.07	2500	544-8888	F		1
14	Fidelity Sel. Indust. Equip. (3%)	Sp. Tech	43.32	1	47	0.74	0.83	2500	544-8888	F		4
15	Fidelity Sel. Leisure (3%)	Sp. Unaligned	39.56	4	26	0.92	0.67	2500	544-8888	F	S W	3
16	Fidelity Sel. Broadcast & Med (3%)	Sp. Unaligned	38.02	8	17	0.99	0.83	2500	544-8888	F		3.5
17	Invesco Strat. Leisure	Sp. Unaligned	35.71	12	4	1.00	0.74	1000	525-8085	S	F W	4
18	Fidelity Sel. Automotive (3%)	Sp. Unaligned	35.37	16	1	0.71	0.54	2500	544-8888	F		2
19	Fidelity Sel. Software/Comp. (3%)	Sp. Tech	32.48	18	1	1.41	1.48	2500	544-8888	F	S W	5
20	Fidelity Sel. Devel. Comm. (3%)	Sp. Tech	31.74	31	5	1.24	1.09	2500	544-8888	F		3.5
21	Benham Target Mat. 2015	Gvt. Treasury	30.51	2	1	3.30	5.17	1000	472-3389	S F W		NA
22	Fidelity Sel. Telecommun. (3%)	Sp. Util	29.65	4	1	0.85	0.74	2500	544-8888	F	S W	5
23	Fidelity Sel. Technology (3%)	Sp. Tech	28.63	45	31	1.40	1.35	2500	544-8888	F		5
24	Fidelity Sel. Home Finance (3%)	Sp. Financ	27.26	7	1	1.28	0.94	2500	544-8888	F		5
25	Vanguard Spec. Energy	Sp. Nat. Res.	26.42	20	33	0.74	1.47	3000	662-7447		S F W	1

*Waived for IRAs maintained at Fidelity
** One to Five "Thumbs Up" (best rating is 5). *Source:* Covenant Investment Management, Copyright 1994.
+ The Donoghue Group, Copyright 1994

S = Charles Schwab & Co.
F = Fidelity FundsNetwork
W = Jack White & Co.

Copyright Morningstar Inc., 1994

volatile sector funds even more difficult to approach. Actually, it has been my observation over the years that the mark of some of the most successful mutual fund portfolios has been their willingness to include a number of carefully selected sector funds. Taking a first look at the Stock and Bond Sector Super-Stars list reveals some tempting choices.

There's Gold in Them Thar Sectors

The eleven top funds are all precious metals or gold mining shares funds (all eleven in the category), which have been enjoying an excellent run of late. They earned an average of 86.94 percent for the year and 27.07 percent for the last quarter of 1993! My feeling is that gold has a way to go and that these funds are worth watching, but only for steel-stomach, patient investors or wise investors who can place five to ten percent in gold funds and live with that.

Which Gold Fund Is Best for You?

Well, United Services Gold Shares has the highest Morningstar Risk by a long shot, being 4.27 times as risky as the average gold fund. After that, you can pretty much take your pick; the rest of the list are about the same risk level. That leaves performance as the last criterion. Here United Services Gold Shares was at the top this past year with a 123.92 percent annual return. Fidelity Select Precious Metals was a close second with a 111.64 percent return.

Weighing against United Services Gold Shares is its high risk; in its favor is its performance. Considering that much of its performance is due to its South African exposure and the fact that the social investment ban on South African stocks has been officially lifted, future performance could be buoyed up by additional demand for those high-performance shares. In addition, the worldwide demand for gold is buoying up the entire market.

On the other hand, United Services World Gold does not invest in South African mining companies and has the best relative (top 6 percent) three-year performance of the eleven gold funds. Still, it did post the second worst record in 1992. Our SuperStar choice should be United Services World Gold for the less aggressive investor, although since I am recommending no more than a 5- to 10-percent position in gold, both are tempting. World Gold is the better pick, however.

The Zeroes Were Positive This Year, Until . . .

As recently as October, the best performer on the list, year-to-date, was Benham Target Maturity 2020, which had posted a return of 44.82 percent in just ten months with a supersonic beta of 3.59! It did end up the year with a total return of 35.62 percent, but what a ride!

If the S&P were to decline only 1.00 percent, this fund would likely plunge three and one-half times as much! The real question is, "Can this fund repeat its superior performance?" I answer, "Yes, but only if interest rates continue their plunge."

In reality, during November 1993, long-term government zero-coupon bond rates rose, and this fund lost 5.5 percent in November alone. No thanks! Not at this point in the interest rate cycle.

I think this roller coaster ride is over for now, but if long bond interest rates are falling (and, who knows, there may be another down leg to this interest rate cycle), this is the place to be. But only if you can stand to watch it fluctuate every day.

Let the Cooler Heads Prevail

There are some very attractive funds that have done nicely this past year. This is a reality check I added to make sure they were still moving in the right direction. With sector funds, it is always valuable to look at their shorter term track records for a reality check.

For the three months ended 12/31/93, the gold funds still top the list but others seem attractive.

No. 12 Evergreen Global Real Estate looks to be a Super-Star fund, earning 51.42 percent for the year and 10.18 percent in the last quarter of 1993. A creative and savvy blend of residential, retail, and commercial real estate holdings, construction companies, mall developers, and apartment managers in the United States and in both developed and underdeveloped emerging markets, this fund looks to be well-tuned to several of the current economic themes.

Fidelity Select Health Care, Vanguard Specialty Health Care, and Invesco Health Science seem to be have found the good news in the Clinton health care package. They placed 15th, 16th, and 17th among the top performers for the last three months of 1993.

While many are tempting, only United Services World Gold and Evergreen Real Estate Fund seem candidates for SuperStar funds.

THE BOTTOM LINE: TOMORROW'S SUPERSTARS?

Let's see how we far we have come. Our list of SuperStar fund candidates is growing. I have included a few worthy higher-beta funds to add some spark to our portfolio after we have concentrated on the low-beta funds (Table 8.6). Remember, these are only the most attractive candidates, we'll do the final sorting later in this book.

TABLE 8.6
Donoghue's Domestic Stock SuperStar Candidates

Fund Name	Type	1993 Return	Mstar Risk (3-Year)
United Services World Gold	Gold	89.78%	2.57
Evergreen Real Estate Fund	Sector	51.42	1.12
PBHG Growth	Growth	46.57	1.52
American Heritage Fund	Blend	41.39	0.94
Safeco Equity	Growth	30.91	1.02
Oakmark Fund	Value	30.50	NA
Mutual Beacon	Value	22.93	0.38

NA = Not available (less that three-year track record)
Source: Morningstar Mutual Funds on Disc and The Donoghue Group

LET'S GET OUT OF THE COUNTRY!

Actually, that's what many diversified domestic stock funds have already done. Most of the funds listed above include in their portfolios at least some foreign stocks. That, obviously, is true of Evergreen Global Real Estate and United Services World Gold. Indeed, it is not uncommon to discover that funds you think are domestic are actually global funds investing in both U.S. and foreign securities.

If you think about it, few domestic funds claim to invest in domestic securities. Rather, they state their goals in their names. They claim to invest for *growth,* or *growth and income,* or they state that they invest in *equities*—without saying they will use only domestic securities to achieve that goal.

In fact, in today's global economy, if you wish to increase the odds of reaching your investment goals, you have to think globally. Hold that thought just a bit and we will, in the next chapter, explore the exciting world of international stock funds.

Get your passport ready, then close your eyes (on second thought, think about closing your eyes), and imagine that we are flying overseas in our sleek, modern "Concorde luxury airplane of the mind." Now, quietly turn the page. Voila! You have arrived.

CHAPTER 9

Can the Overseas Mutual Funds Continue to Soar?

The International Investment Boom Is Just Beginning

If you have not yet discovered international stock or bond Super-Star mutual funds, you are missing out on the investment opportunity of a lifetime. If you love the thrill of seeing "good old American ingenuity" in action, look to China, Southern Europe, and Latin America where they have taken to heart the lessons we taught them.

This is not to put down the American economy—American industry is still the standard of excellence to beat, and there always will be excellent investment opportunities in America. All I am saying is, "A rich patriot is a whole lot more effective than a poor patriot." And the rich patriots are investing abroad.

CHINA, EUROPE, AND LATIN AMERICA ARE LEADING THE WAY

The three most compelling reasons for investing internationally are:

1. ***Chinese Capitalism.*** The triumphant and exhilarating expansion of capitalism in China is having a dramatic impact on the Southeast Asian stock markets, which are supplying construction services, new industry, retail outlets, and other services essential to an ancient agrarian country entering the industrial age in 1994.

2. ***European Recovery.*** The strong but frustrating and slow economic recovery in Europe has been driven by slowly falling German interest rates.

3. ***Emerging Latin American Markets.*** The economic resurgence of the no longer sleepy banana republics in Latin America has been stimulated by the late 1993 passage of NAFTA.

Capitalism Is Alive and Thriving in China

After experimenting with capitalism in a province in South China to study the implications of the return of financial and entrepreneurial giant Hong Kong to Chinese control in 1997, the Chinese have lit a fire that will prove impossible to extinguish. Yet savvy investors understand that it is currently difficult and unwise for individual investors to invest directly in the primitive and undeveloped Chinese stock markets.

It is the companies listed on Southeast Asian markets in Hong Kong, Malaysia, Singapore, Australia, and even on the London stock exchange that hold the true opportunities for investors. The fact that many of these currencies are formally or informally tied to the dollar greatly reduces the currency risks inherent in investing in European stocks.

What's Really Going on in Europe?

European stock and bond funds look to provide especially attractive returns over the next few years. However, the story of a European Common Market is emerging much more slowly than many expected.

Those of you who bought European stock market mutual funds in 1990 and 1991, when "the story" of great opportunities was compelling (and greatly premature), know the sting of investing too early. Now the story is both compelling and true.

It is the no-load funds, where investors typically demand some results before investing their hard-earned money, that are growing. The loaded broker funds are stagnant, since no one believes the story that was told prematurely.

You know the brokers were all saying to themselves, "What is the problem? I made my commissions. My brokerage firm made money. And, well, two out of three is pretty good, isn't it?" Sorry, that's called an opportunistic rip-off, folks.

Germany Is the Engine of European Recovery

The story that is making money for international investors is that Germany has a real economic problem to deal with: East Germany. The Germans are truly challenged in integrating an entire third-world country into their thriving economy.

In fact, it is a twin challenge: Stimulate the economy and provide jobs for East Germans and control inflation in the process. As you remember from the 1980s in America, to keep inflation under control you have to keep interest rates high, and to stimulate growth you have to keep interest rates low.

For years, the Bundesbank, the German "Fed," has been the defender against inflation. Germany has been torn apart before by rampant inflation, and preventing the recurrence of inflation is a major goal for the Bundesbank.

A Wheelbarrow Full of Worthless Cash.   Jim Benham, founder of Capital Preservation Fund and "The Fed Watcher" tells a wonderful story about inflationary Germany. A man goes to the bakery to buy some bread. To buy one loaf of bread, he needs a wheelbarrow full of inflated marks. He goes in to buy the bread leaving the wheelbarrow of money outside. He returns to find the money is there but the wheelbarrow is gone! (The wheelbarrow—symbolic of hard currency or gold—held its value better than the money!)

The German Bundesbank has finally been allowing interest rates to fall in recent years. We can expect further declines in interest rates in the coming years.

The power of declining interest rates to stimulate stock prices can be awesome; witness the effect of falling rates on the U.S. stock market in 1991–1993. So, if you fear rising interest rates decimating the U.S. stock market, why not invest where interest rates are falling?

Forget About Sleepy Banana Republics and Watch an Economic Miracle

If Latin America conjures up images of sleepy banana republics, you are living in the past. Capitalism's triumph over communism is nowhere more evident that in Latin America. I would not be surprised to see workers migrating across the Rio Grande headed south in five years. That may be where the jobs are.

American corporations have been downsizing from the excesses of the 1980s, merging, and consolidating operations in an effort to boost productivity and become more competitive on the international business scene. The resulting layoffs of tens of thousands of workers has undermined consumer confidence in the U.S. economy. This will hold back growth domestically.

On the other hand, in Latin America, the economic recovery is pretty amazing. The investment opportunities in these emerging markets deserve a place in your portfolios.

TWO WAYS MONEY IS MADE ON INTERNATIONAL INVESTMENTS

Understanding what makes international investing unique will help you understand what makes international funds such powerful investments.

First, you can make money because the value of the securities is appreciating in the foreign currency, even if the dollar's value remains unchanged. For example, falling interest rates make European bonds more valuable simply because falling interest rates make all bonds increase in market value. This kind of profit is an economic profit.

Second, you can make money investing in foreign currency-denominated investments—even in stagnant or declining financial markets—when the value of the dollar is weakening or declining against that foreign currency. For example, if you are invested in French franc-denominated stocks on the French stock exchange and the dollar declines against the French franc, when the fund prices that stock's market value in dollars (as it must do each day to determine its net asset value [N.A.V.] per share), it will buy more dollars. Thus, you make a profit (an increase in N.A.V.) on your investment, even if it has not changed value in French francs.

The real key to making international profits is the relative impact of these two factors. A few years ago, the Japanese stock market advanced dramatically while the dollar strengthened (rose) against the yen. Japanese investors made a killing and U.S. investors in yen-denominated stocks lost money.

Finally, the worst thing that can happen is that the dollar rises and the foreign stock market declines. Then, you lose both ways.

SO WHAT DRIVES THE VALUE OF THE DOLLAR? AND WHAT DOES IT MEAN TO AMERICAN INVESTORS?

To grossly oversimplify the currency markets, the value of the currency of the country whose interest rates are rising relative to the country whose interest rates are flat or falling will tend to have a stronger currency (i.e., its currency will buy more of the other country's currency).

The rule of thumb? When the dollar is weakening, don't buy dollars. Invest in foreign currency-denominated investments, instead.

How does this apply to today's investing? Interest rates in Europe, for example, are likely to fall faster than U.S. rates rise in the coming year, so the dollar should remain stable or weaken slightly. This is GOOD news for U.S. investors in international funds whose investments are denominated in foreign currencies (when re-priced in dollars, this adds value in the conversion). Combine that good (or even neutral) news with rising stock markets in Europe and you have a very positive potential for U.S. investors in European stock funds.

If U.S. interest rates should rise dramatically and European rates remain stable, the dollar should strengthen, which would be BAD news for U.S. investors in international funds. Still, the value of European stocks could rise faster than the decline in dollar value and still make American investors a profit.

A rising dollar can have the opposite effect. In 1990, the currency risks more than overcame the dramatic gains in the Japanese stock market to wipe out profits entirely for U.S. investors.

A HEDGE IN TIME SAVES MINE

When the U.S. dollar rises in value (strengthens) against other currencies throughout the world, mutual fund managers can take steps to reduce their losses. They can:

► Keep a larger cash position in U.S. investments when they think the dollar will rise in value.

► Invest more in foreign companies that have good U.S. earnings.

► Hedge against foreign currencies by using options and/or futures.

► Invest in currencies that have a lower correlation with one another.

For example, a manager may invest in Pacific Basin countries even if he thinks the dollar will rise because many Pacific Basin currencies are tied to the movement in the U.S. dollar.

WHEN THE DOLLAR IS WEAKENING, DON'T BUY DOLLARS

That's the rule of thumb you want to follow. But the real answer is: If the value of international stock funds is rising, invest in them, if it is falling, don't.

Performance is the key, as always. That means performance after all the expenses, currency risks, and market profits are factored in as in the total return of a mutual fund.

Remember my favorite refrain, **the guy who manages the fund at the top of the list is right and the guy at the bottom of the list is wrong**. Currently, the new guys at the top of the list are emerging markets funds.

WHAT ARE EMERGING MARKETS?

As the citizens of a less-developed country begin to move from a rural, agricultural society to a more urban, industrialized society, the first three things they invest in are: housing, automobiles, and gold jewelry. In many of these countries (often former communist nations), citizens were denied the right to own property. Their hunger to own their own home must be satisfied first when they begin to accumulate some wealth.

The second purchase is a car. The phenomenon of being able to broaden one's social, educational, shopping, working, and cultural experiences is what changes a narrowly focused agrarian society into a sophisticated urban society. This requires the mobility symbolized and provided by an automobile.

The major purchases of a home and a car require the use of credit. In this way the role of financial institutions begins to take on importance. Combine these experiences with the often high savings rate in developing countries and you can see why financial institutions play a more central role.

As the economy expands at often a very dramatic rate, so does inflation. After acquiring the basis of an inflation hedge in the form of their homes, people discover the need to identify some convenient, portable storehouse of value. That inflation hedge is often 23-carat gold jewelry which has a use, a reliable and plausible gold content, and a reasonably reliable resale value.

THE SCOOP ON EMERGING MARKETS FUNDS

So, you can see why I like three kinds of funds to participate in the emerging markets as well as more established foreign markets. Let's talk a bit about the emerging markets funds that invest in blue chip investments in dozens of less-developed countries.

Emerging Markets Funds invest in housing, automobile, and financial services stocks in underdeveloped but emerging countries: construction companies, lumber companies, banks (as much for their real estate holdings as their business financing, housing, and auto loans), automobile manufacturers, and distributors and the like.

Evergreen Global Real Estate Fund (I hate to be so specific but this is currently the only truly global no-load fund) that invests in REITS, construction companies, apartment owners, shopping center developers, and other housing-related businesses both in the United States and in foreign (including developed and emerging markets) markets.

Gold Mining Share Funds are a less direct investment to take advantage of these trends, but still participating in the growing worldwide demand for 23-carat gold jewelry as an inflation hedge. This is driven strongly by Chinese demand, in particular.

THE INSIDER ROUTE TO BECOMING AN INTERNATIONAL SUPERSTAR INVESTOR

With the investment fundamentals so strong overseas, you would be well advised to invest 50 percent or more internationally. The question is specifically: How? In stocks or bonds? In individual securities or in mutual funds? In specific sectors or in diversified funds? The answers are important to your investment success.

STICK WITH STOCKS AND BEAT THE BONDS

Most of the high yields in declining interest rate debt markets are in Europe where the prospects of continued monetary instability are disturbing as Europeans attempt to form an European Economic Community. Therefore, I prefer investing in stocks rather than bonds because of the high potential.

However, for bond fund devotees, I like the idea of investing in hedged European bond positions where you can earn the capital gains (as interest rates fall and market values rise) without the risks of a rising dollar wiping out your profits. Over time, hedging costs money and, some say, over the long-term is unnecessary. However, if you were in short-term worldwide bonds in recent years assuming they would be as stable as a money fund (they turned out to be vulnerable to a round of European currency devaluations), you learned the value of hedging, even in short-term positions.

If you were in a hedged portfolio, you lost only a little. If you were not, you lost a lot. (Ironically, it was the largely unhedged, mostly loaded funds that lost the most. The few no-load funds were wise enough to hedge and lost the least. This time around, your broker's commission, or load, bought you precious little of value.)

If you feel that you are a long-term investor and are comfortable investing without hedging protection, you might consider an unhedged European bond fund like Benham European Bond Fund (1-800-4-SAFETY). If not, you would do well to choose Blanchard Flexible Income Fund (1-800-922-7771), which includes a hedged European bond position with selected domestic junk and government bond positions.

Personally, I feel that the risk of monetary instability is worth taking for stock-sized profits but not worth it for bond-sized profits, but that decision is yours. If you must invest in international bonds, stick with a flexible fund like Blanchard that knows when to deal itself out of this uncertain bond market. However, investing in stocks outside the United States, where the fundamentals are often much stronger, will likely be safer than investing in stock the good old U.S. of A.

When I say the fundamentals are stronger abroad, what I mean is that, given a tired, aging U.S. bull market in stocks looking forward to a weak recovery, I would opt for the vital, exciting prospects of investing in an emerging underdeveloped country learning the power of capitalism. While young stock markets, like young children, can make some awkward choices, the do grow up to be responsible adults. We did okay, didn't we?

IF YOU WANT YOUR INTERNATIONAL PROFITS TO DANCE, LET YOUR FUND'S PORTFOLIO MANAGER LEAD AND DIVERSIFY YOUR RISKS AROUND THE WORLD

Sometimes it is tempting to concentrate your investments in a few powerful funds focused in specific international financial centers: Southeast Asia, Europe or Latin America or even more specific country funds. It surprises many investors that well-diversified international stock funds and emerging markets funds, while less concentrated in "hot" markets, often return almost as much as the top regional or country funds (and more than most of them) at lower risks.

Managing an international fund is a complex dance that involves choosing individual securities, playing economic trends within the country and between that country's currency and the dollar, picking rising sectors of the securities markets, dealing with foreign custodians, brokers and regulatory agencies, analyzing financial statements maintained on differing accounting standard, and avoiding misjudging financial markets with lower financial disclosure standards, ethical standards and financial discipline. No, folks, this is a dance better left to professionals trained in the field. There are precious few who have the experience to even try.

The best deal for most investors is to stick with either the carefully diversified international stock funds that invest in both developed and emerging markets or the emerging markets funds that spread your risk of investing in dozens of emerging countries. Surprisingly, in international stock fund investing, a broader diversified fund offers a much better risk/reward trade-off than a more narrowly focused country or regional fund.

So, the bottom line is stick with the diversified international stock (and sometimes bond) funds and well-diversified emerging markets funds. You should have more than 50 percent of your money invested overseas. The safest way to invest that much of your money is into the diversified international stock funds.

If you feel more confident, you will want to invest in some of the Pacific Basin, European, or Latin American funds. You will have to develop your "sell" discipline well, however, to keep up with the leaders like Oakmark International, managed by Harris Associates, and Acorn International (run ironically by former Harris Associates partner and fund manager, Ralph Wanger—what happens when you remove an acorn? It leaves an Oakmark!).

WHAT'S IN AND WHAT'S OUT TODAY?

In which type of overseas fund should you invest: *International* (at least 75 percent foreign securities)? *Global* (less than 75 percent foreign securities but both international and domestic U.S. securities)? So-called *domestic* stock funds (which may include between 10 and 50 percent foreign securities), or some *asset allocation* fund that includes foreign securities?

The proof of the pudding is in the performance, and that is why, when we get to building your investment portfolio, we are going to build it with the safest and most consistent top-performing funds in the hottest asset classes. The guy at the top of the list has the right formula and the guy at the bottom has the wrong formula. You know what? Both of their stories are probably equally plausible. Only a few of those stories are true! Performance is truth.

The nice thing about my approach is that you don't have to decide how much to invest internationally or domestically. The right answer is to invest in a few of the top-performing funds on the list. If a domestic stock fund is doing best, invest in that. If a global stock fund is doing best, invest in that. If an international stock fund is doing best, your answer is also obvious; invest in the best, forget about the rest.

Remember my favorite refrain, **the guy who manages the fund at the top of the list is right and the guy at the bottom of the list is wrong**. Right now the international funds are right and the domestic funds are wrong!

TWO WAYS TO WIN—DOMESTICALLY OR INTERNATIONALLY

As I write this, in the short-term, both domestic and international stock funds are doing well. I just think that it's wiser to invest in a young bull market than an old one. While many domestic stock funds are performing very well, it is often in part because of their positions in foreign securities. Why ignore the fact that about two-thirds of the world's capitalization is outside the United States when even the best domestic stock funds haven't?

NOT A NEW FAD BUT A WELL-ESTABLISHED OPPORTUNITY

International equity funds are finding new acceptance after five years of lagging behind U.S. stock funds. In 1993 they hit their stride with a fury.

International stock funds, on average, gained 38.29 percent in 1993. Funds that invest just in the Pacific Rim stocks did even better, gaining an average 57.83 percent. Compare this performance with their five-year track records (Table 9.1).

If you followed the international funds closely as I have, invested in them during periods when the dollar was declining (as it was most of the 1980s), avoided them when the dollar was strengthening, and stuck with the top performers, it added significant total returns as well as valuable diversification to your portfolios.

International Funds for Insurance

In fact, it was international funds which allowed *Donoghue'$ MONEYLETTER* subscribers to *make* money in 1987, the year of the crash, and in 1990, the year of the Gulf War, two years when most managers and investors *lost* money. Granted, it was international *bond* funds that did the trick in both those years. Since 1983 until recently, however, we have recommended investing in the few small international stock funds in existence.

MONEYLETTER'S Untold Story

In case you are about to ascribe to us some great all-seeing vision on our part back in 1983, let me let you in on our deep dark secret. In 1983, when we were converting *Donoghue'$ MONEYLETTER* from a money market mutual fund newsletter (no one cared about the ailing stock markets until the bull

TABLE 9.1
Comparison of 1993 International Stock Returns
with the Five Years Ended 12/31/93

Type of Fund	Average Annual Total Return	
	1989–93	*1993*
Domestic Diversified Stock Funds	14.33%	12.61%
International Stock Funds	9.40	38.29
Pacific Stock Funds	7.39	57.83
Emerging Markets	14.65	72.19

Source: Morningstar Mutual Funds on Disc/The Donoghue Group

market returned in 1982) to an award-winning, full-range mutual fund investment newsletter (the Newsletter Publishers' Association's Best Financial Advisory Newsletter award in 1986),
we naively included international stock funds on the stock
funds list.

Being new to actually recommending individual stock
funds at the time, I simply overlooked the fact that the international stock funds should probably not have been listed with
domestic stock funds at the time. However, we soon recognized
that they were consistent top performers that often offered
lower risk and volatility than domestic stocks. Over the past
decade, we have acquired a valuable respect for and significant
experience with international stock funds, which has since
paid off for our subscribers.

NEW MARKETS AND OPPORTUNITIES WILL EMERGE IN THE 1990s

In the coming years, I suspect that investors will reap profits
from current third-world markets, although not in the near-
term from Eastern Europe or the countries that comprised the
former U.S.S.R. Russia and Eastern Europe are in political tur-
moil, but their longer-term outlook is positive.

Russia and other former states of the splintered Soviet
Union and Eastern European countries are entering the free
market. While they are still poor, underdeveloped countries, the
opportunities to invest in developing businesses in these countries will provide new profit opportunities.

EUROPE 1994 LOOKS A LOT LIKE USA 1982

Europe 1992, the nonfinisher economic union, will probably arrive in the coming years stimulating an already profitable stock
market. Europe is still in a recession. As German interest rates
continue their decline, other European central banks will allow
their rates to drop. After all, they don't have an East Germany to
absorb. As interest rates fall for Spain, Italy, France, and the
rest of Europe—a movement already underway—opportunities
there could be more significant than in Germany.

The parallels between Europe 1994 and the U.S. stock markets in 1982 when our interest rates began their dramatic decline are echoing throughout the financial markets. When U.S.
interest rates declined from 1982 on, the longest bull market in
recent memory ensued, interrupted briefly by rising interest

rates and a stock market crash in 1987. European rates today are high and dropping steadily.

International Bonds Can Wait a While, for Now.   When I started writing the book, international bond funds were yielding over 10 percent. Now they are yielding in the 6 percent range, although they did return on a total return basis 15.97 percent on average over the past year.

THE PACIFIC BASIN IS STIRRING

The Pacific Basin and Far East also are hotbeds of growth. Cheap labor and efficient production in the Pacific Basin are resulting in expanding business.

In the Far East, Thailand's exports have tripled over the last decade and its stock exchange has grown 120 percent in a little more than one year. Malaysia is also going great guns. Foreign investment was up 88 percent last year and manufacturing output increased 11 percent over the past six years. Singapore's economy grew at a 9 percent annual clip over the past several years.

JAPAN IS ALWAYS A PLAYER, BUT INVEST WITH CAUTION

Japan's economy is expected to grow slowly this year. The government is trying to stimulate the economy. If the Japanese central bank keeps lowering interest rates, it will be a big plus for that country's economy and financial markets.

In January, however, the Japanese stock market experienced a meltdown, making Japanese stock fund investing tempting. I, for one, will wait to see improving profits. Investing is seldom the game of playing extremes for "easy" profits. Savvy investors wait for a trend and then follow it until it peters out or another stronger trend tempts them to ride it.

CAVEAT EMPTOR MEANS THE SAME INTERNATIONALLY AS DOMESTICALLY

Regardless of whether you are an aggressive or conservative investor, you assume extra risks when you invest in overseas stock funds.

▶   First, you risk losing money due to an overall decline in a country's stock market or individual stock prices. Bad news about a specific company's financial condition will knock down the price of its stock.

▶ Second, you also face foreign currency risk. If the dollar gains in value against foreign currencies, the market value of your overseas fund will decline since the stocks are purchased in foreign dollars.

▶ Third, a political crisis could lead to a decline in stock prices as well as a weakening of the country's currency on the international markets, a double whammy.

As a savvy investor, you can learn to vote with your feet and switch to a more productive investment or simply switch to the safety of money funds.

AN INFORMAL INTRODUCTION TO SOME WORTHY SUPERSTARS

There are several excellent diversified international funds. I want to introduce you to two of the top international stock funds and two of the top emerging markets (not to be confused with domestic emerging **growth** funds which are ultra-small, capitalization stock funds).

☆ **FIDELITY EMERGING MARKETS FUND** (1-800-544-8888) is a dandy of a fund. It is the No. 1 international stock fund on my list, has been a consistent top-performer (in the top 1 percent of all funds for the past 3-, 6- and 12-month periods), and has a very low Morningstar risk rating (about half the downside risk of its peers). The single detracting characteristic is the 1.5 percent redemption fee if you invest for less than one year, a small price to pay in 1993 when it returned 81.76 percent to investors.

Their international stock funds, all no-load (although Fidelity Emerging Markets will add a 3 percent load in May), are where Fidelity Investments shines. They actually have offices in or near many of these emerging markets. With their well-respected research skills (I have personally visited their unbelievably well-equipped and computerized research library), and their firsthand knowledge, they are experts in this field.

☆ **LEXINGTON WORLDWIDE EMERGING MARKETS** (1-800-526-0056) is another excellent emerging markets fund that has achieved consistent top 10 percent performance in its objective. In 1993, it earned a total return of 63.37 percent for its investors. It did so with two-thirds the risk of its peers, making it another consistent top-performing fund that combines top performance with lower than expected risk.

☆ **OAKMARK INTERNATIONAL** (1-800-OAKMARK), the top-ranked (No. 9 among international stock funds but No. 1 among diversified funds) diversified (non-regional or emerging markets) international stock fund returned 53.58 percent for investors. This stellar performance was achieved in part by avoiding investment in Japan, the Achilles' heel of international stock investing for 1993. A virtual meltdown of the Japanese stock market, a serious problem for many international funds, was avoided by the savvy David Herro, Oakmark's portfolio manager.

A value-oriented (bargain stock) portfolio manager, Herro is a star in a field of growth-oriented (stocks with accelerating earnings growth) international managers. His secret weapon last year? He could find no bargains in Japan, so he refused to invest, a brilliant move in retrospect.

☆ **WARBURG, PINCUS INTERNATIONAL EQUITY COMMON SHARES** (no, don't read the abbreviation as "communications" stocks, although that is an intriguing investment idea) (1-800-257-5614) is a higher risk fund with lower than excellent returns this year but one we expect to be a comer to be watched in 1994. Regardless, it beat all but one diversified international stock fund for the year, no small feat.

WHERE CURRENCY RISK IS HIGHEST AND LOWEST

Currency risk is greatest in Europe and Japan due to monetary instability as Europe moves toward a European Economic Community and Japan tries to recover from its meltdown. Currency risk is a much lesser factor in many of the Pacific Basin (Hong Kong, Malaysia, Singapore, and Australian) stock markets, where many currencies are either formally or informally tied to fluctuations in the value of the dollar. For example, in Hong Kong, there is a fixed exchange rate for U.S. dollars but not for Japanese yen.

WHERE WILL TOMORROW'S WINNERS COME FROM?

Now we come to putting it all together. Which type of domestic mutual fund is best? Which international stock funds are best? Which global stock funds are best? Which areas of the world are best for U.S. investors? Which is best, international, global, or domestic stock fund investing?

INVEST IN THE BEST, FORGET ABOUT THE REST

Our challenge to invest in the best in the world is simplified: Invest in the funds at the top of the list. Don't be worried about the enormity of the universe, the top of the list will include both domestic and international funds most of the time.

If investing internationally seems "foreign" to you, it needn't be. To be brutally honest, as I write this book, international stock funds are topping the list.

LET'S GO TO THE VIDEOTAPE, OOPS, I MEAN THE LISTS

Now that we have a good overall understanding of international investing, it's time to go to the lists. For international funds, we have two lists from which to find our SuperStar candidates. The 25 top-performing direct-marketed international stock funds for 1993 are listed in Table 9.2. The 16 top-performing direct-marketed international bond funds for 1993 are listed in Table 9.3.

In Search of the Ultimate International Stock Fund

Reviewing my international stock list reveals the three strong suits of international investing today (China's impact on the new Asia, a European economic recovery, and emerging Latin American markets) as well as the two Achilles' heels of investing abroad (highly volatile young Latin American markets and a seriously economically unstable Japan).

If you are worried that international funds risk getting caught in a domestic correction, don't worry. They will. If we get a major correction in the S&P 500 (the U.S. stock market) the international funds will correct as well. However, the international stock funds will bounce like a tennis ball and the U.S. stock funds will likely bounce like an egg!

The top of the list is dominated by emerging markets and Pacific Rim stock funds. Until recently, the Pacific Rim funds

TABLE 9.2

Donoghue's International Stock SuperStar Candidates
25 Top-Performing Direct-Marketed International Stock Funds—YTD 12/31/93

Rank	Fund Name	Investment Objective	YTD Total Return (%)	YTD Rank in OBJ	3-Year Rank in OBJ	Mstar Risk (3-Year)	Minimum Initial Purchase ($)	800 #	Availability + No Fee	Fee
1	Fidelity Emerging Markets	Foreign	81.76	1	7	0.54	2500	544-8888	F	S W
2	T. Rowe Price New Asia	Pacific	78.76	24	16	0.83	2500	638-5660		S F W
3	59 Wall St. Pac. Basin Eqty.	Pacific	74.90	31	22	1.11	10000	212-493-8100		
4	Scudder Latin America	Foreign	74.32	5	NA	NA	1000	225-2470		S F W
5	Fidelity Pacific Basin (3%)*	Pacific	63.91	44	38	1.33	2500	544-8888	F	S W
6	Lexington Worldwide Emerging	Foreign	63.37	9	4	0.67	1000	526-0056		F
7	Scudder Pacific Opport.	Pacific	60.08	55	NA	NA	1000	225-2470	S W	S F W
8	Montgomery Emerg. Mkts.	Foreign	58.66	12	NA	NA	2000	572-3863	S	W
9	Oakmark International	Foreign	53.58	13	NA	NA	1000	476-9625	S	W
10	Warburg, Pincus Intl Eq Comm	Foreign	51.26	18	10	0.91	2500	257-5614	W	S F
11	T. Rowe Price Intl Discovery	Foreign	49.85	20	36	1.12	2500	638-5660		S F W
12	Acorn International	Foreign	49.11	21	NA	NA	1000	922-6769		S W
13	Sit International Growth	Foreign	48.37	22	NA	NA	2000	332-5580		W
14	Strong International Stock	Foreign	47.75	23	NA	NA	1000	368-1030	S F	W
15	International Equity	Foreign	45.75	29	47	1.19	2500	344-8332		S
16	Vanguard Intl Growth	Foreign	44.74	31	55	1.22	3000	662-7447		S F W
17	American AAdvantage Intl Eq.	Foreign	42.80	32	NA	NA	None	817-967-3509	W	S
18	20th Century Intl. Equity	Foreign	42.65	34	NA	NA	1000	345-2021	S	F W
19	Preferred International	Foreign	41.53	35	NA	NA	1000	662-4769		
20	Vontobel EuroPacific	Foreign	40.80	36	25	0.75	1000	527-9500		W
21	IAI International	Foreign	40.21	37	41	1.09	5000	945-3863	S W	
22	T. Rowe Price Intl Stock	Foreign	40.11	38	30	1.01	2500	638-5660		S F W
23	Fidelity Overseas (3%)*	Foreign	40.05	39	70	1.38	2500	544-8888	F	S W
24	USAA Investment Intl.	Foreign	39.81	40	28	0.92	1000	382-8722		W
25	Invesco Pacific Basin	Pacific	39.70	62	61	1.64	1000	525-8085	S	F W

S = Charles Schwab & Co.
F = Fidelity FundsNetwork
W = Jack White & Co.

* Waived for IRAs maintained at Fidelity
+ The Donoghue Group, Copyright 1994
Source: Copyright Morningstar Inc., 1994

TABLE 9.3
Donoghue's International Bond SuperStar Candidates
16 Top-Performing Direct-Marketed International Bond Funds—YTD 12/31/93

Rank	Fund Name	Investment Objective	YTD Total Return (%)	YTD Rank in OBJ	3-Year Rank in OBJ	Average Weighted Maturity	Mstar Risk (3-Year)	Minimum Initial Purchase ($)	800 #	Availability* No Fee	Fee
1	Bull & Bear Global Income	Worldwide Bond	24.95	9	2	15.70	0.20	1000	847-4200	W	S
2	Fidelity Global Bond	Worldwide Bond	21.28	14	22	10.00	0.43	2500	544-8888	F	S W
3	T. Rowe Price Intl Bond	Worldwide Bond	19.97	15	17	NA	1.02	2500	638-5660		S F W
4	Scudder International Bond	Worldwide Bond	15.83	37	5	9.90	0.66	1000	225-2470		S F W
5	BB&K International Fixed-Inc	Worldwide Bond	14.80	47	27	12.70	0.49	5000	415-571-5800		
6	Benham European Govt. Bond	Worldwide Bond	12.35	73	NA	10.20	NA	1000	472-3389	S F W	
7	Fidelity S/T World Income	ST World Inc.	11.89	1	NA	2.70	NA	2500	544-8888	F	S
8	BJB Global Income A	Worldwide Bond	11.47	79	NA	NA	NA	25000	435-4659	W	S
9	Blanchard S/T Global Income	ST World Inc.	8.45	12	NA	2.20	NA	3000	922-7771	W	S
10	T. Rowe Price S/T Global Inc	ST World Inc.	7.81	19	NA	2.60	NA	2500	638-5660		S F W
11	Alliance World Income	ST World Inc.	7.13	32	46	0.50	0.80	10000	227-4618		S F W
12	Scudder S/T Global Income	ST World Inc.	6.74	41	NA	1.70	NA	1000	225-2470		S F W
13	Smith Barney Shear W/W Pr A	ST World Inc.	-0.25	96	NA	NA	NA	2500	451-2010		S W
14	Legg Mason Global Government	Worldwide Bond	NA	NA	NA	8.50	NA	1000	822-5544		W
15	Fidelity New Markets Income	Worldwide Bond	NA	NA	NA	9.20	NA	2500	544-8888	F	S W
16	Alliance No. Am. Govt. Inc C	Worldwide Bond	NA	NA	NA	NA	NA	250	227-4618	W	S F

S = Charles Schwab & Co.
F = Fidelity FundsNetwork
W = Jack White & Co.

*The Donoghue Group, Copyright 1994

Source: Copyright Morningstar Inc., 1994

dominated the top of the list. Now it is the emerging markets funds that appear to be coming to the fore.

What Are My Superstar Stock Investment Choices?

You have to just love Fidelity Emerging Markets and Lexington Worldwide Emerging Markets for consistent top performance and Oakmark International and Warburg, Pincus International Equity Common Shares for diversified international choices (although they have shorter track records than the others). In addition, Scudder Latin America is a really outstanding Latin American fund, and—although a sector fund and not on this list—Evergreen Global Real Estate Fund is a fund to watch.

What About a Japanese Stock Recovery?

Does the drastic decline in the stock market (20 percent or more) signal a roaring BUY opportunity for Japanese stocks? Only time will tell, and that is the reason for using the update procedures I am providing you:

▶ Request a FREE Donoghue's Mutual Fund SuperStars Special Update Report by calling 1-800-982-BILL.

▶ Use your FREE Donoghue's SuperStars On-Line software to call 1-800-749-1348 (sophisticated investment software is FREE (a $39.95 value), data updates via modem cost $7 or less, price subject to change).

▶ Visit your business library and review Morningstar Mutual Funds reports.

PUTTING IT ALL IN PERSPECTIVE

Let's face it. For the next few years, it is likely that international stock funds will probably outperform domestic stock funds. The U.S. economy is having significant trouble moving the economy into a recovery and the stock market is, at best, near the end of a very long and tired bull market.

In Europe, the promise and reality of interest rates falling from very high levels, which have favored international bond funds, bring the promise of a long and sustained bull market in stocks. In Southeast Asia and the Pacific Rim, the seemingly unstoppable growth of capitalism in China is driving the stock markets in nearby countries to record levels. While corrections are inevitable from time to time the non-Japanese stock markets hold much more promise than the domestic U.S. stock market.

WHAT CAN GO WRONG?

Exercise caution. Political unrest in China, continued recession in Europe, a reversal of interest rates toward higher rates in the United States, further monetary indecision in Japan and over-speculation in specific countries could cause problems.

For these reasons, I would counsel against investing solely in country or regional international funds. Other than those caveats, the investment truth is **the guy who manages the fund at the top of the list is right and the guy at the bottom of the list is wrong**.

GO FOR IT!

You know my rule: Go with the guy at the top of the list. In the case of international funds, the novice and the experienced investor are well-served by sticking with the diversified international funds. The more aggressive younger investor may want to spice up the stew with some regional or country funds.

But do include international funds in your portfolio. A young bull market is better than an old one, at least for long-term investors.

CHAPTER 10

Should You Trust the Indices or the Managers?

Your Choice: Index, Total Return, or Safe Harbor Funds?

Now that we have looked at the domestic stock funds and the international stock and bond fund alternatives, it's time we satisfied your curiosity about the *easy answer* funds. Easy answer funds are the ones that seem to offer a way around doing the hard work of picking securities, market sectors, or individual mutual funds.

Actually, it hasn't been all that hard, has it? We have already looked at the full range of the most attractive diversified and nondiversified U.S. stock market funds and international funds. Now, we are going to look at potential SuperStar index, total return, and safe harbor funds.

Our goal is very simple. We want to see if we will make more money, more reliably by adding just one more independent middleman to help us pick the right investments. If that doesn't add a lot to the pot, we know that the my SuperStar strategy is the way to go.

SO YOU WANT AN *AVERAGE* INVESTMENT FUND?

Index funds are all the rage. As academics and the financial media love to say, "If something like 70 percent of all mutual funds can't beat the market averages, why not invest in an index fund that represents the overall market average?" The temptation, especially for those who have not yet encountered my SuperStar strategy, is to fall for this argument hook, line, and sinker.

WHAT IS AN INDEX FUND?

An index fund attempts to duplicate the performance of a particular market index. By definition, index funds are average performers.

There are as many kinds of index funds as there are kinds of indices. Some of the indices represented on our potential Super-Stars list are shown in Table 10.1.

TABLE 10.1
Decoding the Index Fund Names

Fund Name (Code)	Index's Real Name
Value Stock Index	S&P/Barra Value Index
Small Capitalization Stock Index	Russell 2000 Small Stocks (the 3000 largest less the 1000 largest stocks.)
Extended Stock Market Index	Wilshire 4500
Mid-Cap Stock Index	S&P Mid-Cap 400
Total Stock Market Index	Wilshire 5000
S&P 500 Stock Index	S&P 500 Largest Stocks
Schwab 1000	Schwab 1000 Largest Stock
S&P 100	S&P 100 Largest Stocks

The Superstar Insider's *Skinny* on Index Funds

The proponents of index funds are as passionate about their investment approach as they come. In fact, they would be right—if there were no such thing as bear markets (when indices like the S&P 500 will fall with the markets) and international investments (for which there are few indices and as many markets as there are countries) and only rising U.S. stock markets existed (so your stock index would be sure to rise in value).

Consider the following:

Index Fund Argument No. 1. It is difficult for average investors, who are unwilling to pay close attention to their investments (buy-and-hold investors), to beat the averages.

MY COMMENTS: We have seen a lot of very consistent, lower risk, attractively performing SuperStar funds whose performance would argue with that contention.

Sure, it *is* probably true that around 70 percent of managed domestic stock funds fail to beat the S&P 500 stock index. If investors are not willing to do any research into fund selection, the odds of beating an index fund are pretty tough. The average guy on the street, unarmed with a mutual fund newsletter to do his sorting for him, is unlikely to beat the index.

However, if you were smart enough to buy this book, you just might find a number of funds that can beat the index funds. If you are unwilling to upgrade your investments from time to time, you have a tough row to hoe.

In our Donoghue Mutual Fund Screens (Table 10.2) we identify more than a few funds that beat the top index fund this year. The No. 1 index fund earned only 18.70 percent this year. That doesn't even match our 20 percent cutoff.

To invest in index funds, you are going to have to decide what to do with your index fund investment when the stock market falls in a bear market. Who is going to shift your money into the international stock markets so you can invest where performance may be better and less risky? Who will shift your money into the safety of money market funds to avoid bear markets? And finally, who is going to shift you to bonds when interest rates are declining?

I can tell you this much. It won't be an index fund manager. Index funds just don't do those things. That is why index funds are not the be-all and end-all that many tout them to be.

Index Fund Argument No. 2. Index funds are cheap, have low expenses, and many of them are no-load.

MY COMMENTS: The low-cost provider, Vanguard, selectively sneaks in a 1 percent, one-time transaction cost and a $10 annual maintenance fee into its index fund accounts. Others, such as Dreyfus, Schwab, and Fidelity, tend to charge a "nuisance"

TABLE 10.2
Donoghue's Index SuperStar Candidates
25 Top-Performing Direct-Marketed Index Stock Funds—YTD 12/31/93

Rank	Fund Name	Investment Objective	YTD Total Return (%)	YTD Rank in OBJ	3-Year Rank in OBJ	Beta (3-Year)	Mstar Risk (3-Year)	Minimum Initial Purchase ($)	800 #	Availability + No Fee	Fee	Covenant Rating*
1	Vanguard Small Cap. Stock	Small Company	18.70	38	40	0.97	0.96	3000	662-7447		S F W	1
2	Vanguard Index Value	Growth-Inc	18.25	11	NA	NA	NA	3000	662-7447		S F W	3.5
3	Federated Mini-Cap	Small Company	15.29	55	NA	NA	NA	25000	245-5000		S W	1
4	Vanguard Index Extended Mkt.	Small Company	14.49	58	68	0.94	0.79	3000	662-7447		S F W	2
5	Vanguard Quantitative	Growth-Inc	13.83	26	34	1.02	0.74	3000	662-7447		S F W	3.5
6	Peoples S&P MidCap Index	Growth	13.52	41	NA	NA	NA	2500	645-6561	S		2
7	IBM Small Company Index	Small Company	11.32	74	70	0.98	0.77	2500	426-9876			2
8	Vanguard Index Tot. Stk. Mkt	Growth-Inc	10.62	47	NA	NA	NA	3000	662-7447		S F W	3.5
9	Vanguard Index 500	Growth-Inc	9.89	53	47	1.00	0.70	3000	662-7447		S F W	4
10	SEI Index S&P 500 Index	Growth-Inc	9.83	54	50	0.99	0.70	None	342-5734		S W	4
11	Woodward Equity Index Retail	Growth-Inc	9.83	54	NA	NA	NA	1000	688-3350			4
12	Capital Market Index	Growth-Inc	9.69	57	NA	NA	NA	10000	328-7408			NA
13	Schwab 1000	Growth-Inc	9.63	57	NA	NA	NA	1000	526-8600	S		4
14	Fidelity Market Index	Growth-Inc	9.62	59	49	1.00	0.71	2500	544-8888	F	S W	4.5
15	PNC Index Equity Instl	Growth-Inc	9.54	60	NA	NA	NA	5000	422-6538			4
16	Peoples Index	Growth-Inc	9.53	61	49	0.99	0.70	2500	645-6561	S		4.5
17	Federated Max-Cap	Growth-Inc	9.52	61	52	1.00	0.71	25000	245-5000	W	S	4
18	IBM Large Company Index	Growth-Inc	9.46	62	59	0.99	0.71	2500	426-9876			4.5
19	T. Rowe Price Equity Index	Growth-Inc	9.42	63	58	0.99	0.70	5000	638-5660		S F W	4
20	Portico Equity Index	Growth-Inc	9.11	66	57	0.99	0.71	1000	228-1024		W	4
21	One Group Equity Index Fid	Growth-Inc	9.09	68	NA	NA	NA	1000	338-4345			4.5
22	Ambassador Indexed Stock Fid	Growth-Inc	9.06	68	NA	NA	NA	None	892-4366			4.5
23	Stagecoach Corporate Stock	Growth-Inc	8.91	69	68	0.99	0.73	1000	222-8222			4.5
24	CoreFund Equity Index A	Growth-Inc	8.66	71	61	1.00	0.73	2500	355-2673			4
25	Seven Seas S&P 500 Index	Growth-Inc	7.99	73	NA	NA	NA	1000	617-654-6089			NA

* One to Five "Thumbs Up" (best rating is 5) Source: Covenant Investment Management, Copyright 1994.
+ The Donoghue Group, Copyright 1994

S = Charles Schwab & Co.
F = Fidelity FundsNetwork
W = Jack White & Co.

Copyright Morningstar Inc., 1994

redemption fee if a fund is sold within 6 months. Index funds often have restrictions or fees that make it more difficult for active investors to upgrade (switch) to other funds. Low expenses may be your tradeoff for more investment restrictions.

Index Fund Argument No. 3. Nearly all index funds have betas very close to 1.00, so there is little extra risk compared to the S&P 500.

MY COMMENTS: This is fascinating, since each index fund says it is tied to a different index, some of which are supposed to be better in one way or another than the S&P 500. If risk really is an issue to you—and it should be—you can find funds with betas much lower than 1.0.

Index Fund Argument No. 4. The best index funds have very low expense ratios. Vanguard has one of the lowest.

MY COMMENTS: Vanguard's funds are six of the top nine funds on our list. On the other hand, our other SuperStar lists have a lot of funds with much better track records. Expenses are important but secondary to performance.

The Kaufmann Fund has been the No. 1 performer since the 1987 crash but has a very high expense ratio—over 2 percent. Expense-sensitive fund buyers often ignore superior funds simply because of their higher-than-average expense ratios.

Index Fund Argument No. 5. Index funds are the best way to play the stock market.

MY COMMENTS: John Bogle of Vanguard has almost made a religion of index funds, and his excellent book, *Bogle on Mutual Funds,* has spread the word. But ask John about the times when the stock market declines and his index funds have losses, albeit average losses, and he'll have to admit that index funds lose money too.

Index Fund Argument No. 6. The academics have written millions of articles recommending index funds.

MY COMMENTS: When was the last time you met an academic who was a professional money manager? You know what they say about those than can and those that can't?

Seriously, it is much easier to rationalize doing studies of index funds over long periods because the index is available for comparisons. It is much harder to find long-term track records of investment advisors who have made judgments. Investing is not simply an investment formula; it is a lot of lost sleep, sweaty hands, and learning from mistakes that improve future performance.

Dozens of sincere and well-educated advisors have made asset allocation decisions, but for the five years ended 12/31/93, only my *Donoghue'$ MONEYLETTER* staff and I have been able to have the best long-term track record of asset allocation timing in *Hulbert Financial Digest.* I can tell you that many of those decisions were far from unanimous, and we wish we could have rethought some, but we put our decisions on the line and the results speak for themselves. Oh, yes, we beat the stock index funds often.

WHY NOT LET SOMEONE WITH ALL THE CHOICES MAKE THEM FOR ME?

That's the question millions of investors ask every day. Standing ready to answer them are the portfolio managers of the total return SuperStar candidates: asset allocation funds, funds of funds, and balanced funds (Table 10.3).

A Word Against Balanced Funds

I can hear the brokers now, "Heck folks, stocks and bonds make money so why don't we buy some of each, and over the long-term, you will make money, too." Balanced funds are typically 40 to 70 percent in stocks and the rest in bonds and/or cash. These are the funds salesmen love to sell when they find investors who know nothing about the investment markets.

Indeed, 1993 was a great year for balanced funds. Of our 25 top-performing total return funds, 14 were balanced funds. (If you ranked the funds on 3-month total returns to 12/31/93, that number would decreases to nine, and only one, Dreyfus Balanced, makes the top ten.)

But there is more to know than recent performance. You see, a balanced investment fund is sort of an asset allocation fund (a fund where the portfolio manager decides how much to invest in each asset class or category) where the basic decision of how much to invest often includes a minimum (typically 25 percent) allocation in high-grade, low-credit-risk, highly interest-rate-sensitive, long-term fixed-income investments.

Over the long-term, balanced funds have done pretty well— if the long term is measured from 1982 to the present when interest rates fell almost in a straight line to today's 25-year lows.

TABLE 10.3
Donoghue's Total Return SuperStar Candidates
25 Top-Performing Direct-Marketed Total Return Funds—YTD 12/31/93

Rank	Fund Name	Investment Objective	YTD Total Return (%)	YTD Rank in OBJ	3-Year Rank in OBJ	Beta (3-Year)	Mstar Risk (3-Year)	Minimum Initial Purchase ($)	800 #	Availability + No Fee	Fee	Covenant Rating*
1	Fidelity Asset Manager: Grth	Asset Alloc	26.32	6	NA	NA	NA	2500	544-8888	F	S W	3.5
2	Blanchard Global Growth	Asset Alloc	24.46	9	79	0.43	0.70	3000	922-7771	W	S	3.5
3	USAA Investment Cornerstone	Asset Alloc	23.73	11	33	0.49	0.66	1000	382-8722	F	S F W	3
4	Fidelity Asset Manager	Asset Alloc	23.29	12	4	0.43	0.29	2500	544-8888		S W	3
5	Founders Balanced	Balanced	21.85	1	17	0.54	0.57	1000	525-2440	S F		NA
6	CGM Mutual	Balanced	21.83	1	2	1.04	1.04	2500	345-4048		W	3.5
7	Fidelity Puritan	Balanced	21.45	2	5	0.62	0.57	2500	544-8888	F	S W	2
8	T. Rowe Price Spectrum Grth.	Growth	20.98	14	38	0.87	0.59	2500	638-5660		S F W	NA
9	Fremont Global	Asset Alloc	19.60	21	45	0.47	0.44	2000	548-4539	W	S	3
10	Fidelity Balanced	Balanced	19.27	4	10	0.41	0.40	2500	544-8888	F	S W	NA
11	Crabbe Huson Asset Alloc.	Asset Alloc	18.21	26	12	0.51	0.42	1000	541-9732	W		3
12	Dodge & Cox Balanced	Balanced	15.96	11	30	0.63	0.62	2500	415-434-0311			4.5
13	Evergreen Foundation	Balanced	15.71	15	1	0.79	0.61	500	235-0064	S F W		3.5
14	Permanent Port	Asset Alloc	15.52	34	95	0.25	0.58	1000	531-5142	W	S	NA
15	American AAdvantage Balanced	Balanced	14.82	18	44	0.54	0.55	None	817-967-3509	W		4
16	Strong Investment	Asset Alloc	14.50	42	77	0.56	0.61	250	368-1030	S F		NA
17	USAA Investment Balanced	Balanced	13.72	26	90	0.41	0.48	1000	382-8722			3
18	Columbia Balanced	Balanced	13.62	27	NA	NA	NA	1000	547-1707		W	3.5
19	Vanguard/Wellington	Balanced	13.52	30	50	0.69	0.63	3000	662-7447		S F W	3
20	Vanguard Asset Allocation	Asset Alloc	13.49	47	29	0.66	0.64	3000	662-7447		S F W	4
21	T. Rowe Price Balanced	Balanced	13.35	31	61	0.58	0.55	2500	638-5660		S F W	3.5
22	Golden Rainbow	Balanced	13.00	34	NA	NA	NA	5000	227-4648			NA
23	T. Rowe Price Spectrum Inc.	Income	12.32	68	74	0.20	0.17	2500	638-5660		S F W	NA
24	Vanguard STAR	Balanced	10.97	51	45	0.61	0.55	500	662-7447		S F W	NA
25	Dreyfus Balanced	Balanced	10.85	54	NA	NA	NA	2500	645-6561	S F	W	NA

* One to Five "Thumbs Up" (best rating is 5). *Source:* Covenant Investment Management, Copyright 1994.
+ The Donoghue Group, Copyright 1994

S = Charles Schwab & Co.
F = Fidelity FundsNetwork
W = Jack White & Co.

Copyright Morningstar Inc., 1994

Wanna bet interest rates won't rise in the next ten years? Neither do I.

So, while I have included balanced funds in the list of total return funds to be objective and all-inclusive, I doubt you will find me recommending a balanced fund. That is especially true when SuperStar candidates like Fidelity Asset Manager, Fidelity Asset Manager-Growth, and USAA Investment Cornerstone are around.

That Leaves Asset Allocation Funds and Funds of Funds

Asset allocation funds and funds of funds are similar in nature. The major difference is that asset allocation funds invest in stocks, bonds, and money market instruments and funds of funds invest in stock funds, bond funds, and money funds.

The object of this game is to beat the odds. When you select a total return SuperStar, you are looking for one that can pick not only the bull markets, but also will be the best investment overall.

THREE GREAT FUNDS TO CHOOSE FROM

☆ **Fidelity Asset Manager** sports a 0.29 beta to the S&P 500, meaning it has only about 29 percent of the risk of the S&P 500. With a return this year of over three times the S&P 500, what can I say? This is one excellent fund and should be in everyone's list of SuperStar candidates.

☆ **Fidelity Asset Manager-Growth** has a shorter track record and slightly (26.32 percent vs. 23.29 percent) out-performed its elder brother/sister fund. It is certainly a fund to watch.

☆ **USAA Investment Cornerstone** is an eclectic asset allocation fund, not so surprisingly hitting on some of today's hot buttons; gold stocks (0 to 10 percent) and 22 to 28 percent in foreign stocks, real-estate stocks, U.S. government securities and basic value stocks. What a clever and insightful asset allocation fund, not just to invest in those categories but to state upfront that those are its choices. (Competitors probably make the same choices, but don't state so upfront.) All of this and a beta of 0.49, or half the risk of the S&P 500.

Have you forgotten the promises of the index funds? Does this sound like a better deal? As a world class asset allocator (being No. 1 does have its ego inflation aspects), I have to say that these total return funds have, and will, beat the pants off of index funds at lower risks.

ONE LAST FUND REVIEW

☆ **Blanchard Global Growth.**   This fund is invested 26 percent in foreign bonds and 10 percent in gold, with the rest of the portfolio in domestic and foreign stocks and domestic bonds. The new manager has made some dramatic changes in the portfolio over recent years and has made a few tactical errors. His recent positions in gold (10 percent) and foreign bonds (26 percent) make the fund a bit riskier than most asset allocation funds. The 0.70 Morningstar risk rating is considerably higher than Fidelity Asset Manager's 0.29 and is in the range of USAA Cornerstone's 0.66.

USAA Cornerstone has a longer-term track record of sticking to its strategy, so I must prefer that fund, and especially Fidelity Asset Manager, over Blanchard Global Growth.

WAIT! THERE ARE MORE CHOICES—

There are three ways to play this game:

1.   Asset Allocation Funds.
2.   Funds of Funds.
3.   Managing a Portfolio of SuperStar Mutual Funds Yourself.

A Frank Preface to This Discussion

Before I begin this discussion, I must, in all candor, reveal where I come from on this subject. I am a confirmed asset allocator. This confession is tempered by the fact that Mark Hulbert of *Hulbert Financial Digest* has ranked the *Donoghue'$ MONEYLETTER* Aggressive Asset Allocation portfolio's timing No. 1 for the past five years. *Donoghue'$ MONEYLETTER* sticks its neck out in public twice a month with advice.

WEDCO, My Money Management Firm, Implements Advice to Clients

Our money management clients put their money where our mouth is. While our portfolios are similar to *Donoghue'$*

MONEYLETTER's, my investment advisory firm, W. E. Donoghue & Co., Incorporated or WEDCO (1-800-642-4276), has more flexibility in its choices. We can use smaller funds, take faster action, be more tax-sensitive for individual clients, and do our own institutional research. WEDCO manages over $200 million dollars of client's no-load mutual fund portfolios.

These portfolios are our clients' own accounts of no-load mutual funds at Charles Schwab & Co. (in their own name and with no commingling of assets with other investors' money). We trade for our clients under a limited power of attorney provided to us by the client and filed with Schwab Institutional. (For this we charge a maximum fee of 1.75 percent per year.)

I feel strongly, as you have no doubt figured out, that over the long-term, a portfolio carefully allocated among the several bull markets, upgraded from time to time, and invested in the SuperStar funds selected as described in this book should provide a successful combination of high returns, lowered risk and lower volatility.

On the other hand, I love to say, "I have no competitors, only friends in similar businesses." With those prejudices in mind, let's search for the total return SuperStars and get a feel for how these fascinating funds work.

THE PERFORMANCE IS ONLY PART OF THE PUZZLE

That total return funds have performed reasonably well in recent years is not the only reason they make sense in many portfolios. Many advisors would argue the real reason is that these returns are accomplished with very low risk.

The funds offer good value. The top funds have returns of 20 percent plus, and betas for four of the top five performers range from 0.43 to 0.54 (meaning equity type returns with considerably less exposure to a market correction).

AN INTRIGUING PROPOSAL

Given the lower-risk, high performance of the top asset allocation funds (Our WEDCO asset allocation portfolios, by the way, performed in the 21 to 23 percent range for 1993), it may well be a reasonable choice to use an asset allocation fund as your home base instead of a money fund or junk bond fund and venture only with those asset funds you feel can outperform the asset allocation fund. Today, those other assets would likely be gold mining share funds, emerging markets funds, diversified international funds (rather than the higher risk regional and country funds), and possibly a few domestic stock funds.

WHAT ABOUT THE SAFE HARBOR FUNDS?

First of all, I will 'fess up and tell you that the *safe harbor* category is nomenclature I invented. I was looking to build a list that included most of the top-performing, low-beta (to minimize stock market risk), relatively non-interest-rate-sensitive (to minimize bond market risk) mutual funds that could serve, along with total return funds, as a *home base* position for investors.

Traditionally, this safe harbor, or home base, function has been performed by a money market mutual fund. However, for a SuperStar portfolio, it makes a lot more sense to learn to live with a bit of volatility and get a whole lot more return.

I then made up a list of all (well, I may have missed some) plausible *storied investments* (investments that have good stories to tell about why they are superior—stories that are not always true or even plausible to the knowledgeable) I could think of that could be described to investors as *no brainers,* safe and high-yielding investment alternatives.

I figured I would throw them all in one big data file, sort them by performance, and see which of the advisors' stories were true. The top-performing safe harbor SuperStar fund candidates would come to the top of the list, and the SupperStars (the ones where you buy their supper and you go home hungry) would be on the bottom.

All of the stories are equally plausible, although most of the time many are simply bad advice. The safe harbor funds at the top delivered valuable performance. If they can pass the common sense test, they are the true safe harbor SuperStar candidates (Table 10.4).

Which Are the *Storied* Safe Harbor Contestants?

I have chosen to include in the safe harbor beauty contest several kinds of mutual funds reputed to be good, safe investments:

- ▶ Worldwide bond funds
- ▶ Short-term world income funds
- ▶ Short-term bond funds
- ▶ Utility stock funds
- ▶ Equity-income funds

TABLE 10.4
Donoghue's "Safe Harbor" SuperStar Candidates
25 Top-Performing Direct-Marketed "Safe Harbor" Funds—YTD 12/31/93

Rank	Fund Name	Investment Objective	YTD Total Return (%)	YTD Rank in OBJ	3-Year Rank in OBJ	Beta (3-Year)	Mstar Risk (3-Year)	Minimum Initial Purchase ($)	800 #	Availability No Fee	Availability Fee	Covenant Rating*
1	Bull & Bear Global Income	Worldwide Bond	24.95	9	2	0.70	0.20	1000	847-4200	W	S	NA
2	Fidelity Capital & Income	Corp Hi Yld	24.19	6	23	-0.17	0.05	2500	544-8888	F	S W	NA
3	Northeast Investors	Corp Hi Yld	23.60	7	69	-0.02	0.18	1000	225-6704		S W	NA
4	PaineWebber High-Income D	Corp Hi Yld	22.24	12	NA	NA	NA	1000	647-1568	W		NA
5	T. Rowe Price High-Yield	Corp Hi Yld	21.82	15	70	0.10	0.09	2500	638-5660		S F W	NA
6	Fidelity Global Bond	Worldwide Bond	21.28	14	22	0.81	0.43	2500	544-8888	F	S W	NA
7	Thomson Equity-Income B	Equity-Inc	21.23	8	14	0.69	0.51	1000	227-7337		F	NA
8	Fidelity Spartan High-Income	Corp Hi Yld	21.13	23	37	-0.10	0.06	10000	544-8888	F	S W	NA
9	Kemper Invmt Diver Inc Prem	Corp Hi Yld	21.11	24	NA	NA	NA	1000	621-1048	W	F	NA
10	Gradison-McDonald Estab.Val.	Growth	20.77	14	53	0.85	0.68	1000	869-5999		S W	1
11	Kemper Invmt High-Yield Prem	Corp Hi Yld	20.10	32	NA	NA	NA	1000	621-1048			NA
12	SBSF Convertible Securities	Convert Bond	20.09	16	50	0.79	0.34	5000	422-7273		S	NA
13	T. Rowe Price Intl Bond	Worldwide Bond	19.97	15	17	1.89	1.02	2500	638-5660		S F W	3
14	Fidelity Equity-Income II	Equity-Inc	18.89	13	1	0.68	0.34	2500	544-8888	F	S W	NA
15	Vanguard F/I High-Yield Corp	Corp Hi Yld	18.13	57	85	0.40	0.12	3000	662-7447		S F W	NA
16	Fidelity Convertible Secs	Convert Bond	17.79	20	13	0.35	0.61	2500	544-8888	F	S W	NA
17	Federated High-Yield	Corp Hi Yld	17.35	68	25	0.02	0.15	25000	245-5000	W	S F	NA
18	Invesco Industrial Income	Equity-Inc	16.69	23	18	0.86	0.63	1000	525-8085	S	F W	3.5
19	Scudder International Bond	Worldwide Bond	15.83	37	5	1.65	0.66	1000	225-2470		S F W	NA
20	Olympic Equity-Income	Equity-Inc	15.76	29	8	0.88	0.62	10000	346-7301		W	3
21	Invesco High-Yield	Corp Hi Yld	15.76	90	90	0.24	0.07	1000	525-8085	S	F W	NA
22	Janus Flexible Income	Income	15.56	21	18	0.15	0.08	1000	525-8983	S F	W	NA
23	Fidelity Asset Manager: Inc	Income	15.39	26	NA	NA	NA	2500	544-8888	F	S W	NA
24	Lindner Dividend	Income	14.92	36	7	0.26	0.10	2000	314-727-5305		S	NA
25	T. Rowe Price Equity-Income	Equity-Inc	14.84	37	26	0.69	0.41	2500	638-5660		S F W	3

* One to five "Thumbs Up" (best rating is 5). *Source:* Covenant Investment Management, Copyright 1994.
+ The Donoghue Group, Copyright 1994

S = Charles Schwab & Co.
F = Fidelity FundsNetwork
W = Jack White & Co.

Copyright Morningstar Inc., 1994

▶ Income funds

▶ Convertible bond funds

▶ Corporate high-yield (junk bond) funds

But Which Safe Harbor Stories Are True Today?

Given all these choices, the types of funds that are the best-performing, direct-marketed safe harbor funds are listed in Table 10.5.

Let's Look at the Two Best Prospects

Corporate High-Yield Junk Bond Funds. No wonder these very attractive funds are doing so well. First of all, in an interest-starved world they are providing very attractive total returns. Second, as we move into a recovery, the prospects for ultimate repayment by these lower investment quality bonds are rising (improving credit ratings), and their values are rising as a consequence. Third, that very appreciation due to improving asset quality will likely offset any depreciation due to rising interest rates.

So, if interest rates stay low, that would be positive for junk bond funds. If interest rates fall lower, these high yields will become even more attractive. Finally, if interest rates rise, these funds could earn even higher returns as their principal appreciation results in a higher total return.

My rationale for the last assertion is that if interest rates rise it is because we will be in a recovery. When the **demand** for money increases, the **price** for money (interest) rises and the credit quality of the junk bonds will likely **increase** and their values **rise.**

TABLE 10.5
The Strongest "Safe Harbor" Stories

Fund Type	Number	Top-Return
Corporate High Yield (Junk Bonds)	10	24.19
Equity-Income	5	21.23
Worldwide Bond	4	24.95
Income	3	15.56
Convertible Bonds	2	20.09
Growth	1	20.77

Source: Morningstar Mutual Funds on Disc/The Donoghue Group

The highly negative but superficial press coverage of junk bonds and the concern about the junk bonds involved in the S&L scandal have scared many investors away. The bonds most junk bond funds hold are issued by what are called "fallen angels" (good companies in temporary bad times) that have to pay a higher interest rate to borrow.

So the top-performing junk bond funds are likely safe harbor SuperStar candidates. Certainly Fidelity Capital & Income is the winner among these attractive funds.

☆   **FIDELITY CAPITAL AND INCOME** is a great example of when bad news for corporations can turn into good news for investors. It is also a great example of the power of the Fidelity research teams.

This fund has about 50 percent of its portfolio in companies that are in default, distress, or bankruptcy. Most cannot even service their debt. That is why the distributed yield is low.

Savvy investors know that they can simply set up a systematic withdrawal plan to access the capital appreciation buildup in the per share value. Surprisingly, the debt management of this fund makes it a low-risk (but not a no-risk) fund.

It's not for the faint of heart but, as part of a portfolio dedicated to low-risk, high-yield investments, this can be an excellent fund for a long-term safe harbor position. Definitely a SuperStar in today's markets.

Worldwide Bond Funds

Worldwide bond funds need two trends to be profitable on the SuperStar level. Interest rates in the country of the bond issues have to be declining, and the value of the dollar relative to overseas currency has to be falling or stable.

While a recovery would benefit junk bond funds, it could hurt the prospects of worldwide income funds. Rising rates in the United States would likely strengthen the dollar and that would hurt the prospects for unhedged worldwide bond funds.

Bull & Bear Global Income.   This fund has done well this year, although it has had some lackluster years. Its positions in European and South American bonds are a case of the "right places at the right time." Still, it is a fund to watch with caution. Not recommended now, but worth watching.

SAFE HARBOR SUMMARY

As you can see, my preference at this time is clearly the junk bond funds, which offer attractive returns and little interest rate risk (Table 10.6).

The Easy Answers Weren't So Easy, Were They?

Quite frankly, when I started this research, I expected that if we built an asset allocation portfolio with the right mix of the right index funds, we could have a safe and powerful portfolio. It didn't turn out that way.

In a year when international and domestic stocks and bonds made money, using an index fund meant missing a whole lot of opportunity. Frankly, when the domestic stock market is strong and rising and risks are low, it is easy to identify above average funds. When the stock market is threatened by higher interest rates and is likely to correct, just how much money do you want in a stock index fund that is correlated 0 percent with the S&P 500?

So, it wasn't the index funds that won the day. The safe harbor fund search only unearthed the junk bonds we already knew about. Even junk bond funds can have their problems, but they certainly are safer than government bond funds. In February 1994, the AAA-rated, government-guaranteed 30-year Treasury bonds lost 7 percent of their market value—in a single month.

Much to my relief but not to my surprise, the class act was asset allocation funds, which demonstrated both mid-20 percent returns and reduced risk. Fidelity Asset Manager earned 23.73 percent with a Morningstar risk rating of only 0.29. This is exactly what we were looking for.

TABLE 10.6
Easy Answer SuperStar Candidates Summary

Fund Name	YTD 12/31/93	Mstar Risk
USAA Investment Trust Cornerstone Fund	23.73	0.66
Fidelity Capital & Income	24.19	0.05
Fidelity Asset Manager: Growth	26.32	NA
Fidelity Asset Manager	23.29	0.29

Source: Morningstar Mutual Funds on Disc/The Donoghue Group

The asset allocation portfolios of *Donoghue's MONEY-LETTER* and WEDCO are more than competitive with the best. After all, the *Hulbert Financial Digest* rates our past five-year track record in asset allocation timing as No. 1 among investment newsletters. (Watch you don't step in my modesty!)

At this point, I want to caution you that the portfolios we are going to develop reflect the best information available as of December 31, 1993. If you want our latest info, you can call 1-800-982-BILL.

Now, let's get on to building *your* SuperStar portfolio.

CHAPTER 11

Are You Ready to Put Your Money Where Your Mouth Is?

The Right Funds at the Right Time Equals SuperStar Profits

I hope you have enjoyed our journey through the world of direct-marketed (as opposed to salesperson-sold mutual funds), no-load, and low-load mutual funds. We have reviewed the entire scope of long-term diversified stock and bond mutual funds, domestic and international, and many nondiversified specialty mutual funds.

Oh yes, I did overlook most bond funds (other than international bonds, long-term zero-coupon bonds and junk bonds). It is now the time to sit down and write the prescription for the portfolio that will make this whole process pay off.

FREEBIE NO. 1

CAVEAT: Remember, however, this is the prescription that was in our minds, yours and mine, with information current as of

December 31, 1993. Now, you know me by now. I wouldn't ever leave you hanging. Call me toll-free at 1-800-982-BILL, and I will send you a free special report, *Donoghue's Mutual Fund Super-Star Update,* which updates the recommendations in this book.

TODAY'S CHOICES MAY NOT BE TOMORROW'S

The screening process is the focus of this book, and I suspect that in the spring of 1994, when most of you will be reading this book, these recommendations will still hold true. They should hold true for most investors, barring unforeseen circumstances, for most of 1994.

The most important point to remember is that you need a well researched and viable strategy to manage your money. You have learned such an imaginative process from this book.

The second most important point to remember is that the secret of success is not to be an active trader who tries to get in just before the market's big move and get out before the correction. That's speculation and impossible to do consistently. However, learning to invest in the right types of funds or asset classes and then selecting the lower risk, consistent, high-performance funds in those classes will get you in the Super-Star ball park, which is a long way from where you started.

The key element to understand is that there is no *ultimate investment,* there is only a series of attractive opportunities. You cannot predict every time what will be the next big investment winners, but you can recognize which classes of asset (types of funds) are performing well and invest in lower risk examples of that investment type. Invest in the best and forget about the rest!

That said, let's take the next logical step to financial investment success.

LET'S GET THIS PROCESS DOWN TO A SIMPLE CHECKLIST

Prepare or Obtain a List of All of the Funds Conveniently Available to You

For the purposes of this book, I am defining the screening criteria as no-load mutual funds (or Fidelity Investment Group direct-marketed funds with loads of 3 percent or less) with $50 million or more in assets and minimum initial investments of $25,000 or less, the Donoghue Direct-Marketed Mutual Fund Universe. You may choose to screen this list even further to include only the funds available at Charles Schwab & Co. where you can buy 52 of the 64 fund finalists.

Review the All-Fund SuperStars for Important Investment Themes Among the Most Successful Funds

This would get you to Donoghue's All-Fund SuperStar Candidates, the 100 best-performing direct-marketed mutual funds (Table 11.2). But first, let's look a little closer at the composition of these top 100 funds (Table 11.1).

As you can see, the asset classes that you would have wanted to be in recently are Pacific, Foreign, Gold, World (Global), Europe, (Domestic) Aggressive Growth, and Growth Stock Funds. In addition, it is comforting and encouraging to see that the less well-diversified funds made the Top 100.

These are the asset classes that you want to include in your portfolio. As we progress in this chapter, we will identify for you the most consistent and lower risk top performers in each asset class.

TABLE 11.1
Composition of
100 Top Performing Direct-Marketed Mutual Funds

(Based on total return during the three- and twelve-month periods ended December 31, 1993, listed in the order of proximity to the top of the list—fund types that placed only one fund in the top 100 are deleted.)

Type of Fund	Fourth Quarter 1993		Full Year 1993		
	Top 50	*2nd 50*	*Rank*	*Top 50*	*2nd 50*
Pacific	5	1	3	6	1
Foreign	24	9	2	24	12
Gold	11		1	11	
World	6	5	7	2	6
Europe	1	4			5
Aggressive growth		2	6	1	2
Growth		10			7
Asset allocation		4			1
Small company		3	4	1	2
Technology		1	5	1	3
Junk bonds		3			
Zero coupon bonds					2

Sources: Data: Morningstar Mutual Fund on Disc
　　　　　 Analysis: The Donoghue Group

TABLE 11.2
Donoghue's All-Fund SuperStar Candidates
The 100 Best-Performing Direct-Marketed Funds (YTD 12/31/93)

Rank	Fund Name	Investment Objective	1993 Total Return (%)	1993 Rank in OBJ	3-Year Rank in OBJ	Beta (3-Year)	Mstar Risk (3-Year)	Minimum Initial Purchase ($)	800 #
1	United Svcs. Gold Shares	Sp. Metals	123.92	3	93	-0.74	4.27	1000	873-8637
2	Fidelity Sel. Prec. Metals (3%)	Sp. Metals	111.64	9	10	-0.42	2.40	2500	544-8888
3	Blanchard Precious Metals	Sp. Metals	100.42	16	24	-0.34	2.50	3000	922-7771
4	Vanguard Spec. Gold & Prec.	Sp. Metals	93.36	22	17	-0.30	2.17	3000	662-7447
5	United Svcs. World Gold	Sp. Metals	89.78	29	6	-0.44	2.57	1000	873-8637
6	Lexington Goldfund	Sp. Metals	86.96	38	65	-0.41	2.44	1000	526-0056
7	Fidelity Emerging Markets	Foreign	81.76	1	7	0.30	0.54	2500	544-8888
8	Benham Gold Equities Index	Sp. Metals	81.22	41	51	-0.31	2.76	1000	472-3389
9	T. Rowe Price New Asia	Pacific	78.76	24	16	0.36	0.83	2500	638-5660
10	Fidelity Sel. American Gold (3%)	Sp. Metals	78.68	51	20	-0.19	2.27	2500	544-8888
11	59 Wall St. Pac. Basin Eqty.	Pacific	74.90	31	22	0.32	1.11	10000	212-493-8100
12	Scudder Latin America	Foreign	74.32	5	NA	NA	NA	1000	225-2470
13	Invesco Strat. Gold	Sp. Metals	72.63	61	48	-0.37	2.64	1000	525-8085
14	Fidelity Pacific Basin (3%)*	Pacific	63.91	44	38	0.27	1.33	2500	544-8888
15	Lexington Worldwide Emerging	Foreign	63.37	9	4	0.68	0.67	1000	526-0056
16	Scudder Pacific Opport.	Pacific	60.08	55	NA	NA	NA	1000	225-2470
17	Scudder Gold	Sp. Metals	59.35	77	75	-0.24	2.10	1000	225-2470
18	Montgomery Emerg. Mkts.	Foreign	58.66	12	NA	NA	NA	2000	572-3863
19	USAA Investment Gold	Sp. Metals	58.33	80	68	-0.30	2.41	1000	382-8722
20	Oakmark International	Foreign	53.58	13	NA	NA	NA	1000	476-9625
21	Evergreen Global Real Estate	Sp. Unaligned	51.42	1	34	0.64	1.12	2000	235-0064
22	Warburg, Pincus Intl Eq Comm	Foreign	51.26	18	10	0.49	0.91	2500	257-5614
23	T. Rowe Price Intl Discovery	Foreign	49.85	20	36	0.37	1.12	2500	638-5660
24	Fidelity Sel. Brokerage& Inv (3%)	Sp. Financ	49.30	1	20	1.34	1.07	2500	544-8888
25	Acorn International	Foreign	49.11	21	NA	NA	NA	1000	922-6769
26	SIT International Growth	Foreign	48.37	22	NA	NA	NA	2000	332-5580
27	Strong International Stock	Foreign	47.75	23	NA	NA	NA	1000	368-1030
28	PBHG Growth	Small Company	46.57	1	3	1.40	1.52	1000	809-8008
29	International Equity	Foreign	45.75	29	47	0.43	1.19	2500	344-8332
30	Vanguard Intl Growth	Foreign	44.74	31	55	0.52	1.22	3000	662-7447
31	Fidelity Sel. Indust. Equip. (3%)	Sp. Tech	43.32	1	47	0.74	0.83	2500	544-8888

#	Fund	Category							Phone
32	American AAdvantage Intl Eq.	Foreign	42.80	32	NA	NA	NA	None	817-967-3509
33	20th Century Intl. Equity	Foreign	42.65	34	NA	NA	NA	1000	345-2021
34	Preferred International	Foreign	41.53	35	NA	NA	NA	1000	662-4769
35	American Heritage	Aggr Growth	41.39	1	1	1.20	0.94	5000	828-5050
36	Vontobel EuroPacific	Foreign	40.80	36	25	0.51	0.75	1000	527-9500
37	IAI International	Foreign	40.21	37	41	0.49	1.09	5000	945-3863
38	T. Rowe Price Intl Stock	Foreign	40.11	38	30	0.57	1.01	2500	638-5660
39	Fidelity Overseas (3%)*	Foreign	40.05	39	70	0.41	1.38	2500	544-8888
40	USAA Investment Intl.	Foreign	39.81	40	28	0.49	0.92	1000	382-8722
41	Invesco Pacific Basin	Pacific	39.70	62	61	0.53	1.64	1000	525-8085
42	Fidelity Sel. Leisure (3%)	Sp. Unaligned	39.56	4	26	0.92	0.67	2500	544-8888
43	Loomis Sayles Intl. Equity	Foreign	38.54	41	NA	NA	NA	2500	633-3330
44	Managers Intl. Equity	Foreign	38.23	43	17	0.55	0.67	10000	835-3879
45	Nomura Pacific Basin	Pacific	38.21	65	66	0.31	1.70	1000	833-0018
46	Scudder Global Small Company	World	38.18	16	NA	NA	NA	1000	225-2470
47	Fidelity Sel. Broadcast& Med (3%)	Sp. Unaligned	38.02	8	17	0.99	0.83	2500	544-8888
48	BB&K International Equity	World	37.84	19	97	0.46	1.23	5000	415-571-5800
49	CoreFund Intl. Growth A	Foreign	37.71	44	46	0.47	1.24	2500	355-2673
50	PNC Internatl Equity Instl	Foreign	36.85	49	NA	NA	NA	5000	441-7762
51	Fidelity Diversified Intl	Foreign	36.67	51	NA	NA	NA	2500	544-8888
52	Fidelity Worldwide (3%)	World	36.55	25	38	0.66	0.91	2500	544-8888
53	Scudder International	Foreign	36.50	53	44	0.45	1.04	1000	225-2470
54	Invesco Strat. Leisure	Sp. Unaligned	35.71	12	4	1.00	0.74	1000	525-8085
55	Vanguard Intl Equity Pacific	Pacific	35.46	68	72	0.46	2.50	3000	662-7447
56	Fidelity Sel. Automotive (3%)	Sp. Unaligned	35.37	16	1	0.71	0.54	2500	544-8888
57	Fidelity Intl. Growth & Inc (2%)	Foreign	35.08	56	57	0.41	1.02	2500	544-8888
58	Bernstein Intl Value	Foreign	34.63	58	NA	NA	NA	25000	212-756-4097
59	Thomson International B	Foreign	33.47	65	39	0.81	1.03	1000	227-7337
60	Fidelity Capital Apprec (3%)*	Aggr. Growth	33.41	6	64	0.55	0.67	2500	544-8888
61	Columbia International Stock	Foreign	33.37	66	NA	NA	NA	1000	547-1707
62	Ambassador Intl Stock Fid	Foreign	32.50	68	NA	NA	NA	None	892-4366
63	Fidelity Sel. Software/Comp. (3%)	Sp. Tech	32.48	18	1	1.41	1.48	2500	544-8888
64	Elfun Global	World	31.88	38	31	0.64	0.78	100	242-0134
65	Lexington Global	World	31.88	40	65	0.72	1.03	1000	526-0056
66	Fidelity Sel. Devel. Comm. (3%)	Sp. Tech	31.74	31	5	1.24	1.09	2500	544-8888
67	20th Century Giftrust Inv.	Small Company	31.41	6	2	1.68	1.76	250	345-2021
68	Scudder Global	World	31.10	44	29	0.63	0.58	1000	225-2470
69	SAFECO Equity	Growth-Inc	30.91	1	7	1.07	1.02	1000	426-6730
70	Benham Target Mat. 2015	Gvt Treasury	30.51	2	1	3.30	5.17	1000	472-3389

TABLE 11.2 (continued)

Rank	Fund Name	Investment Objective	1993 Total Return (%)	1993 Rank in OBJ	3-Year Rank in OBJ	Beta (3-Year)	Mstar Risk (3-Year)	Minimum Initial Purchase ($)	800 #
71	Oakmark	Growth	30.50	2	NA	NA	NA	1000	476-9625
72	Vanguard/Trustees' Eqty.Intl	Foreign	30.49	77	81	0.49	1.23	10000	662-7447
73	Founders Worldwide Growth	World	29.89	53	19	0.84	0.89	1000	525-2440
74	Fidelity Sel. Telecommun. (3%)	Sp. Util	29.65	4	1	0.85	0.74	2500	544-8888
75	One Group Intl Equity Fid	Foreign	29.59	82	NA	NA	NA	1000	338-4345
76	Vanguard Intl Equity Euro	Europe	29.13	34	22	0.75	1.23	3000	662-7447
77	Nations Intl Equity Tr A	Foreign	28.83	85	NA	NA	NA	1000	321-7854
78	Fidelity Sel. Technology (3%)	Sp. Tech	28.63	45	31	1.40	1.35	2500	544-8888
79	Janus Worldwide	World	28.41	58	NA	NA	NA	1000	525-8983
80	Wright Intl Blue Chip Eq	Foreign	28.22	87	49	0.53	1.04	1000	232-0013
81	Invesco International Growth	Foreign	27.87	89	96	0.61	1.60	1000	525-8085
82	SteinRoe Capital Opport.	Aggr. Growth	27.52	10	22	1.10	0.94	1000	338-2550
83	Fidelity Sel. Home Finance (3%)	Sp. Financ	27.26	7	1	1.28	0.94	2500	544-8888
84	T. Rowe Price European Stock	Europe	27.24	42	40	0.65	1.21	2500	638-5660
85	Fidelity Europe (3%)*	Europe	27.16	46	31	0.64	1.27	2500	544-8888
86	59 Wall St. European Equity	Europe	27.12	50	1	0.62	0.94	10000	212-493-8100
87	Vanguard Spec. Energy	Sp. Nat. Res.	26.42	20	33	0.74	1.47	3000	662-7447
88	Fidelity Asset Manager: Grth	Asset Alloc	26.32	6	NA	NA	NA	2500	544-8888
89	Benham Target Mat. 2010	Gvt. Treasury	26.28	4	3	2.81	3.55	1000	472-3389
90	T. Rowe Price Mid-Cap Growth	Growth	26.24	5	NA	NA	NA	2500	638-5660
91	Pierpont Intl Equity	Foreign	26.20	92	89	0.59	1.74	25000	521-5412
92	Invesco European	Europe	25.88	53	50	0.74	1.35	1000	525-8085
93	Founders Growth	Growth	25.53	6	13	1.17	1.16	1000	525-2440
94	Fidelity Canada (3%)	Foreign	25.47	95	52	0.47	0.97	2500	544-8888
95	Bull & Bear Global Income	Worldwide Bond	24.95	9	2	0.70	0.20	1000	847-4200
96	Loomis Sayles Small Cap	Small Company	24.68	10	NA	NA	NA	2500	633-3330
97	Fidelity New Millennium (3%)	Growth	24.67	6	NA	NA	NA	2500	544-8888
98	Fidelity Magellan (3%)	Growth	24.66	7	16	1.06	0.65	2500	544-8888
99	Thomson Target B	Growth	24.52	7	NA	NA	NA	1000	227-7337
100	Fidelity Blue Chip Growth (3%)*	Growth	24.50	7	8	1.20	0.73	2500	544-8888

*Waived for IRAs maintained at Fidelity

Copyright Morningstar Inc., 1994

THE THEMES DEFINE THE ASSET ALLOCATION

It is quite clear that the strong themes in 1993 were:

► Gold funds (the rising demand for gold).

► Emerging markets.

► Pacific and international (foreign) stock funds (the growth of the less developed countries).

► An attractive global real estate fund (another international asset class play).

► Investment trading, strategy-driven domestic stock funds (aggressive growth and small company).

The highly interest rate-sensitive zero-coupon bond funds have done well simply because interest rates have plummeted, a trend unlikely to repeat itself. Similarly, it is easy to dismiss the stock sector funds as highly volatile, narrowly focused, nondiversified funds that always show up among the top performing funds. I have never felt comfortable recommending such nondiversified domestic sector funds when equally attractive, higher return, diversified international stock funds exist.

BUILDING YOUR ASSET ALLOCATION PORTFOLIO

Translating these themes into an investment portfolio that almost defines itself should be easy. Your first thought is that you want to include the following types of funds into your portfolio:

► Gold funds.

► International stock funds (with good Pacific coverage).

► Domestic stock funds.

► Sector funds.

A REALITY TEST—SAGE ADVICE FROM AN EXPERIENCED INVESTOR

Gold Funds

Your first reaction may be, "I want a lot of that gold action!" Don't jump into gold mining stock funds "in size" that is, by investing a lot of your portfolio. Studies indicate that a 5 to 10 percent position in gold funds, acquired after a market pullback or gradually on over a six- to twelve-month period (assuming no transaction costs), will probably add to your return. If your 10 percent position doubles—and that takes only a small movement in the price of gold—it will make a dramatic improvement in your total return and lower your portfolio's risk.

Gold funds seldom invest in gold. Gold funds invest in common stock shares of gold mining companies whose values fluctuate due to many factors, only one of which is the price of gold.

You will notice that gold funds have negative betas. That means the fund usually makes money when the S&P declines, a factor that can add stability to your investment portfolio. However, you should expect a very low correlation with the S&P 500 because there are no or very few gold mining shares in the S&P 500. However the low beta does demonstrate that adding gold adds noncorrelated diversification to your portfolio.

Gold funds have several "Achilles' heels"—political instability in South Africa (for funds that invest in South Africa), low or declining inflation levels, as well as the general volatility of gold mining shares. So, a 5 to 10 percent maximum position in gold mining shares funds is a wise choice. Studies indicate that anything above that increases risks and reduces returns.

My recommended choice for a gold fund is shown in Table 11.3.

TABLE 11.3
Donoghue's Gold Fund SuperStars

Fund Name	Total Return (%)	Rank in OBJ	Mstar Risk (3-Year)	Minimum Purchase ($)	800 #
United Services World Gold	89.78	5	2.22	1000	873-8637

While there are other gold funds on both our long-term and short-term screens, this fund appears to have the stamina to stay at the top of its objective sufficiently well and to do so with a lower Morningstar Risk rating than its peers. Therefore, it is my favorite choice. However, when gold is moving, all gold funds move. If you have a stronger stomach and South African investment risk is something you are comfortable with, then you might as well go with United Services Gold Shares, which have both greater risk and greater potential.

International Stock Funds

International stock funds are an especially wise choice for 1994. The opportunity to invest in the exciting Southeast Asian stock markets that are benefiting from the growth of capitalism in China, the emerging markets in Latin America and the falling interest rate-driven recovery in Europe, are much more exciting that trying to squeeze the last few dollars out of the domestic stock market.

The beauty of international markets today is that the focus has shifted from the developed countries (Europe and Japan), where currency fluctuation is a major investment risk, to the lesser developed and rapidly emerging markets of Latin America and Southeast Asia. The European and Japanese currencies are so dominant that they float independently of the dollar. The dollar rises, and returns in those countries decline in dollar terms.

Many Latin American and Southeast Asian currencies are tied to the dollar, greatly reducing currency risks and allowing a direct relationship between the performance of the underlying stocks and the performance of the fund without the arbitrary distortion of the currency risks. This reduced risk profile is a whole new dimension to international investing which works to your advantage.

One can argue—and I do—that international stock fund investing, especially if you focus on the widely diversified international stock funds rather than the regional funds, reduces the overall risk of your portfolio. My favorite types of funds are both highly diversified international stock funds, rather than regional or country funds:

▶   Fully-diversified **international stock funds**, whose portfolios are carefully balanced to take advantage of sector, country, market, and currency trends.

▶   Well-diversified **emerging market funds**, which are essentially funds investing in blue chip investments (housing, financial, and automotive industries) in literally dozens of small countries with emerging economies.

My favorite funds in those categories are:

☆   **Fidelity Emerging Markets Fund.**   Who can turn down a fund that has been a consistent leader in its field for over three years and still emerges at the top of the list of all international stock funds for 1993 with a 81.76 percent return and a low 0.54 Morningstar Risk rating. the lowest among the top 25 funds? Amazingly, it is one of only three Fidelity Investments funds (No. 5 Fidelity Pacific Basin, and No. 23 Fidelity Overseas are the others) to make the top 25 international stock fund list.

☆ **Lexington Worldwide Emerging Markets** is yet another excellent fund with a low Morningstar Risk rating (0.67) that is well worth your consideration. Its No. 6 finish is excellent, with a 1993 total return of 63.37 percent. (These returns are so high this year that it makes little sense to differentiate among the top funds on a return basis, a risk basis is a more useful separation of the wheat from the chaff.)

On that basis, we must give an honorable mention to a regional fund, **T. Rowe Price New Asia** which placed No. 2 for the year before the correction in Southeast Asia in early 1994, from which it emerged almost unscathed.

☆ **Oakmark International** finished the year as the No. 1 diversified international fund and cannot be ignored.

   ▶ I have been investing my money and my clients' money in this fund and have been impressed by its potential to make money, even when the S&P 500 and other international stock funds decline. I don't have to see a three-year total return to know this fund is highly ranked among its peers. It is, and there is good reason.

   ▶ I am also impressed by the portfolio manager's value-oriented discipline.

☆ **Warburg, Pincus International Equity Common** at No. 10 is a close second to Oakmark International and should be included on your international fund candidate list.

My recommended choices among international funds are shown in Table 11.4 on page 185.

Domestic Funds

Domestically, we are nearing the end of a bull market that is still strong enough to hold our attention. That does not mean there are no more profits to be made in this bull market; it does mean that international stock funds are providing higher returns at arguably lower risks.

TABLE 11.4
Donoghue's International Fund SuperStars

Fund Name	12-Mo. Total Return (%)	Rank in OBJ (3-Year)	Mstar Risk	Minimum Purchase ($)	800 #
Warburg, Pincus Int'l Eq. Comm.	51.26	10	0.92	2500	257-5614
Fidelity Emerging Markets	81.78	7	0.54	2500	544-8888
Lexington Worldwide Em. Mkts.	63.37	4	0.67	1000	526-0056
Oakmark International	53.58	13	NA	1000	476-9625
HONORABLE MENTION					
T. Rowe Price New Asia	78.76	16	0.83	2500	638-5660
Montgomery Emerging Markets	58.66	2	NA	2000	572-3863

This is one man's opinion, so make your own judgment. Empowering you to make more informed judgments is the very purpose of this book. Providing you with the opportunity to follow me as I perform my analysis, with all my foibles and shortcomings, is designed to give you a sound basis to disagree with me if you wish. That disagreement would, of course, be an informed disagreement.

My recommended choices among diversified domestic stock funds are shown in Table 11.5.

Here are some excellent choices. What I like about American Heritage and PBHG Growth is the fact that they have strong three-year track records when ranked within their objectives. They both have strategies that provide the returns that make the risks of owning them worth taking.

Oakmark, although it does not yet have a three-year track record, has a low beta relative to the S&P 500, which makes it

TABLE 11.5
Donoghue's Diversified Domestic Stock SuperStars

Fund Name	12-Mo. Total Return (%)	Rank in OBJ (3-Year)	Mstar Risk	Minimum Purchase ($)	800 #
PBHG Growth	46.57	1	1.53	1000	809-8008
American Heritage	41.39	1	0.97	5000	828-5050
SAFECO Equity	30.91	1	1.03	1000	426-6730
Oakmark	30.50	NA	NA	1000	476-9625
Mutual Beacon	22.93	2	0.38	5000	553-3014

TABLE 11.6
Donoghue's Sector Fund SuperStar

Fund Name	12-Mo. Total Return (%)	Rank in OBJ (3-Year)	Mstar Risk	Minimum Purchase ($)	800 #
Evergreen Global Real Est.	42.29	1	1.13	2000	235-0064

very attractive. It can brag being the No. 1 diversified stock fund in America in 1992 and the No. 6 direct-marketed, diversified stock fund in 1993, a record not to be ignored.

Sector Funds

My recommended choice among sector funds is shown in Table 11.6.

I discovered this very attractive fund in the midst of a series of high-beta, narrowly defined sector funds. This is truly a superior return for a fund with a beta of 0.64.

Real estate has been beaten down in recent years and is only now beginning to recover. The real estate portfolio we are talking about, however, is not raw real estate or buildings but corporations whose business is related to real estate: mortgage companies, construction companies, developers, and so on. This is really a global fund with holdings in emerging markets and developed countries, the United States and foreign countries, and residential, shopping mall, and commercial real estate.

Safe Harbor Funds

For funds that provide a high-yield, low-beta, relatively non-interest-rate sensitive alternative, and which may serve as a "home base" for an investment portfolio, there are a few attractive choices.

Fidelity Capital & Income, a high-yield junk bond fund, does have a 1.5 percent redemption charge, but its return is well worth that risk. This fund will serve as an excellent home base for investors. By *home base*, I mean a fund whose presence reduces the risk of the portfolio to match the investor's

TABLE 11.7
Donoghue's "Safe Harbor" SuperStar

Fund Name	Total Return (%)	Rank in OBJ	Mstar Risk (3-Year)	Minimum Purchase ($)	800 #
Fidelity Capital & Income	21.86	17	0.05	2500	544-8888

risk tolerance, or that allows an attractive alternative investment when the investor wishes to side step a bear market, or is waiting for a new better opportunity.

My recommended choice for a safe harbor fund is shown in Table 11.7.

Total Return Funds—Safe Harbor Alternatives

There are two ways to provides the safety necessary for a home base or safe harbor investment:

▶ Find a fund that invests in individual securities with a strategy that provides for stable growth with low principal risk.

▶ Find a fund that invests in classes of securities that does the same thing.

I tend to prefer the latter, if it can deliver attractive returns, since in a down market it has more viable options to choose from. "You make your choice and you take your risks."

My recommended choices among total return funds are shown in Table 11.8.

TABLE 11.8
Donoghue's Total Return SuperStars

Fund Name	Total Return (%)	Rank in OBJ	Mstar Risk (3-Year)	Minimum Purchase ($)	800 #
Fidelity Asset Manager: Grth	26.32	NA	NA	2500	544-8888
USAA Investment Cornerstone	23.73	11	0.67	1000	382-8722
Fidelity Asset Manager	23.29	12	0.29	2500	544-8888

That completes our roll call of the fund sub-universes for SuperStar candidates, so let's go back to our short-term screen list of candidates (Table 11.9) and see if we can come to a more focused closure on this process.

Now that we have looked at all the choices, let's get down to the final picks. First, we rejected many of the top performers (see R next to their ranks) because they were higher-than-average Morningstar risks and we had excellent choices who were lower than average risks. Second, we gave others honorable mentions because we already had better choices.

TABLE 11.9
Donoghue's Mutual Fund SuperStar Finalists

(Direct-marketed funds that ranked in top 30 percent in their objective for the past 3-, 6-, and 12-month periods ended 12/31/93. Highlighted funds in Bold Type are recommended funds.)

Rank	Fund Name	Investment Objective	3-Month Total Return (%)	1993 Total Return (%)	Mstar Risk (3-Year)
1	***Fidelity Emerging Markets**	**Foreign**	**39.73**	**81.76**	**0.54**
2	***Lexington Worldwide Emerging**	**Foreign**	**31.81**	**63.37**	**0.67**
3R	United Svcs. Gold Shares	Sp. Metals	31.67	123.92	4.27
4R	Vanguard Spec. Gold & Prec.	Sp. Metals	31.20	93.36	2.17
5R	Fidelity Sel. Prec. Metals	Sp. Metals	30.88	111.64	2.40
6	Montgomery Emerging Mkts.	Foreign	29.14	58.66	NA
7	Scudder Latin America	Foreign	26.98	74.32	NA
8	Strong International Stock	Foreign	18.70	47.75	NA
9	Sit International Growth	Foreign	18.57	48.37	NA
10	***Warburg, Pincus Int'l Eq. Comm.**	**Foreign**	**17.28**	**51.26**	**0.91**
11	**Oakmark International**	**Foreign**	**15.21**	**53.58**	**NA**
12R	BB&K International Equity	World	15.19	37.84	1.23
13R	T. Rowe Price Int'l Discovery	Foreign	15.07	49.85	1.12
14R	Strong Discovery	Aggr. Grth	10.72	22.21	1.22
15R	**Evergreen Global Real Estate**	**Sp. R/E**	**10.18**	**51.42**	**1.12**
16	**Oakmark**	**Growth**	**9.54**	**30.50**	**NA**
17	Blanchard Global Growth	Asset All.	8.63	24.46	0.70
18	Fidelity Asset Manager: Grth.	Asset All.	7.97	26.32	NA
19R	SAFECO Growth	Small Co.	7.33	22.19	1.86
20	Fidelity Sel. Indust. Equip.	Sp. Tech	7.25	43.32	0.83
21	***Fidelity Asset Manager**	**Asset All.**	**7.17**	**23.29**	**0.29**
22	T. Rowe Price Growth Stock	Growth	6.96	15.56	0.78
23	Fremont Global	Asset All.	6.92	19.60	0.44
24	Fidelity Low-Priced Stock	Small Co.	6.92	20.21	0.60
25	T. Rowe Price Spectrum Grth.	Growth	6.53	20.98	0.59

Rank	Fund Name	Investment Objective	3-Month Total Return (%)	1993 Total Return (%)	Mstar Risk (3-Year)
26	Kemper Invmt. Diver. Inc. Prem.	Corp. HiYld	6.31	21.11	NA
27	T. Rowe Price Mid-Cap Growth	Growth	6.24	26.24	NA
28	*Berger 101	Growth-Inc	6.18	23.57	0.70
29	Northeast Investors	Corp HiYld	6.09	23.60	0.18
30	*Fidelity Retirement Growth	Growth	5.95	22.13	0.72
31R	**Fidelity Sel. Brokerage & Inv.**	**Sp. Finance**	**5.92**	**49.30**	**1.07**
32R	SAFECO Equity	Growth-Inc	5.68	30.91	1.02
33	Crabbe Huson Asset Alloc.	Asset All.	5.38	18.21	0.42
34R	T. Rowe Price New Horizons	Small Co.	5.33	22.01	1.28
35	*Fidelity Global Bond	Worldwide Bond	5.24	21.28	0.43
36	Invesco Growth	Growth	5.10	19.02	0.92
37	Neuberger & Berman Sel Sectors	Growth	5.04	16.33	0.79
38	Olympic Equity-Income	Equity-Inc	5.04	15.76	0.62
39	Legg Mason Special Invstmt.	Small Co.	4.95	24.13	0.80
40	SteinRoe Capital Opport.	Aggr. Grth	4.93	27.52	0.94
41	Janus Enterprise	Growth	4.90	15.64	NA
42	*Fidelity Value	Growth	4.64	22.94	0.58
43R	**PBHG Growth**	**Small Co.**	**4.16**	**46.57**	**1.52**
44R	20th Century Giftrust Inv.	Small Co.	4.15	31.41	1.76
45	Dreyfus Growth & Income	Growth-Inc	4.09	18.59	NA
46	*SteinRoe Special	Growth	4.02	20.42	0.76
47	**USAA Investment Cornerstone**	**Asset All.**	**3.98**	**23.73**	**0.66**
48R	Vanguard/PRIMECAP	Growth	3.92	18.03	1.08
49	***Mutual Beacon**	**Growth-Inc**	**3.86**	**22.93**	**0.38**
50	*Bull & Bear Global Income	Worldwide Bond	3.83	24.95	0.20
51R	Scudder Capital Growth	Growth	3.67	20.07	1.08
52	Homestead Value	Growth-Inc	3.65	18.83	0.57
53	Weitz Value	Growth	3.46	19.98	0.43
54	*Fidelity Equity-Income	Equity-Inc	3.37	21.31	0.49
55	*Founders Balanced	Balanced	3.33	21.85	0.57
56	*Invesco Industrial Income	Equity-Inc	3.32	16.69	0.63
57	SBSF	Growth-Inc	3.32	20.41	0.49
58	*Fidelity Puritan	Balanced	3.26	21.45	0.57
59	Loomis Sayles Bond	Corp Bond	3.20	22.22	NA
60	Salomon Brothers Investors	Growth-Inc	3.14	15.19	0.71
61	*Fidelity Equity-Income II	Equity-Inc	2.60	18.89	0.34
62	*Strong Income	Corp Bond	1.96	16.81	0.66
63	Fidelity Invest. Grade Bond	Corp Bond	0.59	15.59	0.71
64	*Fidelity Sel. Home Finance	Sp.Finance	−0.73	27.26	0.94

*Also met qualifications for Donoghue's Long-Term Fund Screen.

R Rejected on initial screening due to higher than average Morningstar (downside) risk (Some funds are recommended in spite of higher risk.)

Finally, we worked from the top of the list until we filled out the asset classes we were looking for. We didn't need more domestic stock choices, any balanced choices, any bond choices nor did we need all of the gold or international choices.

The envelope please!

LET'S ROLL THE VIDEOTAPE—I MEAN, LET'S BRING BACK THE FINALISTS ONE MORE TIME

The funds in the top portion of the table are recommended on all counts. All but the two Oakmark funds met the demanding three-year criteria. Oakmark, while having a shorter than three-year track record does have an excellent record as a value-oriented stock fund. It was the No. 1 diversified stock fund of all in 1992 and No. 6 among direct-marketed diversified stock funds for 1993! Oakmark International, a still younger fund, was the No. 1 performing direct-marketed diversified international stock fund for 1993, if you exclude the emerging markets funds.

In the second part of the table, Evergreen Global Real Estate is added to the list solely on my own judgment rather than on the strict quantitative criteria. It adds a very attractive high return opportunity to selectively participate in the global real estate recovery. It seems too good to be ignored. In addition, USAA Cornerstone's electic but "right on the money" asset mix adds additional diversification potential, although you probably

TABLE 11.10
Donoghue's Mutual Fund SuperStars Portfolio Picks

Rank	Fund Name	Investment Objective	3-Month Total Return (%)	1993 Total Return (%)	Mstar Risk (3-Year)
1	*Fidelity Emerging Markets	Foreign	39.73	81.76	0.54
2	*Lexington Worldwide Emerging	Foreign	31.81	63.37	0.67
10	*Warburg, Pincus Intl Eq Comm	Foreign	17.28	51.26	0.91
11	Oakmark International	Foreign	15.21	53.58	NA
16	Oakmark	Growth	9.54	30.50	NA
21	*Fidelity Asset Manager	Asset All.	7.17	23.29	0.29
49	*Mutual Beacon	Growth-Inc	3.86	22.93	0.38
15	Evergreen Global Real Estate	Sp. R/E	10.18	51.42	1.12
47	USAA Investment Cornerstone	Asset All.	3.98	23.73	0.66
32R	SAFECO Equity	Growth-Inc	5.68	30.91	1.02
43R	PBHG Growth	Small Co.	4.16	46.57	1.52

R Rejected on initial screening due to higher than average Morningstar (downside) risk (Some funds are recommended in spite of higher risk.)

don't need two asset allocation funds in a dynamic global asset allocation portfolio. If you feel strongly about having a domestic equity position and are willing to take a bit higher risk because the rest of your portfolio is so much below average downside risk, than these funds make some sense.

Three other attractive funds that made the three-year list but appear to have dropped off the pace of late (and could likely recover their momentum) are:

T. Rowe Price New Asia which, even with a slackened pace, could outperform the domestic stock funds easily. Early 1994 could be an excellent buying opportunity, as it rebounds from the recent market correction in Southeast Asia (the location of the bulk of "New" Asia) and continue to flourish as "the emerging China" scenario plays out.

American Heritage, with an excellent three-year track record and a dynamic and eclectic manger remains a fund to watch. After the past three years, it is certainly reasonable to forgive a slow quarter, especially as the fund experienced a significant cash flow due to being discovered by the press.

Fidelity Capital & Income, my favorite high-yield bond fund, is worthy of the same consideration you should accord to American Heritage, and for the same reasons.

THE ASSET ALLOCATION DECISIONS

To remind you, the markets in which we will currently want to participate are:

Gold Funds

We only need a 5 to 10 percent position, so we would aggressively recommend that you acquire a position gradually in gold funds, thus:

United Services World Gold

International Stock Funds (with good Pacific coverage)

You would have a problem investing too much in this very attractive kind of fund. So, let's say:

Fidelity Emerging Markets

Lexington Worldwide Emerging Markets

Oakmark International

Domestic Stock Funds

American Heritage or PBHG Growth

Oakmark

SAFECO Equity

Mutual Beacon

Sector Funds

Evergreen Global Real Estate

Total Return Funds

Fidelity Asset Manager

Let's put our portfolios together from our choices. Remember, these are simply examples of logical portfolios of the top, consistent low-risk, high-performance funds at the end of 1993. I highly recommend that you call 1-800-982-BILL to get an updated copy of my current recommendations before you commit your money.

THE BIG THREE PORTFOLIOS

I am assuming that you will want to be more assertive with your tax-sheltered investment program, concentrating it in eight funds or fewer (Table 11.11). You will then review your portfolio progress monthly or quarterly, review updated lists of the latest SuperStars, and decide if your portfolio needs upgrading. Remember, you have no tax consequences trading tax-sheltered money. Since you will be willing to trade more frequently, you

TABLE 11.11
Portfolio A—Your Tax-Sheltered Retirement Savings

10 percent United Services World Gold
15 percent Fidelity Emerging Markets
15 percent Lexington Worldwide Emerging Markets
20 percent Oakmark International
10 percent PBHG
10 percent Oakmark Fund
10 percent Fidelity Asset Manager
10 percent Evergreen Global Real Estate
100 percent

can afford to concentrate a portion (20 percent) of your money in the super-high-performance domestic equity funds (American Heritage and PBHG).

This portfolio is best established at Charles Schwab & Co. A $10,000 minimum balance will mean no annual IRA fee. Furthermore, Oakmark International, United Services World Gold, and Evergreen Real Estate are available at no transaction fee at Schwab. The reason to maintain your account at Schwab is that they have available, in a single account, the widest choice of no-load funds in the most useful fund families (Table 11.12).

What's the difference between these two portfolios? Gold and global real estate, which I have emphasized more. Since I feel you will be happier with these funds longer than you will with the domestic stock funds, we hope you will take a long-term position for both portfolios.

Because this is a long-term taxable portfolio, with tax consequences for upgrading, I have emphasized funds with excellent long-term, consistent track records to minimize upgrading needs. Choosing positions you can hold on to for the long term reduces the risk of having to sell, realize taxable capital gains, pay the taxes, and reinvest your money.

You will notice that we have eliminated funds that may not be good investments one or two years from now. T. Rowe Price New Asia, American Heritage, and PBHG Growth may be excellent funds to hold if you are willing to sell them if a better deal emerges or their investment performance deteriorates. For long-term holds, however, the alternative choices are better bets.

If this portfolio is too concentrated in equity investments for your tastes at this time, I suggest that you reduce the domestic equity positions (the least likely to be long-term successes) and replace them with an investment in Fidelity Asset Manager.

TABLE 11.12
Portfolio B—Your Long-Term Taxable Long-Term Savings

10 percent United Services World Gold
25 percent Fidelity Emerging Markets
25 percent Oakmark International
10 percent Fidelity Asset Manager
10 percent Oakmark or Mutual Beacon
20 percent Evergreen Global Real Estate
100 percent

Portfolio C—Portfolio A or B with Cash Flow Generation

To add cash flow to your portfolio, you can simply add a 10 percent money fund position to your portfolio. If you are at Schwab, you have few choices, but you should look at Schwab's U.S. Treasury money fund because most of the income will be state and local tax-exempt.

The cash flow tap can be turned on either by writing a check each month as you need it or by arranging for a check-a-month program to provide the cash flow. Don't be worried about running out of cash in the money fund. Each time you rebalance your investments, make sure you bring it back to a 10 to 15 percent position so you have enough for your needs. Then reinvest the dividends and interest in all of the investments to make sure you reinvest in the most productive portions of your portfolio. It's that simple.

Well, now you are on your way to becoming a successful investor. I hope that I have inspired you to take the risk, overcome your fear of the unknown, and become a confident assertive investor.

THE CLOCK IS TICKING—ARE YOU WATCHING?

Face it folks, if you are saving for retirement, you don't have time to "play it safe" and still build up enough retirement reserves in the time you have left. Too many people are being laid off from high paying jobs too early for Americans to count on being able to work until they wish to retire.

If you are already retired, you already understand that the wonders of medical science have improved the odds of your outliving your savings. You cannot afford the luxury of "playing it safe."

A FINAL SOBERING COMMENT TO PLAY-IT-SAFE MUNICIPAL BOND FUND INVESTORS

As I was finishing writing this book, my attention was drawn to a recent research study from Weiss Research, the insurance safety rating people (1-800-289-9222 for information) regarding insured municipal bonds. All insured municipal bonds (and few uninsured municipal bonds) are rated AAA, not because they are strong issues but because that is the rating given by all agencies to the insurance companies that insure municipal bonds.

Weiss' research indicates that those ratings are much higher than is justified. They probably deserve around a C rating on his tough scale or BBB on S&P or Moody's scales. In any case, if the rating agencies are overrated, the bonds are overpriced. If the market accepts this fact, a lot of people investing in insured municipal bonds will see the values of their bonds declining.

The losses will come from realistic ratings of the insurers and not new failures, which may be a decade or so later if Weiss' research is correct. I give Weiss' rating agency research a lot of credibility and I must say I am pleased to see yet another reason to get out of bonds before interest rates rise. This adds yet one more nail to the coffin of what appear to be *play it safe* investments.

PLAY IT SAFE OR PLAY IT SMART?

Playing it safe is the riskiest choice you can make! The traditional play it safe investments are too risky. Rising rates will wipe out profits in bonds; bank CDs are no longer competitive; guaranteed investment contracts (GICs) are one of the only insurance policies that are specifically *not* covered by state guaranty funds; tax-free muni-bond funds will find aggressively rising rates the impetus for a blood bath; and money funds just don't pay enough.

Playing it safe, in traditional terms, will be a disaster. What you need to do is play it smart and you are well on your way to true financial security.

CHAPTER 12

Can You Do Well and Do Good Too?

Make a Covenant with Your Society and Prosper

Just how can you do well (be a responsible steward of your family's money) and still do good (support enterprises that enhance the quality of life in our over-stressed world)? You can do just that, and do VERY well giving up little return in the process, while having a more satisfying investment experience.

DOING GOOD IS EASIER THAN YOU THINK; DOING WELL IS MORE SATISFYING THAN YOU CAN IMAGINE!

We all sense that responsible corporate citizenship should translate into good business and that socially conscious businesses should also, in the best of worlds, be good investments.

As responsible citizens, we would prefer to channel our money into companies whose presence in the marketplace enhances our quality of life. However, as responsible family members, we have to be concerned that we earn sufficiently high returns on our investments to fulfill our obligations to provide for ourselves and our families.

Reconciling these two goals—social responsibility and successful investing—has been a very real a challenge that I have long felt could be addressed, in my mind at least, in two practical ways:

Strategy #1:   Invest in companies that are socially responsible, giving up some "doing well" for "doing good," and provide for you and your family's welfare some other way.

Strategy #2:   Invest in whatever makes you the most money, and then share the wealth with charities and causes in whose goals you believe.

Strategy Two Always Seemed the Easier to Implement

I have always thought the second strategy—make the most money and share it—made the most sense since so few so-called social investment mutual funds had a strategy that made much investment sense or provided consistently competitive returns.

On the other hand, I recognized that this approach is only a partial solution to the problem since social responsibility goes far beyond just charitable giving.

SOCIALLY CONSCIOUS FUNDS DON'T WORK WELL

Too many social investment funds seemed to be just a "soap-box" for the managers' social agenda. While I would be the last to criticize their motivation or restrict their right to express their sincere returns, investment management carries other responsibilities.

Often, the goals are expressed in exclusionary terms: Calvert Social Investment funds (a load fund family) would not buy Treasury bills because the federal government financed the making of "weapons of mass destruction"; Amana Income Fund invests along Islamic principles (invest in nothing that pays interest, or is involved with liquor, wine, casinos, pornography, or gambling); a new "women's fund" manager has stated publicly that the fund will invest in a company because the company has a female treasurer.

While many of these goals are laudatory, they simply lack financial relevance. Their exclusionary criteria so narrow the

TABLE 12.1
Socially Conscious Mutual Funds

Rank	Fund Name	Investment Objective	1993 Total Return (%)	Rank in OBJ	Assets ($MM)	Covenant "Thumbs Up"
1	Pimco	Total Return III	12.67	21	76	5.0
2	Amana	Income	11.60	67	10	3.0
3	Parnassus	Income Fixed-Inc	10.99	39	4	5.0
4	Domini	Social Equity	6.53	80	21	5.0
5	Dreyfus	Third Century	5.26	77	511	4.0
6	Pax World		−1.05	100	477	5.0

Source: Morningstar Mutual Funds on Disc/Covenant Investment Management

investment options that it is extremely difficult to construct an adequately and prudently diversified investment portfolio. Entire industries are excluded. Surely, in any industry there are corporations that are sincere about and are acting prudently to express their social responsibilities.

In short, many social fund managers fail to address the need to invest in companies that will make attractive profits for investors. Other social investment funds have more carefully thought-out philosophies or strategies but still revolve around a "whistle blower" mentality.

Until recently, this widely respected investment movement seemed to produce lackluster returns. Look at the track records of the six no-load retail Socially Conscious Mutual Funds shown in Table 12.1.

As you can see, the no-load socially conscious funds available may all have a story compelling to some, but none have returns competitive with other funds in their peer group (Rank in Objective). Nor do they have the assets under their control to make a real impact on a corporation's social consciousness.

A great idea but poor results.

A FRESH NEW APPROACH

Covenant Investment Management (1-312-443-8472), a Chicago-based investment firm, has developed a socially conscious, corporate responsibility rating system that makes sense and makes money.

The Covenant 200™ Index, a capitalization-weighted index of 200 large U.S. companies Covenant determined to be the most socially responsible, has consistently outperformed

TABLE 12.2
The Five-Year Track Record

	Average Annualized Total Return
The Covenant 200	15.1%
Standard & Poor's 500	4.5%
Average Domestic Stock Mutual Fund	14.3%

the S&P 500 over the five years ended June 30, 1993. Just take a look at Table 12.2.

The Wall Street Journal reported on a Covenant analysis that looked at how a company's equal opportunity practices impacted its financial returns. Over five years, the 200 companies with the best equal opportunity records beat the market by 2.8 percent a year. The 200 companies with the poorest track records under-performed the market by 8.0 percent over the same five years. Talk about poor equal opportunity practices being an "Achilles' Heel"!

A MORE RATIONAL WAY TO MEASURE SOCIAL CONSCIOUSNESS: BUILDING THE STANDARDS

Covenant surveyed leaders across the social, political, academic, corporate, and religious sectors (individuals whose influence and authority shape the playing field on which corporations compete) to arrive at 36 corporate social responsibility criteria.

Given the active, political, social, and regulatory agendas now being developed and implemented by the Clinton Administration in Washington, DC, these could well be the leading indicators of future financial performance. In fact, the Covenant 200 began to significantly outperform the S&P 500 as the reality of a Clinton Administration unfolded.

These socially conscious leaders told Covenant that responsible companies need to be primarily concerned with the needs of their customers, employees, and shareholders. Once those needs are met, companies should be attentive to the needs of their communities and environment.

To measure social consciousness, Covenant currently rates the 1000 largest companies in America on the following criteria.

The Social Covenant

It is society that grants the right to conduct business. In accepting this privilege, each American corporation, in effect, enters into a contract with each of the many societies in which it exists. With social contracts come responsibilities. These social responsibilities extend to relationships with their customers, employees, shareholders, suppliers, competitors, communities, and the environment, as well as responsibility to address specific social issues (see avoidance issues, below).

Covenant corporate responsibility rating analyses measure the following criteria (in order of greatest weighting in determining ratings):

Customer Responsibility. Fair pricing, product safety, and product quality.
Maximum Possible Score: 181

Employee Responsibility. Training programs, benefits, equal opportunity, work place safety, union representation, and retirement plan funding.
Maximum Possible Score: 166

Shareholder Responsiveness. Takeover defenses, independence of board of directors, management stock ownership, and employee stock ownership.
Maximum Possible Score: 157

Community Responsibility. Civic involvement, employee voluntarism, and corporate philanthropy.
Maximum Possible Score: 143

Environmental Sensitivity. Compliance, recycling and waste reduction initiatives, responsible packaging, financial contributions to environmental causes, and research and development activities.
Maximum Possible Score: 126

Avoidance Issues. Animal testing, gambling, tobacco, liquor, defensive contracting, business practices in Northern Ireland, and nuclear power. (Gone is the avoidance of South Africa. Recently a group of social investment fund managers voted South African

interests and investments to be a *positive* factor ending the boy-cott of South Africa and celebrating the end of apartheid.)
Maximum Possible Score: 99

Supplier Relations. Litigation, joint venture initiatives, and co-operative supplier relations.
Maximum Possible Score: 80

Competitive Practices. Regulatory compliance, litigation, and distribution tactics.
Maximum Possible Score: 48

As you can see, there are many issues—many objective and subjective issues—that make up a quantitative evaluation of a company's relationship with its many communities.

SOCIAL INVESTING IN REAL LIFE

At a recent national meeting involving officials of a major labor union (who had invited Covenant executives to explain the re-search behind their ratings to the labor union's pension plan money managers), a former U.S. Secretary of Labor spoke to the money managers:

> You all tell me you can beat the market. Look around, you are the market. What I want you to do is to raise the level of the marketplace for everyone. And the way to do that is to invest in companies that invest in their employees. Invest in companies that provide training, safe work places, a healthy community environment, and productive supplier relations.

A union official summed up the meeting with the follow-ing caution to the money managers, "Your portfolios' Covenant scores will be watched closely."
They got the point. Socially conscious investing can make money and encourage responsible corporate behavior.

HOW RATINGS ARE DETERMINED

Corporations are rated one to five "Thumbs Up" for their social consciousness, with five "Thumbs Up" being the top rating. In addition, corporations can have one to eight "Achilles' Heels," identifying their areas of vulnerability. As Covenant expands the number of corporations it reviews from 1000 to 2000 or more, more funds that hold stocks in smaller companies will qualify for Covenant ratings.

Mutual funds are portfolios of many stocks. Covenant examines the corporations whose stocks are held by mutual funds. Therefore, it rates mutual funds based on the fund's corporate stock holdings. Like the underlying companies, funds can receive up to five "Thumbs Up" or up to eight "Achilles' Heels."

Translating these ratings into mutual fund ratings is yet another process.

First, Covenant gathers data from several hundred public and private sources on an ongoing basis. Each company is scored on each of the 36 criteria. The scores are aggregated to an overall Covenant Corporate Responsibility Rating.

Next, Covenant compiles the holdings of all stock funds with assets of more than $25 million, plus all socially responsible funds, and environmental funds. To qualify for a rating, each fund must be at least 40 percent invested in equities, have at least ten holdings of top 1000 companies, or at least 40 percent of the dollar value of all holdings in the top 1000 corporations.

Then Covenant develops a score for each fund in each category by calculating a weighted average of each holding multiplied by its Covenant score to arrive at an overall score for the fund. Based on the dollar-weighted ratings, a rating of one to five "Thumbs Up" is assigned to the fund.

THERE ARE LIMITS

The ratings are best applied to the types of funds that are most likely to hold positions in the 1000 largest corporations. The "hit ratio" of matches between the largest 1000 corporations and the fund's portfolio is going to be higher on large cap than small cap funds, on stock funds than balanced funds, on domestic funds than international funds, and on equity funds than fixed-income funds.

However, if you want to invest in domestic stock funds, there are a lot of socially responsible winners out there, more than you ever suspected. Take a look at Table 12.3.

TABLE 12.3
Selected Top-Performing Funds for 1993 with High Covenant Ratings
(All Over $50 MM in Assets, 3 Percent or Less Load,
and $25,000 or Less Minimum Initial Investment)

Rank	Fund Name	1993 Total Return (%)	Beta	Covenant Rating ("Thumbs Up")
1	American Heritage	41.39	1.20	3.5
2	Invesco Strategic Leisure	35.71	1.00	4.0
3	Fidelity Select—software	32.48	1.41	5.0
4	Fidelity Select—telecomm	29.65	0.85	5.0
5	Fidelity Select—technology	28.63	1.40	5.0
6	Janus Worldwide	28.41	Na	5.0
7	Steinroe Capital Opportunity	27.52	1.10	3.5
8	Fidelity Select—home Finance	27.26	1.28	5.0

Source: Morningstar Mutual Funds on Disc/Covenant Investment Management

THIS GROUP OF FUNDS PRESENTS A CHALLENGE FOR INVESTORS

As you have probably noticed, in each of the nine Mutual Fund SuperStar Candidates lists (with the exception of the All Fund SuperStars table), we have included the Covenant ratings where available. (Remember the very nature of the ratings applies only to corporate stock fund portfolios.)

You will be surprised, as I was, to see top performers with high Covenant ratings, including American Heritage (4 "Thumbs Up"), up 41.39 percent in 1993, Vanguard Index Value (3.5 "Thumbs Up"), up 18.25 percent, Fidelity Asset Manager—Growth (3.5 "Thumbs Up"), up 26.32 percent, and Blanchard Global Growth (3.5 "Thumbs Up"), up 24.46 percent.

As the corporate ratings base is expanded in the coming year and the number of rated funds expands, we will be pleased to include a greater number of socially conscious funds in our portfolios.

CHAPTER 13

Is the Government Taking Too Much of Your Profits?

18 Legal Tax-Avoidance Strategies to Keep Clinton at Bay

It's not the money you make, it's the money you **keep** that counts. Today, with a new Democratic administration aiming to reorganize the national health care system and reduce the deficit and, at the same time, tax those of us who have somehow amassed some wealth—and all of us seem to be rich—keeping your share is an increasingly difficult effort.

THEY GOT ME, THEY'LL GET YOU TOO

Folks, I don't know about your tax bracket, but my marginal federal tax rate just jumped up nearly 28 percent in a day—from 31 percent to 39.6 percent—and, to add insult to injury, the increase was retroactive to January 1, 1993! In 1994, with the earnings cap removed from the 1.45 percent Medicare tax, that increase will be expanded to 32 percent and, for those of you stuck with the 2.90 percent Medicare tax for the self-employed, nearly 37 percent!

So, with the new 36 percent top tax bracket, the 10 percent surcharge for those of us earning over $250,000 adding an additional 3.6 percentage points to the bill and, in 1994, the removal of the $135,000 cap on earned income eligible for the 1.45 percent Medicare tax (2.90 percent for the self-employed like me), my tax bracket jumped from 31 percent to 42.50 percent. That will be a 37 percent increase in my tax rate in 1994. Thank God, I live in Seattle, Washington, where at least we have no state income taxes—so far.

Now you understand why frazzled tax accountants across the country have become frustrated beyond endurance. How can accounting professionals responsibly advise their clients about tax planning when Congress keeps tax policy such a punitive, arbitrary, and moving target?

Back to the Drawing Board

The shocking new tax increases were all I needed to sit down and take a close look at each of my investment strategies and a few I had shelved when tax rates were cut in the 1980s.

If your investment strategies are sensitive to, but not driven by tax considerations, you can keep considerably more of your investment dollars longer. If you are ready to improve your investment portfolio strategies tax sensitivity, here we go!

THE VERY WORST CLINTON TAX SHELTERS

Investing Naively in Tax-Exempt Bond Funds

The first gut reaction from many investors is to say to yourself, "If income taxes are going up, then the obvious strategy is to invest to earn more tax-exempt income." It may sound obvious, but it can be a treacherous money trap, especially if you decide this is the easy way out and forget to keep a very close eye on your investments.

If you invest in tax-free municipal bond funds whose yields are high enough to provide you with a significant improvement over money funds and bank CDs, you have to stretch for greater credit risk, market risk, and/or longer average maturities—and there's the rub. Those are all strategies that increase your vulnerability to principal losses due to rising interest rates.

I recently interviewed a young and astute portfolio manager of a conservatively managed intermediate-term municipal bond fund for *Donoghue's MONEYTALK*, my monthly audio cassette advisory service. The fund was paying slightly over 6 percent with an average maturity of ten years and a duration (an important statistic) of six years. The rule of thumb with duration is that if interest rates rise 1 percent and the duration is X, then you will lose X percent in principal.

I asked the manager, "Now, let me get this straight. If interest rates in your market rise only a single percentage point it would wipe out your entire annual return? Right?"

"I guess so," she acknowledged. I saw no reason to continue the interview. With rates this low the risk of a rate turnaround is simply too high.

If that happened, investors would have to pay state income taxes on the dividends (in the case of national tax-free funds, which are only federal income tax free) and get no tax break for their 6 percent loss of value unless they sold their shares. That's like paying taxes on your losses! That is a risk not worth taking in my book, especially with interest rates so low.

With interest rates at or near 25-year lows, investing in bonds of any kind doesn't really make much sense. Although the tax-exemption of muni-bond fund dividends does cushion the risk a bit, investors who take this route will likely lose money and pay taxes on their losses.

In addition, investors in so-called "insured municipal bonds" or bond funds should be aware of a disturbing study from the well-respected insurance company rating agency Weiss Research. According to Weiss, the major insurance companies that insure "insured" municipal bonds have underestimated the default risk of such bonds.

Since the rating of all "insured" municipal bonds (and few noninsured municipal bonds) is AAA, the current ratings of the insurers and, in Weiss' opinion, these major insurers are grossly overrated, the bonds are overpriced. Once the financial world recognizes that these bonds are overrated, the price of these bonds will decline to a more realistic valuation. Thus, insured municipal bond investors are in for a surprise decline in the market value of their bond investments.

The next step in a savvy investment strategy is likely to *sell*—not buy—bonds, especially "insured" bonds.

Investing in Tax-Exempt Money Funds

While there is little principal risk in tax-exempt money funds, the yields are so low as not to be significantly competitive. Often, but not always, it makes more sense to invest in arguably safer (state and local income tax-free) 100 percent U.S. government securities (federal income) taxable money funds.

The top choice has to be United Services Government Securities Savings Fund (1-800-US-FUNDS), often in recent years the highest-yielding money fund, even before taking its state and local income, franchise, and intangibles tax exclusions.

Donoghue'$ MONEYLETTER will keep you up to date on the best money funds for you, including the tax-exempt money funds.

DONOGHUE'S CLINTON TAX-BUSTER STRATEGY #1

Capture Long-Term Capital Gains in Fixed-Income Investments

Millions of investors have dramatic capital gains built into the resale value of their holdings of CMOs (Collateralized Mortgage Obligations), zero-coupon, long-term government and corporate bonds, tax-exempt municipal bonds, and bond fund and unit investment trusts. I predict that when interest rates rise— and they most assuredly will eventually (certainly **before** you expect and **after** you have experienced losses)—that the bond market and especially the municipal bond market could see a bloodbath, even the five-star and AAA-rated investments.

The inevitable risk of rising rates wiping out all or part of those profits and the fact that many of those fixed-income investments are in tax-sheltered retirement plans with no tax consequences if they are sold make it wise to capture those tax-preferred capital gains in the near future. Of course, it's up to **you** to decide how long you will hold on and when you will sell. Even if your bonds or bond funds are held in a taxable account, the current maximum 28 percent tax bracket on long-term capital gains makes it attractive to take long-term (generally held over one year) capital gains before Congress changes its mind about their tax-preferred status.

There are over 3,000,000 different tax-free issues outstanding, and for the most part they are not required to provide financial information to the SEC. Most muni-bond funds have rarely had to sell these securities in a secondary market and then at the significant disadvantage of insufficient financial information. Also, most muni-bond funds portfolio managers have never had to sell a portfolio security, and millions of investors have never seen a rising rate market (except briefly in 1987).

When the bond funds see investors' redemptions exceeding their new investments and are forced to sell, the brokers will ask in amazement, "Sell? To whom? You are the only one who has ever bought this issue!" There will be buyers, of course, but at fire sale prices. Don't get into something that could be that risky.

DONOGHUE'S CLINTON TAX-BUSTER STRATEGY #2

Capital Losses Are Great Tax Shelters—Use the Ones You Have—Don't Buy New Ones

If you have capital losses, you would be wise to sell, realize the losses, and start getting your tax breaks immediately. Remember that after you have offset capital losses against capital gains, you can only deduct $3,000 per year against ordinary income. Consult your tax advisor for details.

First, ultimately rising interest rates will likely increase your stock and bond losses as markets react negatively. Second, if you have realized your losses, even if you have a large loss carry-forward, you can use those losses to offset against future gains giving you greater freedom to upgrade and reposition your taxable portfolio holdings without having to worry about the tax consequences.

DONOGHUE'S CLINTON TAX-BUSTER STRATEGY #3

Pay Down Your Credit Card Balances

Always a high priority and a riskless yet often overlooked tax-shelter strategy, paying down your credit card balances pays off handsomely. While this is not specifically a tax-savings strategy, the new higher tax rates put this strategy at the top of your "must do" list.

For example, if you are in, say, a 40 percent federal, state, and local income tax bracket (and millions of taxpayers like you would like to be in that *low* a tax bracket) and you are paying the national average rate of, say, around 19 percent on your credit card balances, paying down your credit card balances is like discovering a 31.7 percent risk-free government-guaranteed (it's their tax rules that make this transaction riskless) investment.

Why such a high return? Two simple reasons: (a) your credit card interest is no longer deductible and (b) to pay $1.00 of interest you have to earn $1.67 before taxes in our example.

As you can see, it even makes sense (if you cannot afford to pay off all of your credit card balances immediately) to place your taxable investments into a discount brokerage account like Schwab One and borrow on margin at cheap interest rates to pay off those pesky credit card balances.

Donoghue's Clinton Tax-Busters for Fully Taxable Accounts

To fully understand how to tax-manage fully taxable mutual fund portfolios, you need to understand exactly how taxable events occur. Mutual funds can earn you taxable profits in three ways:

Dividends.   At least 98 percent of all of the interest and dividend income earned by the fund on its portfolio securities during the calendar year must be distributed by year-end each year or the fund itself must pay income taxes as well as the shareholders.

Bond funds tend to distribute income as *dividends* monthly, money funds do so daily, and stock funds tend to do so quarterly or semi-annually. Dividends are reported to the IRS on a Form 1099 DIV.

Realized Capital Gains.   At least 98 percent of the net capital gains (after deducting capital losses) from actual sales of port-folio securities for the year ended 10/31 must be distributed by 12/31 each year. Most funds distribute annually in December or semi-annually.

In recent years, tax management has been a real challenge for even savvy investors because some important mutual fund families refused to inform even the press, much less their share-holders, with the amount of the *capital gains distributions* early enough for investors to implement tax-minimization tactics, such as the year-end tax swap strategy I reinvented. (See Strat-egy #9.)

Fidelity Investments, previously reluctant to provide early notice of capital gain distributions, announced recently that it would give investors an estimate by Thanksgiving, giving in-vestors time for tax-minimization tactics. Their action repre-sented another victory for *Donoghue'$ MONEYLETTER* readers as your editors were the among the first to campaign for early disclosure.

Realized capital gain distributions are reported to the IRS on a Form 1099. Most funds report the net long-term gains and combine short-term gains and dividends.

Unrealized Capital Gains.   The increase in market value over their cost of securities that are still in the funds' portfolio and not yet sold (hence **un**realized capital gains) is reflected in the net asset value per share (price of no-load funds) of the fund. These capital gains are tax-deferred until either the fund sells the security and realizes the gain (it must then be distributed as a taxable capital gain as noted above) or fund investors sell the shares of the fund at a price above their cost basis.

It is then up to the investors to report *their* realized capital gains on their tax return. Investors should take care to note that they have already paid taxes on both reinvested dividends and capital gain distributions for the years in which they are received (and reinvested) so that those distributions and dividends are not taxed twice, a common mistake taxpayers make (for more details, see Strategy #17).

Taxes are due on these profits on April 15 of the following year or possibly during the year if the taxpayer files quarterly returns. This provides an additional short-term tax-deferral benefit of mutual fund investing.

DONOGHUE'S CLINTON TAX-BUSTER STRATEGY #4

Exercise Care to Exclude State and Local Income Tax-Exempt Dividends from State and Local Returns

Dividends derived from interest on Treasury bills and certain specific government agencies' direct obligations (not Ginnie Mae pass-throughs but Ginnie Mae notes, for example) are exempt from state and local income, intangible, and franchise taxes in most states. One hundred percent (qualified) government money funds, such as the current top after-tax yielding United Services Government Securities Savings Fund, will indicate the exemption in their annual shareholder statements.

DONOGHUE'S CLINTON TAX-BUSTER STRATEGY #5

Exercise Care to Take Advantage of Foreign Income Tax Credits Paid by Global and International Funds

Taxes withheld by or paid to foreign governments by the funds can rightfully be deducted from federal and state income taxes. Normally, the funds will report such payments (which are common among global and international funds) and will explain the complex alternatives for your reporting same on your tax returns.

It is usually best to take a credit rather than a deduction since that is a 100 percent offset against your tax liability. Don't be bashful about asking your fund for more detailed tax-preparation instructions.

Investors with international fund investments in tax-sheltered accounts, such as IRAs, cannot, however, use the deductions or credits. They are tax-deferred, and all withdrawals are taxed as fully taxable ordinary income.

DONOGHUE'S CLINTON TAX-BUSTER STRATEGY #6

Watch for Alternative Minimum Tax Problems Before Investing in a Tax-Exempt Money or Bond Fund

Many tax-exempt funds invest in securities whose interest is not tax-exempt if you must pay the alternative minimum tax (AMT). Consult with your tax advisor before investing in such a fund if there is any chance that you will be subject to the alternative minimum tax.

It is not uncommon for affluent investors to opt for large investments in "tax-free" investments only to discover that they have triggered the alternative minimum tax and they would have been better off, on an after-tax basis, in a fully taxable fund. Your best protection is to check the prospectus for the percentage breakdown between fully tax-exempt and AMT taxable dividends in the most recent year and talk with the customer service representatives about any changes in policy. Caution: Remember that just because a fund can invest in AMT paper does not mean it *does* invest in such paper.

DONOGHUE'S CLINTON TAX-BUSTER STRATEGY #7

Check Out the Morningstar Tax Analysis on Each Stock Fund Before Investing

In August 1993, Morningstar Mutual Funds initiated an intriguing and potentially valuable tax analysis statistical service that we will be watching closely. In an attempt to begin developing a strategy to address the tax sensitivity of stock funds (especially), Morningstar Mutual Funds has begun to calculate two statistics:

Percent of Pre-Tax Return.   The percentage of the fund's total return (dividends plus realized and unrealized capital gains) that was left after the maximum federal (but not state) income taxes calculated at the tax rates in effect at the time—before income tax rates were raised in the 1993 tax bill. The closer to 100 percent, the better.

Noting that "those funds that have paid the fewest recent capital gains [a positive attribute by itself] are likely to be those sitting on the greatest future taxable gains," Morningstar calculates a second statistic:

Potential Capital Gains Tax Exposure.   Defined as "the maximum percentage of a fund's current assets that might be paid out as a taxable [realized] gain were the fund to liquidate all its holdings today [a highly unlikely event]."

The percentage is not actually the tax *liability* but the *unrealized capital gains* remaining in the fund's price per share. For example, a fund with a 33 percent estimated tax liability would have a cost basis of its portfolio, on average, equivalent to 67 percent of the current market value. The actual maximum possible capital gains tax liability would, of course, be only 28 percent of the 33 percent or 9.2 percent of the net asset value.

At WEDCO our managers review these statistics carefully in light of market conditions before investing in stock funds. If we are viewing this position as a long-term, core position, we would prefer a fund with a high percentage of pre-tax return because it means that, barring an unexpected event, this fund understands the value of tax-deferring capital gains for its investors.

If we thought of the investment position as a shorter-term "take advantage of an opportunity" [like the post-crash opportunity] investment, we would avoid a fund with a high pre-crash estimated tax liability, especially if we were near the year-end when capital gains distributions are made, so we would not be forced to accept a high and unwanted capital gain distribution.

DONOGHUE'S CLINTON TAX-BUSTER STRATEGY #8

Try Mom's CD-Beater Cash Flow Investment Strategy

This "old favorite" strategy, which I used to manage my mother's investment portfolio, is a natural dividend tax shelter. Our strategy was simple:

▶   Invest the portfolio for growth not income.

▶   Maximize investments in funds that pay smaller dividends.

▶ Maximize investments in funds with a track record of tax sensitivity (minimizing capital gains distributions by tax-sensitive portfolio management).

▶ Maximize tax-free return of principal withdrawals to maximize spendable cash.

▶ Reinvest dividends and capital gain distributions when received.

Although the last are, of course, taxable, it is normally simplest to reinvest them at the source, usually the most productive place for them to be reinvested, and withdraw all cash flow from a single fund, usually the least productive fund in the portfolio. That way cash flow is in a predictable (timing and amount), single check-a-month format. This is fairly simple since nearly all fund families will arrange for regular monthly redemptions to generate a monthly check in the amount the client requests.

Mom liked it since it gave her more spendable cash and the emphasis on target growth rates in excess of withdrawals meant, in her words, "I won't run out of money before I run out of life." Unfortunately, for Mom, that did not turn out to be the case, as she died soon after she entered the program. However, she slept more peacefully and enjoyed her life more fully because she had fewer money worries.

DONOGHUE'S CLINTON TAX-BUSTER STRATEGY #9

Use Donoghue's Year-End Tax Swap Strategy

This is a strategy I practically invented in 1987, the year of the Big Crash. Actually, I was one of the few who saw its application to the unique situation mutual funds found themselves in 1987. Tax swaps were not new, but few investors had ever experienced a scenario such as 1987, and even fewer were willing to find out if tax swaps were necessary—in time to save investors' money that year.

The Wall Street Journal that year and again in 1989 devoted significant space to cover my research, which I shared with the world, although probably only our private money management clients and *Donoghue'$ MONEYLETTER* subscribers were able to take full advantage of the swaps before the end of the tax year. Others, no doubt, waited to see if someone else would follow this strategy and paid dearly for the wait.

That year, many investors, caught up in the euphoria of the summer's highs, came into December with mutual fund accounts considerably below the amount they had originally invested. The problem was that many of the stock funds had realized more capital gains than they would have otherwise as they sold off older portfolio holdings to reposition their portfolios to take advantage of the radically different post-crash markets.

The result was underwater (accounts with unrealized losses) investor stock fund accounts and 25 to 30 percent taxable capital gains distributions. The investors had lost money and then gotten 25 to 30 percent of their own principal back in the form of realized capital gains distributions. Further complicating this mess was the dramatic profit potential in the post-crash markets that were just beginning to rebound as year-end approached.

Investors did not want to be hit with unnecessary taxes on what was essentially a return of principal, but they also didn't want to sell and get out of the market and miss the rebound from the crash. What we did was to contact the funds involved to determine when they were going to distribute their capital gains and how large the distribution would be.

First, we sold the underwater positions before the capital gains distribution was made (it works just as well if you do so after the capital gains distributions, but with last minute year-end distributions, that is very difficult to do in time), avoiding the taxable event and realizing some capital losses to offset against other gains from earlier in the year or carried forward to future years.

Second, we reinvested the client's money in similar stock funds (carefully avoiding the "wash" sale rule, which would have invalidated the tax losses we realized), but not until *after* they had declared their year-end capital gains distributions. Hence, my privately managed accounts avoided a very expensive and unnecessary taxable event and were in the right place to enjoy the post-crash markets.

The tax savings were mammoth, and we have carefully watched the stock markets for similar tax-saving opportunities in subsequent years. Astute competitors watch *Donoghue'$ MONEYLETTER* for our annual analysis.

DONOGHUE'S CLINTON TAX-BUSTER STRATEGY #10

Invest for the Long Term Using the Donoghue Signal

The Donoghue Signal Strategy increases the amount of long-term holds in your investment portfolio. The long-term holds maximize the long-term capital gains tax deferral benefits. It is precisely that long-term discipline and its rewards for which The Donoghue Signal Strategy was created. I wanted to devise an investment discipline that would allow me to invest 100 percent long-term in a few specific growth stock mutual funds and also one that would let me be 100 percent out of the market when the risks of rising interest rates were too high.

It worked well. For example, over the decade ended 5/31/91, the strategy, which is based on interest rate trends, required only 15 trades and improved buy-and-hold performance of forty top-performing no-load stock mutual funds by 101.9 percent. Returns since then have been equally attractive.

Our last *BUY* signal was on July 14, 1989, and the Donoghue Signal generated a *SELL* signal on December 6, 1993. Thus, we are 100 percent in cash or money funds in our Donoghue Signal Portfolios as of February 28, 1994. During the period between *BUY* and *SELL* signals, our portfolios earned an average of 74 percent or 20 percent higher than the S&P 500 with all dividends reinvested (the tougher standard to beat).

From a tax-sheltering perspective, we have been able to defer most unrealized capital gains for over four years (although we did trade up a bit to take advantage of excellent new funds such as Oakmark Fund).

The Donoghue Signal is an outstanding example of how to address maximization of tax-deferral of unrealized capital gains.

DONOGHUE'S TAX-BUSTERS FOR TAX-SHELTERED ACCOUNTS

When you have the opportunity to invest in a tax-sheltered account, you want to understand that the opportunities of this investment experience are significantly different than investing in taxable accounts. The U.S. government feels so strongly about the benefits of tax-sheltered investing that it most frequently allows you to deduct your contributions to the account.

DONOGHUE'S CLINTON TAX-BUSTER STRATEGY #11

Invest Assertively in Tax-Sheltered Accounts

The single biggest advantage of tax-sheltered accounts is that there is no reason *NOT* to *GO FOR IT!* anymore. Given the easy availability of lifetime free IRAs, a choice of over 200 no-transaction-fee mutual funds, and the inherent no-tax-consequences nature of tax-sheltered accounts, the constant surveillance of your accounts for opportunities to upgrade portfolio holdings results in extra profits.

In fact, the single-statement, no-transaction-fee, no-load mutual fund programs at Charles Schwab & Co., Fidelity Brokerage, Waterhouse Securities, and Jack White & Co. offer over 500 no-load funds to choose from, although no single discount broker currently offers more than 240. That's quite a choice of funds to work with.

Tax-sheltered retirement accounts are Congress's special gift to American savers because they provide investors the opportunity to trade without having to be concerned about tax consequences. This allows investors to invest their retirement savings much more aggressively than nonsheltered savings in order to take full advantage of the tax-deferral of their profits.

If you can tax defer your profits, it makes sense to maximize those profits. If there are no transaction costs to hold you back, it makes sense, within the limits of the Schwab Mutual Fund OneSource™ program, for example (maximum four short-term trades a year), to concentrate your tax-sheltered money in a few funds (to avoid being kicked out of the no-transaction-fee program for too many short-term trades) and to be willing to upgrade your portfolio as new leaders emerge.

An excellent example of how this might work is the shift in profit opportunities from domestic to international stock funds. For the full year of 1993, the top ten international stock funds outperformed the top ten domestic stock funds by a factor of almost two to one. International stock markets are just beginning their bull market while the domestic stock markets are slowly hitting new peaks in a very old and tired bull market.

Upgrading your portfolio to include greater concentrations in international funds would be a wise decision in this case.

DONOGHUE'S CLINTON TAX-BUSTER STRATEGY #12

Request That Your Employer Offer a More Appropriate Range of Investment Choices in Your Retirement Savings Program

Many employers know their employees as workers and individuals, but few employers know you as an investor. Consequently, they do not know that you need sophisticated investment choices in their employee retirement plans.

Thinking they are doing a "good enough" job by establishing an employee savings plan, they have probably provided a fixed-income choice (probably a guaranteed investment contract, or GIC), a stock market and a bond market option, a money fund, and possibly a company stock option.

As you get more serious about your retirement savings and accumulate more and more money in the plan, you will want to and should get more demanding about the choices. You should question if the insurance company behind the GIC is rated highly (at least a B) by the most demanding insurance rating agency, Weiss Research (1-800-289-9222 for a $15 rating). You should request a diversified international stock market option to avoid the eventual correction in our domestic stock markets. You should request a short-term money market alternative to avoid the risks of rising interest rates to the bond markets. In short, you should be more selective.

Few responsible employers would refuse reasonable requests from their employees. Some employers have even chosen a WEDCO-managed portfolio as one diversified and actively managed option (1-800-642-4276).

Make a request for a wider and more sophisticated choice of investment options. You have everything to gain and nothing to lose.

DONOGHUE'S CLINTON TAX-BUSTER STRATEGY #13

Maximize Your Contribution to Your Employer's Retirement Savings Plan

Considering that most employer retirement savings plans allow you to invest more than $2,000, are fully deductible, and provide for generous employer-matching contributions, you want to make sure you have maxed out your employer's plan before you invest in an IRA. If your employer contributes, say, a 50 percent matching contribution, that makes your investment even safer since you would have to lose 33 percent of your total investment (assuming you are fully vested) before you are as bad off as if you put the same money in an IRA.

A 50 percent gain on the first day you invest is hard to turn down. On top of that, you can probably invest more in your 401(k) than in an IRA, making it the better deal.

DONOGHUE'S CLINTON TAX-BUSTER STRATEGY #14

Invest Unlimited Amounts in Variable Insurance Policies

Once you have maximized your contributions to your employer's retirement plan and funded your personal individual retirement account, you are ready to learn the limitations of government retirement accounts:

▶ TOO SOON: Withdrawals before age 59½ carry a 10 percent tax penalty.

▶ TOO LATE: Withdrawals that do not start after age 70½ carry a 50 percent tax penalty.

▶ TOO MUCH: Withdrawals in excess of $150,000 in a single year carry a 15 percent tax penalty.

To get around these restrictive limits, many individuals who wish to invest for the long-term choose to invest instead in annuities that permit unlimited amounts to be invested and have no requirements that you ever withdraw at all.

Many investors choose variable annuities, which allow the money to be invested in mutual fund-like separate accounts rather than the general account of the life insurance company, which could be subject to claims by other creditors in the event of a financial failure.

Of course, in all fairness, it is appropriate to note that the investment choices in tax-deferred employee retirement programs are broader and the expenses much lower than in variable annuities. In addition, having the government as your partner in an IRA also means having the IRS as your partner when you withdraw. As with other retirement plans, money withdrawn from annuities is subject to federal, state, and local income taxes.

Still other investors choose variable life insurance, which, if funded in at least four substantially equal payments over a seven-year period, allows investors to borrow rather than withdraw from the policy tax-free, with the loans repaid before the cash value plus the remaining profits are paid tax-free to your heirs. Currently, most annuities and life policies are overly expensive, have too few investment choices, and are sold by commission-hungry agents with much to gain and little to offer.

However, if you have already invested in such a variable annuity or variable life policy, you might want to consider doing a Section 1035 tax-free transfer to either Fidelity Investments' no-load variable annuity or Nationwide Insurances' Best of America IV variable annuity of variable life insurance programs, which do offer attractive investment opportunities.

DONOGHUE'S CLINTON TAX-BUSTER STRATEGY #15

Carefully Avoid Unnecessary Investment Costs in Tax-Sheltered Accounts

Because the eventual post-retirement withdrawal value (down the road 20 or 30 years or so) of even small amounts is magnified so dramatically through the magic of compounding, it is wise to minimize *friction* costs at the time of investing. Friction costs come in three flavors: annual trustee fees, transaction or trading costs, and continuing asset management fees. Annual trustee fees, often referred to as IRA *account charges,* can be totally eliminated by the use of Schwab's Lifetime FREE IRA program for accounts over $10,000 or Fidelity Brokerage's similar program for active traders.

Transaction costs can be avoided by using either the Schwab Mutual Fund OneSource™ program or the Fidelity Brokerage's FundsNetwork program. Each offers over 200 no-load mutual funds (although not the same 200 funds) from several fund families at no transaction charge. Both programs have similar trading frequency limits (four short-term—less than six months' hold—sales per year).

Account management fees, such as those charged by WEDCO and other money managers, can be prepaid directly rather than deducted from your tax-sheltered account. The advantage is that the money you have in your tax-sheltered account is increased, resulting in more dollars compounding to your benefit, and the fees paid directly may be tax deductible if, when combined with other miscellaneous tax-deductible expenses, such as your *Donoghue'$ MONEY-LETTER* subscription, they exceed 2 percent of your adjusted gross income.

When Charles Schwab & Co. offers NO-load funds (over 650), some with NO-transaction fees (over 200), NO annual IRA fees and NO tax consequences for active trading, you are wise to KNOW about your opportunities and ACT on them.

DONOGHUE'S CLINTON TAX-BUSTER STRATEGY #16

Extra Leverage Can Backfire on You

If you are one of those extra-aggressive and confident investors who invests mostly in small cap stock funds on margin, you should sit down with your tax advisor and take a close look at the tax deductibility of your investment interest. Under the new law, to deduct your investment interest against your capital gains, you may have to elect to have your long-term capital gains taxed at the full 39.6 percent rate rather than the 28 percent capital gains rate.

Since this strategy is quite complex and applies only to those in the top tax brackets who also invest on margin to earn primarily long-term capital gains, we simply suggest that if that describes you, you should consult your tax advisor before investing on margin.

DONOGHUE'S CLINTON TAX-BUSTER STRATEGY #17

Don't Pay Taxes on Your Dividends and Capital Gains Distributions—Twice

The single most frequent mistake investors make is to forget to increase the cost basis of your mutual funds positions when you reinvest dividends and capital gains distributions. When you sell your fund shares, you often subtract the original cost of the shares from the sales price and pay capital gains taxes on the difference. Doing so, you're paying taxes on their reinvested dividends and capital gains distributions TWICE—when they are received and when you sell the shares.

Be careful, this is a mistake so easy to make. After all, we are paying more than enough in taxes as it is!

And, finally, one bonus from the government . . .

DONOGHUE'S CLINTON TAX-BUSTER STRATEGY #18

Tax Defer Your Tax Increase—If You Are Careful

To soften the blow of the tax increase, the "rich"—yes, that is probably you—get to spread their actual payment of the tax increase (not the full tax, just the increase) over the next three years. However, be aware that you must know approximately how much you are deferring by April 15, or you risk losing the benefit of the deferral. If you are used to requesting an extension for your return, you would be wise to plan to file on time this year. You can always file an amended return, which may result in losing the deferral.

For example, if your taxes went up $12,000 because of the increase in the tax rates, you can pay $4,000 on April 15, 1994, and again on April 15, 1995, and April 15, 1996. This small break is to make up for the fact that the taxes are retroactive to January 1, 1993, but at least it's a break from an increasingly hostile and demanding federal government.

THE BOTTOM LINE . . .

The Clinton tax increases are probably not the last we will see during the coming year. They are just the warning shot over the bow. Keep your eyes peeled for additional new and increased taxes at both the state and federal levels as others join in this attack on your wealth.

What Are You Going to Do When Interest Rates Rise?

Get Out of Their Way, I Hope. Doing Nothing Can Be Frightening

Have you ever tried to boil a frog? (I sense a vast and curious silence out there.) Let me tell you how. If you put it in hot water, any sensible frog will jump right out, just as you or I would. No, the way to boil a frog is to put it in tepid water, and heat the water up slowly until the frog boils to death. This works quite well.

RISING INTEREST RATES LIKE RISING WATER TEMPERATURES CAN "BOIL YOUR FROG"

Rising interest rates can be as sneaky as our recipe for boiling a live frog. At the first increase (and resulting loss in market or resale value of your principal), you start thinking that you are indeed a wise long-term investor and you are receiving a nice return and you intend to hold this fund to maturity and every-thing is as you wished . . . almost.

As interest rates continue to rise and you lose more princi-pal, you say to yourself, "Interest rates fluctuate all the time. I'll stick in until I break even. Heck, this has happened before. I can stand this any time. I am an experienced and savvy investor and I'm not going to panic at the bottom of this move. I'm okay . . . almost."

As interest rates continue to rise, you realize that the inter-est rates markets are "boiling your frog." You will soon experi-ence enough losses to your principal to wipe out one, two, or maybe three years' returns. You also realize that you will have to pay taxes on your dividend income (remember I warned you about income?) and that you can't take your losses un-less you sell at a loss, which you are currently unwilling to do. You are not O.K.—not even almost!

Then you start hearing that others are beginning to bail out of the bond funds, especially the muni-bond funds whose lower returns went underwater first. People tried to bail out anyway, and for days the muni-bond markets didn't trade because there were no bids. (This really happened in 1987 when interest rates rose just a little!)

The bottom line? Rising rates are not a pretty thing for fixed-income investors: The lower the credit risk, the greater the market risk; the longer the interest rate guarantee, the greater the market risk. It ain't pretty.

LIMBO ECONOMICS, OR HOW LOW CAN INTEREST RATES GO?

Many interest rates are at or near 30-year lows. All the easy profits already have been made in bond funds. Over the past 10 years, the average taxable bond fund has grown at an 11 percent annual rate. Over the past six decades, bonds have grown at an annual rate of just 5 percent.

We are not likely to see the average bond fund grow at an annual rate of 11 percent in the foreseeable future. Interest rates have gone through a full cycle. We saw double-digit yields in the late 1970s and early 1980s. Since that time, rates have dropped from a high of 14 percent on three-month T-bills to about 2.5 percent today. Just a few years ago, you could lock into a 10 percent long-term Treasury bond. Today, you are lucky to get 6 percent.

The next major move in interest rates likely will be higher. No one knows for sure when rates will move up. There are no simple answers. One thing I do know: Rising interest rates will hurt the returns on both stock and bond funds.

What Is the Big Deal About Rising Rates?

The fact is that both stock and bond markets are directly impacted by rising interest rates. When interest rates rise, the bond market is absolutely hit with market value or price declines. If interest rates rise, bond values fall.

In a period of rising interest rates, the stock market becomes riskier, and stocks that are sensitive to interest rates, such as utility stocks and income-oriented stocks with steady dividend streams, decline.

Growth stock funds will eventually decline because of the rising interest rates (as evidenced by the success of the Donoghue Signal, which invests in growth stock funds when interest rates are falling and in cash when rates rise). Although this relationship is not absolute, it is highly predictable over the longer term. Rising interest rates add significant risk of loss to the stock funds and real losses in bond funds.

Of course, the markets fluctuate. That's the name of the game. A blip up in short-or long-term rates over the next 6 months isn't anything to worry about. Such changes are considered "noise." You can hold your ground, keep your current asset allocation mixes and invest in the best performing funds.

Is Inflation Just Around the Corner?

One of my greatest fears is that inflation will rear its ugly head. Under threat of inflation, the Federal Reserve most likely will increase rates. The Fed is said to have considered raising rates in February 1994, which would have marked a reversal of its monetary policy for the first time in four years. If the economy grows faster than most expect and inflation rises, I'll bet you dollars to donuts the Fed raises rates.

What If Interest Rates Stay Low?

This would be excellent for small company stocks that thrive under low interest rates. For fixed-income investments, it will mean a serious struggle to keep your assets above water, taxes, and inflation. The bottom line is that low rates are low rates, and bond funds just don't produce significant returns when rates are low. The after-tax and inflation returns are just not worth the risk you are facing. Just when it looks like you are getting a reasonable return, your "frog is boiled."

WHAT CAN YOU DO TO PREPARE YOURSELF FOR RISING INTEREST RATES?

1. Losses are wonderful tax shelters. Use the ones you have. Don't buy new losses. Take your losses and use them as tax shelters, perhaps getting money back in your next paycheck if you choose to adjust your withholding to reflect your deductible tax losses.

2. Stay short and safe. Stick with short-term investments and avoid the risks. Money funds are your safest investment. Remember: No one has ever lost money in a money fund investment.

Money funds' yields will rise with interest rates, and their principals will stay intact. Short-term bonds funds can be suitable money fund substitutes if interest rates rise slowly. Short-term bond funds restrict themselves to bonds with maturities of less than five years and often have an average maturity of one or two years. This short maturity protects you against rising interest rates while offering slightly higher returns than money market funds.

3. Invest in junk bond funds. For the savvy investor, junk bond funds will likely be very safe and profitable investments a good while into the interest rate rise.

Despite the improved average credit quality of junk bonds since their bad experience in 1989-1990, junk bond asset values should be surprisingly insensitive to rising interest rates. This insensitivity is due to the expectation that rising interest rates will be the first signal of a recovery and will result in an improvement in the conditions that caused many "fallen angel" companies (strong companies in temporary bad times) to see their creditworthiness improve and the values of their junk bonds rise.

4. Invest where interest rates are falling. One of the strong reasons to invest in international stock funds is that at least part of most of the diversified international stock funds is invested in Europe. European interest rates are high and falling, ideal times for stock market investing. So, if rising domestic rates worry you, don't worry. Invest in international stock funds and benefit from falling European interest rates.

5. Follow the Donoghue Signal into cash. One of our best long-running investment strategies is the Donoghue Signal Strategy, which on December 6, 1993, switched back into a 100 percent cash position in the face of rising interest rates. That means this system—which only applies to domestic U.S. growth stocks or money funds—is in its "hibernation" phase, waiting for a rising rate "winter" to pass. Don't feel sorry for these investors; their money is in the ultimate safe investment—money funds—and they have grown an average of 74 percent since the last stock fund BUY signal in 1989. This rate is 20 percent higher than the S&P 500 adjusted for reinvested dividends. They deserve a peaceful rest before jumping totally back into the stock market.

6. Build a solid asset allocation portfolio. As you have learned, the Donoghue SuperStar Portfolio is currently allocated among international stock funds, emerging markets funds, a gold fund, an asset allocation fund, and a global real estate fund. Only the domestic holdings are vulnerable to rising interest rates, and then only a small portion of the portfolio is exposed to rate loss.

Although I should warn you that if we have a major correction domestically, many types of funds, including international funds, could "correct" as well. Keep some cash aside to take advantage of those opportunities. The odds are that we will find other sectors of the economy among the top performers and will simply replace the domestic stock "weak sibling" (are we still politically correct?) position with a stronger alternative. The other possibility is that lackluster performance will drop some of the weaker funds from our approved list.

7. Consider international bond funds. If domestic interest rates rise, you will see some new SuperStar funds rising to the top of the list. You will see international funds that are performing well in a high domestic interest rate environment.

When interest rates are rising in the United States, they may be falling in other countries. Therefore, international bond funds may be the best place to invest. If an international bond fund comes to the top of the SuperStar list because rates are declining abroad, we will invest. My favorite and best performing international bond funds are Bull & Bear Global Income (1-800-847-4200) and Fidelity Global Bond (1-800-544-8888).

8. Watch for SuperStar value stock funds. In a rising interest rate environment, funds that buy on value and own low price/earnings stocks may perform well. Some fund managers may be picking the right stocks in the right industry in businesses that will do well regardless of where interest rates are headed. By contrast, aggressive stock funds, which do well in a falling interest rate market, get hit hard when interest rates rise and the stock market tumbles. Be especially leery of high beta funds, that is, those with betas of 1.10 or higher.

9.   Some bond funds may hedge against rising rates or have unique flexibility or strategies.   This country's market does not move in tandem with the stock markets of other countries, so some international stock and bond funds may perform well. Some bond funds may hedge against part of the risk of rising rates or invest overseas where interest rates are high and falling. It takes a flexible bond fund to make the moves necessary to avoid vulnerability to rising interest rates. My favorites are Blanchard Flexible Income Fund (1-800-922-7771) and Janus Flexible Income Fund (1-800-525-8983). There also are many funds, such as the Gateway Index Plus Fund (1-800-345-6339), a unique no-load option income fund, that employ hedging techniques to protect investors in bear markets for stocks.

10.   Invest in funds that automatically capture rising interest rates.   Traditional bond funds invest in traditional bonds—bonds that pay a fixed rate of return for a fixed period of time. A fairly new breed of bond funds invest in a new breed of bonds—adjustable-rate bonds. Adjustable-rate bonds are like adjustable-rate mortgages. Periodically, the interest rate of adjustable-rate bonds resets to reflect current interest rates. When rates decline, the interest rate of the bond declines. Conversely, when rates increase, the rate of the bond increases. To adjustable-rate bond fund investors, this means that their returns will adjust upward.

However, there can be a significant lag in this adjustment because some adjustable-rate bonds may adjust quarterly, semi-annually, or annually. In the meantime, your principal values will decline, albeit less than traditional bonds. Of course, these funds only yield 100 to 200 basis points over money funds, so the advantage can be eliminated temporarily.

WHAT TO DO IF INTEREST RATES STAY LOW

If interest rates stay low or head lower, we will stay invested in the top-performing stock funds. If you are a market timer, the Donoghue Signal will again give you the green light to invest.

Asset allocators will add to their stock funds rather than safe harbors.

SuperStar Investors Know What to Do if Rates Go Up

The best performing funds, whether they are stock or bond funds, are the place to invest. Invest in different kinds of funds during different economic cycles. If and when rates move up, make the adjustments. Sitting still isn't the thing to do. You have to be an active manager of your investments. That's what it means to be a SuperStar investor. Stick with the SuperStars Portfolio and prosper.

CHAPTER 15

How Should You Invest After You Retire?

So You Don't Run Out of More Money Before You Run Out of Life

The two most dangerous pieces of post-retirement investment advice ever spoken—at least in terms of today's financial realities—are:

1. "Invest in bonds and CDs. You will need the income."

2. "You should 'play it safe' with your retirement money. After all you can't earn this money again."

The cumulative impact of these two "tried and true" pieces of traditional advice is that many of today's retirees will likely live retirement life significantly less comfortably than their parents.

INVEST IN BONDS AND CDS—YOU WILL NEED THE INCOME

I am convinced that every broker sits down for his first day on the job and with his supervisor does two things:

▶ First, he is handed a three-page sales manual:

—Page one says, "Sell what you understand."

—He quickly turns to page two.

—Page two says, "Sell Yield."

—He turns to page three, which reads, "Read Page Two Again."

—(Please note there is nothing said about discussing the risks involved in fixed-income investing.)

▶ Second, he is given "the brokers briefing," which goes something like this:

"At exactly 3:32 P.M. on the day a person becomes age 65, he or she becomes senile and must march down to their broker and immediately sell all their investments (commission opportunity # 1) and buy government bond funds (commission opportunity # 2) and in the process pay their broker three to five percent of their life's savings in commissions.

When interest rates rise and they lose money (as they inevitably will in today's environment), they must return in panic and trade those investments for something else safe (commission opportunity # 3), and so it goes."

Think about this a bit. What research did the broker do to justify his 5 percent commission? How many governments did he research for you? (I only know one—the federal government!) Do you really want to know what his research revealed? (I don't.)

The bottom line is that there is no more terrifying experience than cashing in your CDs, buying a government bond fund at the bottom of an interest rate cycle, and watching the principal value decline. You don't need that experience. If you did, you could have bought a no-load government bond fund just as easily.

In recent years, declining interest rates rewarded naive bond fund investors with rising market values rather than losses. It was a lovely time. Sorry, those times are over and the next experience facing us is rising interest rates.

"YOU SHOULD PLAY IT SAFE WITH YOUR RETIREMENT MONEY. AFTER ALL, YOU CAN'T EARN THAT MONEY AGAIN," YOUR FRIENDS TELL YOU

The reality is that most of us don't have enough time left or enough money to afford to "play it safe." You've got to take charge of your investment life *now* and think long term if you want to live comfortably for the long life ahead of you.

Longevity is a triumph of modern medicine, but it has heavy costs for the unprepared. You should make sure your savings are growing, not just throwing off an income, if you want to settle into a long and comfortable retirement.

The Wealthy Can Afford to Play It Safe

Playing it safe may still be good advice if you have more than enough money to live on. But few have that luxury. Retirement is when you have the time to manage your investments, something you may have neglected during your working years. It is a time of leisure to read a few good investment books (like this one), study the not-so-difficult skills of investing, and get on with your life.

The Myth of Playing It Safe Was Created to Distract You

Safe is a very powerful word. Behind the cloak of the "safety" of FDIC and FSLIC was hidden the greatest financial scandal and most expensive bailout of all time. Never has money been squandered so foolishly at a worse time in our history while we naively trusted the savings and loan institutions to manage our savings.

Americans are only beginning to appreciate the financial devastation of that S&L bailout: the lack of federal funds to provide jobs to get us through this recession, the cost of rising state income taxes (the not-so-hidden cost of the S&L bailout), the devastation brought on our real estate investments and homes, and the destruction of honest professionals' banking careers. The cloak of "safety" has covered a dramatic shift of financial risks from banks, S&Ls, and insurance companies to individuals.

THE INSTITUTIONS ONCE TOOK THE RISK, NOW THE RISK IS YOURS

First, it was the banks. Remember the late 1970s? The banks and S&Ls were complaining about the burden of having to pay double-digit interest rates on savings accounts while holding on to low single-digit mortgages? They faced the fact that if they had to sell off their losing mortgages in a double-digit market-place, they would have to realize accounting losses that would have pulled many a thrift institution under water.

Rates are low again, and now what has happened to those risky mortgages? Banks and thrifts sold off mortgages to un-suspecting savers as quickly as they could make them. Holding the mortgages was too risky for the banks' safety and sound-ness. Meanwhile, little old ladies were being sold AAA-rated, government-guaranteed collateralized mortgage obligations, which will almost certainly lose substantial market value in the coming years, or even months, when interest rates begin to rise.

Think again about money market deposit accounts with fluctuating rates that replaced the old dependence on CDs with real rate guarantees, about the Adjustable Rate Mort-gages (ARMs) with rates that fell with the marketplace. They were good for many, but today only a fool chooses an ARM when he or she can get a fixed-rate mortgage at historically low interest rates.

Insurance companies used to take the risks of investing your money for you. Traditional insurance companies, because of the economic downturn and some poor investments, are hard pressed to meet all of their obligations. Several major insurers have failed already, and those that did survive rely on the cash flow from fixed annuities to keep up with their obligations to policyholders. Now they want to sell variable insurance, not a bad deal in itself, but the risk of making investments is being passed on to you the investor because the insurance companies are unwilling to assume the risks themselves.

The Banks Forgot to Tell You About Interest Rate Benefits

Reliance on so-called safe investments led many investors to count on insured CDs, whose returns plummeted from double digits to less than 3 percent a year. Millions of well-meaning savers trusted the banks to provide them with needed income only to see their interest income shrink 70 percent or more.

Only belatedly are the banks telling trusting savers they could have invested in long-term bond funds and profited, as the decline in interest rates increased the value of their bonds. Now it's too late to invest safely in all but the shortest-term bonds. The sad legacy of this whole craving for safety is that investors have played it safe because their bank advisors, unwilling to give more assertive and intelligent investment guidance, took the easy way out.

WHEN A "GUARANTEED" INVESTMENT ISN'T GUARANTEED

The bottom line? Investors in defined contribution plans (401(k)s, profit sharing, SEPs) have 35 percent of their money in apparently high-yielding, fixed-income accounts called guaranteed investment contracts (GICs) from life insurance companies.

Few investors, especially those with Executive Life of California GICs, realized that despite the high income, they might not get their principal back intact or on time. Even professionals don't get the point and still rely on overly optimistic ratings of life insurance companies that may not outlive their policyholders. That employers selected these risky policies on behalf of their employees is a sad commentary on their fiduciary responsibility to their employees.

Ironically, guaranteed investment contracts are one of the few insurance policies that are specifically *not* guaranteed by state guaranty funds. The other thing you need to know is that state guaranty funds make few reliable guarantees, are not guaranteed by the state, and have no funds of their own. They simply assess the remaining insurance companies to bail out the policyholders of failed insurance companies, a process that can take years.

I can only hope for retirees who rely on their retirement savings in GICs, that their employers have chosen safe and sound insurance companies. If you are not sure, call Weiss Research (1-800-289-9222 for a $15 rating) to get the inside and accurate story on your insurer.

Tax-Free Is Not Risk-Free

Unfortunately, many people think tax-free means risk-free. Tax-free municipal bond investments today have a great deal more risk than they did before we, as a nation, squandered hundreds of billions of dollars bailing out the depositors of the nation's abominably managed savings and loan institutions. As a consequence, there's little federal money to assist cash-strapped state and local governments.

Rising interest rates could result in a blood bath as investors redeem shares of shrinking-value munibond funds and as portfolio managers try to sell off municipal securities in a thinly traded market. Wise investors remember that the tax-free securities markets operate without most of the protections from full disclosure rules and SEC oversight. They also understand that buying tax-free investments is often a lot easier than selling them.

As I described in an earlier chapter, there is currently a very special risk associated with "insured" municipal bonds and bond funds. These "insured" bonds are uniformly rated AAA as are their insurers, the insurance companies that back the bonds.

A recent Weiss Research study of default rates among insured municipal bonds (Yes, they do default; that's why they need the insurance!) revealed that the insurers are overrated, which means the bonds are overvalued. If the marketplace has not yet accepted this study—and the insurers will no doubt debate it—it would be wise to get out before the overvaluation is recognized. Discretion is the better part of valor. You heard it here!

WHAT ELSE DOESN'T WORK THAT YOU THINK DOES

What investments do you commonly hear recommended for retired investors—preferred stock, utility stocks, government bond funds? Most of what you think will work, won't.

Utility Stocks. Utility stocks are popular investments for retirees. The dependability of quarterly dividend checks and the opportunity for capital appreciation are enticing characteristics.

What many investors don't realize is that utility stocks behave a lot like bonds. The same interest rate risks we discussed for long-term bonds also apply to utility stocks since they are priced in much the same manner. So, when rates rise, utility stocks go down in value just like bonds. When rates decline, they go up in value.

With interest rates near 25-year lows, how likely is it that interest rates will go lower? Not very. How likely is it that they will go higher? Very good. That means that utility stock buyers have a greater probability of losing money than making money from interest rate movements.

I certainly agree that utility stocks are better choices than long-term bonds. Utility companies have the opportunity to raise rates to their customers and ultimately pass on higher dividends to their shareholders. Over time, this increasing dividend should compensate against rising interest rates, but in the short term, utility stocks will be beaten down just like bonds.

Government Bond Funds. Again, investors confuse the risk of default with the risk of rising interest rates. Sure, government bonds are guaranteed, but they still have exposure to interest rate risk. In fact, government bonds have the highest amount of interest rate risk of all types of bonds.

A bond matures or repays its principal at a specific time in the future. With government bonds, the maturity could be as long as 30 years or as short as one year or less. Bonds with under five-year maturities are called *notes* and those with under one-year maturities are called *bills.*

Does the table make sense to you? It might not, intuitively, since you probably equate credit risk (the risk of repayment) with safety, but the rationale is sound. The most dramatic and imminent risk for investors is not repayment but resale risk (the risk of having to sell your investment for less than it cost you).

However, the two most risky types of fixed-income investments are not on the list—zero-coupon bonds and bond funds and collateralized mortgage obligations (CMOs).

▶ **The zeros have got to go.** If you bought zero coupon bonds or bond funds a few years ago when interest rates were higher, ask your broker or fund family what your investment is worth. Chances are it is worth a lot. Then ask what it was worth in October 1993, and I suspect you will be told that is worth much less today because interest rates bottomed out in that month. Now you know how much you lost by holding on this long. Sell your zero-coupon bonds; rising rates will only reduce your profits.

▶ **The CMOs are the sneaky ones.** They are manmade artificial investments that are constructed from the principal

TABLE 15.1
Least to Most Interest-Rate-Sensitive Bond Funds

1. Junk Bond Funds
2. Corporate Bond Funds
3. Ginnie Mae Funds
4. Municipal Bond Funds
5. Government Bond Funds

and interest payments of mortgages. When a bank or thrift institution lends money in the form of a mortgage, it is often unwise for that institution to hold on to the mortgage because if interest rates were to rise and the institution were forced to sell its mortgages at a loss, it could impair the capital of the institution. So, the federal banking regulators frown on an institution that holds on to too many risky mortgages.

The institution then sells off the mortgage to a securities firm, which breaks up the principal and interest payments into a series of tranches (French for "slices") and resells the safest tranches, often referred to as the *A* tranches, back to the institution, the *B* tranches to pension plans and other institutional investors, and the riskiest investments, the so-called *Z* tranches, to the public through stockbrokers.

The unsuspecting public buys these Z tranches because they offer higher returns than CDs, and they are all rated AAA. A triple-A rating is given because in many cases the government guarantees the eventual repayment of principal and interest. These Z tranches are sold with estimated maturities. For example, you might buy one with a seven-year estimated maturity—if nothing happens.

If something happens, such as interest rates rising, the borrowers don't refinance their mortgages, because they have locked in such a low rate and because the eventual repayment might be 20 to 25 years later. Since the low rate is locked in for so long, making the CMO unattractive to investors, rising interest rates could wipe out a large part the current resale or market value of the investment. After all, a 20- to 25-year mortgage is a lot riskier than a five-year mortgage.

So, if your broker sold you something that was collateralized by mortgages a few years ago, ask him what he will pay for it now. You may want to consider selling, even at a loss, because it may be worth less later. Don't be surprised if your broker doesn't offer you a good price; he doesn't want to sit on that dog of an investment either.

The riskiest CMOs turned out to be those collateralized by interest payments only. The government guarantee extended only to contractual payments. If the mortgagees repay their mortgages early in order to refinance them, the future interest payments that collateralized your CMO disappear. Since the government only guaranteed that you would receive all of the interest from the mortgage, the refinancing redefined what you were entitled to receive. So, you only receive the refinanced amount, not the original amount. The government guarantee just didn't work out right, did it? Sorry, Charlie!

JUNK BONDS ARE MORE COMPLEX

Junk, muni, and corporate bonds, however, are affected by a number of factors, including interest rates. Junk bonds, however, could actually go up in value even though interest rates rise. For example, a junk bond could receive a credit rating upgrade from BB to BBB, which would make it more valuable. One positive (the upgrade) could more than offset the one negative (rising rates). The bonds with the least credit risk (governments) are the most risky because they have the most interest rate risk (interest rate sensitivity).

BOND FUNDS IN GENERAL

Bond fund managers must replace bonds that mature with new bonds, which means that the bond fund has an endless life without a specific maturity date. Unlike individual bonds, bond funds (except occasionally for zero-coupon bond funds) do not have a maturity date, so you never have the assurance that you will get back your principal.

In a rising interest rate environment, bond buyers are better served by buying individual short-term bonds instead of a bond fund. By buying individual bonds, you are assured of getting your full principal back upon maturity of the bond(s). Bond funds give you no such assurance of return of principal intact. This only applies, of course, to government bonds, which don't have default risk.

The research you would have to do on individual corporate (both investment grade and junk) and municipal bonds would be quite challenging for individual investors. Therefore, the safest way to invest in corporate or junk bonds is to buy funds. The safest way to invest in government bonds is to buy the actual bonds.

Bottom line advice? Buy short-term Treasury bills and notes directly in individual issues. If you decide to buy junk, corporate, or municipal bonds, stick with bond funds.

A Donoghue tip for bond fund buyers: When evaluating bond funds on the basis of interest rate risk, the best measure of interest rate sensitivity is *duration*. Duration refers to how long it will take you to get your principal back from the interest payments. The lower the duration, the lower the volatility.

The often cited "average maturity" statistic is a misleading indicator of interest rate risk. Very simply put, if a bond fund has a duration of six years, a 1 percent rise in interest rates would cost you 6 percent in loss of value and could easily wipe out a whole year's returns in an intermediate-term munibond fund.

Let me show you three strategies that you can use.

STRATEGY #1: IF YOU HAVE SOME BUILT-IN BOND CAPITAL GAINS, TAKE THEM NOW

Ask your broker about the market value of your zero-coupon, government, or other bonds or bond funds, and you will likely discover they are worth significantly more than you paid for them. Why? Interest rates have fallen and resale values have risen.

Guess what? You have a long-term capital gain, and if you sell, you will pay no more than 28 percent capital gains tax and will protect that gain from a loss.

Don't get flustered about your tax liability here. If you bought a bond at 100 and its value has risen say 40 percent to 140, you only pay 28 percent taxes on the 40. You pay taxes of 11.2, or only 8 percent of your investment. If you lose 8 percent to the market, you still have the tax losses to worry about.

Easing into earning capital gains is safer than forcing high income. Most attractive income investments are long term or "higher risk than you would wish" investments when you consider the impact on your principal of losses resulting from the inevitable rise in interest rates.

It's Time to Rethink Risks

It's time we rethought what risk is all about. Astute investors know that the way to become a successful investor is not to avoid risk but to learn how to manage it. Learn how to manage risk, and you can build and enjoy a secure retirement.

How Do You Measure the Risk You Want to Manage? Safety is described by a risk/reward ratio. Unfortunately, you have to take a lot more risk to earn high rewards today. For example, money funds are very safe, but the reward for investing today is minuscule. Taking a little risk and getting a whole lot more reward is a better choice.

As we rethink risk/reward ratios, we need to begin to think about what kind of rewards might justify taking some risks. For example, are you willing to have an investment that could fluctuate in value plus or minus 5 percent to earn an average return of 15 percent annually over the next two years? Sounds like a good deal to me. While you're thinking about it, are you willing to take the time to recognize that last year's advice is no longer on target?

Threats to Your Financial Security in Retirement

Interest Rate Risk. Interest rate risk is the risk of loss to bond fund principal caused by rising interest rates. For example, if you purchased an 8 percent, ten-year U.S. Treasury note at par ($10,000) and market interest rates on new or resold ten-year U.S. Treasury notes rise only 1 percent to 0 percent, the bond will fall $617 (or 6.17 percent) in value to $9,383 resale value (not including brokerage costs).

Rising interest rates in February 1994 alone cost investors in 30-year Treasury bonds a full 7 percent decline in market value. Thus, the threat of losses in bond funds is very real and very recent.

Falling interest rates, not a very real short-term expectation, would, of course, have a positive effect on bond values. Don't count on falling rates making you much money in the near term, folks. Study Table 15.2 for a few minutes.

TABLE 15.2
Interest Rate Sensitivity of Bonds

Treasury Securities	Increase/Decrease in Market Value Due to One Percentage Point Change in Market Yield	
	Up 1.0%	*Down 1.0%*
3-Month Treasury Bill	−0.24	+0.24
1-Year Treasury Bill	−0.93	+0.94
5-Year Treasury Note	−3.80	+4.01
10-Year Treasury Note	−6.17	+6.72
30-Year Treasury Bond	−9.40	+11.23
30-Year Zero Coupon Bond	−19.89	+26.65

Think of bonds as a seesaw with interest rates on one end and bond values on the other. If interest rates rise, bond values decline; if interest rates fall, bond values rise. Retirees who insist in investing in bonds were spoiled by the high returns of the 1980s and the subsequent decline in interest rates that produced a corresponding increase in values. That experience is over, and the next experience is a lot less attractive. Sell your bonds and protect your principal.

Staying Too Short. Investors were spoiled by the high interest rates of the 1980s. High rates conditioned retirees to invest all their money short term because rates kept rising, year after year. Investing all your assets under one strategy is always dangerous, no matter what asset class. I wouldn't advise anyone to put everything into long-term bonds, nor would I advise them to put everything into short-term CDs; the same goes for stocks, real estate, or anything else.

Whenever you put all your eggs in one basket, you create extra risks for yourself that you may not have realized. The only time a short-term strategy is beneficial is when interest rates are rising, because you can quickly reinvest your money at higher rates upon maturity.

Just the opposite has happened recently. Interest rates have declined to 25-year lows, so short-term investors have had to reinvest their money at lower rates upon maturity.

For those living on their interest earnings, this short-term CD and T-bill strategy sliced their income by as much as 70 percent. A strategy of buying short-term CDs and T-bills is an aggressive and risky strategy.

Purchasing Power Risk. Retirees face the very real danger of slowly seeing the purchasing power of their savings erode over time. This is also known as inflation risk. Everyone knows that goods and services will cost more in the future due to inflation. Unless you have a growing pool of money to compensate for rising prices, you are certain to see your purchasing power decline as you grow older.

What Is the Best Kind of Income?

When you retire at age 65, you are likely to live longer. At age 65 you have over one-third of your life still ahead of you. You are still a long-term investor, so you must prepare for the long term. This means investing, rather than saving, and living on a limited fixed income.

STRATEGY #2: HOW I MANAGED MY MOTHER'S MONEY

The rule of thumb that many advisors love to quote is, "The percentage of your portfolio that should be exposed to the stock market should be 100 minus your age." For example, if you are 30, you should have 70 percent of your portfolio in the stock market. If you are 70, only 30 percent.

Sounds like good advice, right? After all, the stock market does include some significant short-term risks for naive investors. There were the stock market crashes, such as the one in 1987, and long-term bear markets, such as those in the mid-1970s.

However, this advice assumes that you know nothing about investing and that you are a buy-and-hold investor, considerations that are probably *not* true for *you*, my reader, because you have that extra edge—relevant and available statistical information, an understanding of the financial markets, and the strategies I am teaching you in this book.

Now what about Mom? Well, Mom (or Pop, as it may be) needs cash flow now and a growing portfolio that assures that, when she or he lives longer than ever expected, the assets necessary to generate the cash flow needed later will be there. Since the bulk of retirees can reasonably expect to be alive at least 5 years from now and probably 20 years from now, it is reasonable to invest as if you did not need a large part of your money for 5 years or more.

With that kind of time frame, you can risk some short-term market fluctuation. When you agree to accept that small risk, you can pick investment choices that have significantly greater investment potential.

Which Portfolio should you use to manage Mom's or Pop's or your post-retirement savings? Portfolio C, *Mom's CD-Beater Cash Flow Portfolio*, is actually Portfolio A (your tax-sheltered portfolio) or Portfolio B (your taxable portfolio) with a cash flow provision added. The strategy is simple. Invest for growth, reinvest all your dividends and capital gains distributions, and set up a systematic redemption program.

Why should you reinvest all your dividends and capital gains distributions (on which you had to pay taxes) and then set up a systematic redemption program to get a check-a-month? For the following good reasons:

▶   To create order from chaos, you need the check-a-month to be reliable and in a fixed amount (which you can change at any time, of course) because, unlike your bills, dividends and capital gains distributions do not come every month.

▶ If you establish a *Mom's CD-Beater Cash Flow Portfolio* and pick investments that are likely to increase in value over time, a large portion of the growth of your portfolio will be unrealized (neither you nor the fund sold shares that have increased in value, so you did not *realize* your profits and they are not yet taxable) capital gains on which the taxes are deferred until you sell or realize your profits.

If you follow this strategy, you will, over time, be able to watch your portfolio grow most of the time and still withdraw, for example, 8 percent or higher returns from a portfolio that may only be generating an average of 5 percent in taxable profits (which can change dramatically from year to year, of course).

Three Keys to a Secure Retirement

Here are a few tips I've developed to help you get started to become a post-retirement SuperStar investor:

1. **Maximize your retirement savings power.** Invest your tax-qualified (tax-sheltered) retirement savings assertively. Use your taxable money first, and then withdraw from your tax-sheltered money, making sure that after age 70½ you do withdraw the minimum required by the IRS. Allow the tax shelter to help you build up your retirement kitty, compounding on a tax-deferred basis.

2. **Invest your taxable savings well.** Invest your taxable money assertively. Reinvest all dividends and interest in your stock or bond funds. If you need a check-a-month plan, you can always arrange that with your fund family.

3. **Invest large lump sums or catch-up retirement savings in variable life insurance policies.** Tax shelter your remaining unsheltered investment capital in a variable life insurance policy. (You don't want a variable annuity because you pay taxes on 100 percent of your withdrawals until you have withdrawn all your profits.)

    Fund your variable life insurance in at least four substantially similar payments over four to seven years (ask your insurance company how long it will take), and you will be able to borrow the cash value plus your profits tax-free during your lifetime and still leave the balance to your heirs as an income tax-free death benefit. (See Chapter 16 for more on this subject.)

If you do not have to waste your hard-earned dollars on taxes, you only need about half the principal to produce the same amount of spendable cash. That makes retirement savings goals much more attainable. Use lots of stock funds, avoid the bond fund trap baited by rising interest rates, and avoid investing in money funds because rates are so low.

Remember, annual IRA withdrawals over $150,000 cost a penalty tax of 15 percent in addition to state and local income taxes. I caution my clients in that category to keep careful records of their IRA money. That way, they will not overfund the account.

Invest for Growth, Withdraw Cash Flow

If you put all your money in CDs, utility stocks, Treasury or municipal bonds, you will have a difficult time beating inflation. You'll lose purchasing power mighty fast. It will cost you more to live and you will still have to pay the tax man. Go for more investment growth and invest in top-performing domestic and international stock funds. You have to manage risk; don't let it manage you. Don't let your best friend's lack of investment expertise or cautious nature distract you from doing what you understand best.

STRATEGY #3: SOMETIMES JUNK IS BETTER THAN QUALITY

Over the past decade, junk bond funds in the Donoghue's Mutual Fund SuperStars Universe have delivered double-digit returns in seven years. The bad years were in 1987, when the stock market crashed (and the funds averaged only 2.21 percent), and, in 1989 and 1990, when junk bond funds produced returns of −5.9 percent and 0.8 percent, respectively. The stock market correction in 1990 and the junk bond market correction in 1989 took their toll.

The rest of the decade has been another story and reflects the more typical junk bond fund experience. Consider Table 15.3.

What will happen to junk bond funds as interest rates rise? Ironically, at least for the initial stages of the rise in interest rates, the total returns should remain attractive. These are bonds but are likely to be less interest rate sensitive. However, if the price of money (interest rates) is rising, it will likely

TABLE 15.3
Junk Bond Fund Total Returns, 1984–1993
(average for 81 funds)

Year	Total Return
1984	8.39%
1985	21.81
1986	13.01
1987	1.57
1988	13.02
1989	−0.24
1990	−10.20
1991	37.31
1992	17.48
1993	18.92

Source: Morningstar, Inc. Mutual Funds on Disc

be because the economy and the credit quality of the bonds are improving and that will result in enough appreciation in the bonds to offset any market depreciation due to rising interest rates.

Another Perspective on Junk Bond Funds

Whenever my research staff works on optimizing a portfolio, finding the best asset allocation to give you the best risk-adjusted rate of return, junk bonds always pop up. A junk bond fund is a dominating asset, which means that its return and risk mix well with other kinds of stock funds and money market funds.

To make a long story short, you can get a better total return with less price volatility by substituting a junk bond fund for a government bond fund in a portfolio that also includes domestic stock funds, international stock funds, and money funds. Most well-informed advisors I've talked to agree that junk bond funds will provide significantly higher, safer returns in the coming years than long-term U.S. government bonds, which will lose value in the face of rising interest rates. In fact, most expect high-quality junk bond funds to significantly outperform government bond funds.

Some of my picks for the best junk bond funds are:

Fidelity Capital and Income	(1-800-544-8888)
T. Rowe Price High Yield	(1-800-638-5660)

Vanguard Fixed Income High Yield   (1-800-662-7447)

INVESCO High Yield   (1-800-525-8085).

TURN YOUR FULLY PAID-FOR HOME INTO RETIREMENT CASH

Much of what I've been writing about is for those of you who have accumulated a nice retirement nest egg. Some of you, however, may be cash poor and house rich, with most of your net worth tied up in the market value of your home.

I get many letters from my readers asking what they can do to release some of their home equity to pay the bills. If your first reaction is the obvious, a home equity loan, remember most senior citizens don't have the income to qualify for a home equity loan, which requires repayment during their lives. What they need is a loan that allows them to borrow and never make a loan payment as long as they live in their homes—which could be the rest of their lives.

Picture this: An elderly widow, whose only income is a small $300 monthly Social Security check, lives in a beautiful $450,000 home in California that she owns absolutely free and clear. She and her deceased husband raised their children in the house, and her deepest desire is to spend the rest of her life in her own home.

This is a true and not uncommon story. A once elegant California woman lived in poverty despite her comfortable net worth. With only $300 a month cash to live on, she was forced to live exclusively in her kitchen, with an open oven to keep herself warm to minimize her heating bills. The rest of her spacious home was sealed off because she could not afford to heat it. After paying even that minimal heating bill, all she could afford to eat was hot dogs, noodles, and beans and rice. She was house rich and cash poor, and, unfortunately, her children could not afford to pay both their bills and hers.

A Lifetime Reverse Mortgage to the Rescue

I recently talked to Bill Texido of Providential Home Income Plan (1-800-441-4428), and he explained to me how a *lifetime reverse mortgage* was the ideal solution to this woman's problem.

Here is what a lifetime reverse mortgage did for her. Due to the high equity value in her home, she was eligible to receive as much as $3,000 a month for the rest of her life and still live in her home until the day she died or entered a nursing home. Since she didn't need $3,000 a month, she chose to take only $1,500 a month, which she felt would transform her life. She suddenly went from poverty to dignity while still remaining in the home she loved.

Lifetime reverse mortgages, as the name applies, are the opposite of traditional mortgages you take out when you buy a home. Instead of making payments each month, you get paid each month for the lifetimes of you and your spouse. You will receive your monthly payments until you die or enter a nursing home for at least one year. At that time, your house is sold by you or your estate and, from the sale of the proceeds, the loan is paid back. Any profits above the outstanding loan balance go to you or your heirs.

Just like a regular mortgage, your house is appraised, and you pay some mortgage origination fees. Then you close on the reverse mortgage. This time, however, you get money instead of paying out money. Unfortunately, this private loan program is only available in a few states, and the interest rate is relatively high (around 10 percent) because of the real estate recession, which depressed real estate values.

YOUR GOVERNMENT IS HERE TO HELP YOU—A LITTLE

The government offers a limited lifetime reverse mortgage. You can take out a Federal Housing Authority (FHA) reverse mortgage, although the FHA loan limits are lower than conventional financing. Currently, the FHA maximum home value eligible for reverse mortgages is $124,000. For mortgage amounts higher than the FHA limits, you will need to use conventional financing. Just like the traditional mortgage market, not all reverse mortgages are the same. So shop around.

The Risks to Watch For

A word to the wise. There are two things that could make your reverse mortgage undesirable. The first is living too long. The second is a dramatic decline in the value of your home below the equity required to pay off the loan. Either case could trigger a forced sale. If this is true, the lenders cannot call them *lifetime* reverse mortgages. In a real lifetime reverse mortgage, the lender takes the risk of your living too long or the value of your home declining. The latter has indeed happened in California in recent years.

The Providential Home Income Plan's customers do not face these risks; however, they pay a higher mortgage rate. Of course, when you consider that the loan balance starts out very low and builds up, the benefits dramatically can clearly outweigh the cost. Shop carefully before you sign a reverse mortgage contract.

I would suggest hiring an attorney to take a close look at the deal. You will pay interest rates and fees. The rate may be fixed or variable. There is frequently an insurance fee that averages about 4 percent. The insurance protects the lender in the event you die and the value of your home does not cover the loan when it matures. Closing costs may also be added to your loan balance.

For more information on reverse mortgages and who is offering them, write to:

National Center for Home Equity Conversion
Suite 115
7373 147 Street West
Apple Valley, MN 55124

MAKING SURE YOU DON'T RUN OUT OF MONEY BEFORE YOU RUN OUT OF LIFE

I have to keep going back to the way my mother kept describing her financial plan because it is the essence of post-retirement investment strategies. When you retire, your goal is simple—you have to make your retirement kitty last. Social security certainly isn't going to help you very much. You may have a pension to help a little. You may still want to or have to work.

LET THE CASH FLOW AND THE IRS GO

If you have worked all your life and are used to a salary, I can understand your desire for *income*. Income, however, is a designation attached to money on which you have to pay taxes. If you can make the semantic switch to thinking *cash flow*, you can empower yourself to managing your money as if you were going to live for 20 years or more, which is likely.

Investors with a 20-year time horizon invest in assets that will grow over time. These investors can take advantage of the wonders of compounding of their returns. Rather than paying taxes every year on every penny of income they can earn, they

can defer those taxes and reinvest the tax money for their benefit, not the government's.

So, Mom's CD-Beater Cash Flow Strategy (Chapter 15) is
the way to go.

Let Your Home Take Care of You, It's Time It Returned the Favor

Later, if you need to dip into the equity in your home without
leaving it, you can look at supplementing your cash flow with a
Lifetime Reverse Mortgage—live in your home, let it pay you
tax-free cash flow as you paid the mortgage for years, and never
have to repay a dollar back until you choose to or have to leave
your home to go to a retirement home or that dire second
choice. You could well live out your life in your home and still
get extra cash to live on.

Enjoy Fully the Retirement for Which You Saved—You Earned It!

My major goal in writing this chapter was to demonstrate to
you that with some creative lower-risk investing you can life a
fuller life in retirement. After all, you worked hard to build a
retirement savings kitty, you should enjoy your retirement to
the fullest. You have earned it.

Become a SuperStar Retirement Investor and send me a
thank you card at Christmas time!

CHAPTER

When Would You Like to Stop Paying Taxes on Your Investment Profits?

You Could Double Your Retirement Income and Retire with Dignity

YOUR ADVISOR'S BEST ADVICE—EVER

Imagine you are sitting down with your investment advisor one evening. After coffee and pleasantries, the subject turns to taxes.

"You know, with state and local taxes, your total income tax bracket is rapidly approaching 50 percent. I know that in the early 1980s the top tax bracket was 90 percent, but this is still getting pushy because so many deductions are being eliminated. What can we do to reduce my income tax burden?"

Your investment advisor has been waiting for you to ask this question. To your surprise, he asks calmly, "How soon would you like to stop paying taxes on your investment income?"

You sit back, thinking to yourself, "Right now, of course, but what is he getting at?"

"I can hardly wait!" you finally respond.

"What I want to suggest is that you invest the bulk of your savings in a variable life insurance policy." You sit back again. "We could start with the money that you have already entrusted to me."

Not Variable Annuities . . .

"I've heard about variable annuities. Tell me more."

"I'm not talking about variable *annuities*. Most variable annuities are expensive ways to turn tax-preferred long-term capital gains into highly taxed ordinary income!"

"What do you mean by that?" you ask in surprise.

"By the time you pay the agents' commissions, the hefty annual expenses, invest in the watered-down funds most have available, and then withdraw your profits at ordinary income tax rates, it could take 10 to 15 years to earn enough to get ahead of the same investment outside of the annuity. No, I mean variable *life* insurance. Actually, because it gives you the most flexibility in arranging your investment, I like *variable universal life insurance.*"

Take a Breather for a Minute and Read On

At this point, the MEGO principle takes over. When people hear the word "insurance" they get the "mine eyes glaze over" or MEGO look. But, humor me a bit here. When I say "insurance," think "investment" for now. Trust me, you'll love this investment angle. Are you still awake? O. K., stick with me.

"Variable life insurance, huh?" you say. "Why variable life insurance?"

"For two reasons:

First, inside a variable life insurance policy are a number of no-load mutual funds (even load funds are no-load within an insurance policy), so investing inside the policy is very similar to investing outside the policy. Some policies have some great funds from great managers.

Second, if you invest in this policy in at least four substantially equal payments over a seven-year period, you can borrow the cash value including your profits out of the policy—tax-free.

We could make those payments directly from the long-term investment money you have already entrusted to me.

In fact, after a while you can withdraw your principal (although you probably will not want to do that since this is the most powerful investment you will have in your portfolio!)."

"DAWN COMES TO MARBLEHEAD"

"You mean that I can invest in a variable life insurance policy, invest in a series of mutual funds offered within the policy, have the taxes on my profits deferred until I withdraw (which may be never) and then borrow the cash value and profits out whenever I want? What's the catch?"

"Well, there are a few minor 'catches':"

1. The loans are at a low interest rate but most of that is credited to your account. So except for a .5 percent to 2.0 percent spread, you are paying interest to yourself.

2. There is a built-in commission to the insurance broker and annual maintenance fees.

3. The funds offered are often watered-down "clones" of mutual funds with similar names (they are specifically, by law, NOT the same funds). As a matter of fact, a responsible agent will disclose that fact to you. If an agent doesn't, he just doesn't understand the policy from an investors' point of view and may just mislead you.

4. You will have to pay taxes on any profits you withdraw (but none on any money you borrow out)."

After absorbing those concerns, you reply, "With all those fees is it really worth it?"

The "Perfect" Tax Shelter?

"You bet, especially if you are willing to actively manage your money or allow me to do it for you. An actively updated tax-deferred account has all the benefits of active management without the tax consequences. Maximizing pre-tax compounding of returns is a major benefit. If you are *un*willing to actively manage, you are right, it is a bit expensive."

"Explain to me more about the funds I can use," you ask.

"First of all, the IRS forbids variable insurance separate accounts from investing directly in mutual funds available directly to the public. As a result, special funds are created specifically for variable insurance separate accounts.

"Separate Accounts" Are Profit Accounts

In fact, there are a total of 1,651 separate accounts (combination of funds and policies; a fund may be offered in several policies) to choose from (532 of these separate accounts are available in variable life policies), although no single policy offers more than

22 different choices. The more choices you have, the better for you.

Second, many of the funds offered suffer from the paternalism of the insurance companies that desire to create funds with middle-of-the-road performance to discourage having to process too many transactions. They are a bit lazy on this issue. Only a few funds have consistent top performance.

Third, many policies offer only a limited number of choices, with international and precious metals funds—two of my current favorite investments—being the most frequently mentioned funds NOT available in most policies.

Picking a Winner of a Policy

"What should I look for in choosing a policy?" you ask, as this idea has piqued your curiosity.

One essential element is that you have a wide enough range of investment choices to build a successful SuperStar portfolio. As you have seen elsewhere in the book, a SuperStar portfolio needs a gold mining shares fund, an international stock fund, some top-performing domestic stock funds, a solid junk bond fund, some attractive sector funds (like a global real estate fund), and maybe an international bond fund for good measure.

A second attractive feature is a reasonable annual fee, as low as possible. A fixed fee would be preferable if you want to put a lot of money in this program.

A third attractive feature would be a low or no-load program. If YOU are going to select the program, why should you have to pay a high fee?

Borrow from Yourself at Low Rates

In addition, you might want to look for a policy that has a low net loan cost (the interest rate you pay minus the amount credited to the policy) especially if you will want to borrow out your money tax-free later on, a low surrender charge although, if you can pick the right policy up-front and plan to leave the money for at least eight years, the surrender charge should not be much of a problem, and finally, you will want to decide if you want to manage the money or your insurer will work with a professional money manager.

Ironically, some of the most attractive policies are with insurers that will not work directly with any managers who are not also insurance agents. Ask your investment advisor who he or she can work with."

DO YOU THINK THAT THIS ISN'T FOR YOU?
THINK AGAIN

As many of my clients would have to say, "But Bill, I am 55 and I have a pre-existing illness, I got turned down for an insurance policy and I can't buy new life insurance, anyway. I guess I can't participate, right?"

"Wrong, why don't we insure the lives of your children or buy a 'last to die' or 'second to die' policy?" your advisor suggests.

"I get it. If we insure my children and I own the policy, we can tax-defer the profits even after I die, and I can still use the policy as my savings account while I am alive," you say.

Borrow Tax-Free or Withdraw after Taxes?

"You are getting the idea. Now comes the best part; not only can you borrow the money out tax-free, but you can pass on the 'death benefits' (What a strange combinations of words. Only an insurance executive could make up that phrase.) to your heirs tax-free. You can own the policy during your life, make your children the contingent owners so they have the choice to continue to invest tax-free during their lives, borrow out the proceeds tax-free during their lives, and pass it on to their children tax-free when they die."

NOW IS THE TIME TO ASK THE HARD QUESTIONS

That's the investment pitch that you should be hearing from your investment advisor/insurance agent—one you seldom ever hear. It is my goal that in the future more advisors will be asking these questions.

However, about this time, I will bet that you want to ask me a few questions. I hope I have anticipated most of the questions you needed to ask.

First to Die? What's the Hurry?

Q. What about the *first* to die?

A. You can set up a trust for your heirs to receive the proceeds (as a loan) without liquidating the policy. That way the rest of your children don't have to give up the continuing tax-shelter of the policy.

Q. How much can I borrow out of the policy?

A. Realistically, you can borrow about 80 percent of its value before you risk triggering a surrender, which would trigger taxes on most of the past, present, and future distributions (including the tax-free loans). Remember, however, that, if you were to pay income taxes on the amount you borrowed, you would have been lucky to get 50 cents on the dollar after taxes. So anything over that is practically gravy.

Investment Limits?

Q. Are there limits on the amount I can invest?

A. Basically, for most folks, no. But if the IRS says the economic or insurable value of any child's life is far below the insurance policy's cash value, the tax benefits may be disallowed. Of course, you can invest more if you invest smaller amounts in several insurers' policies.

Trading Limits?

Q. Are there limits on trading the funds in the program?

A. In many cases, no, although the insurer may place some discouraging barriers in your way. There are no legal limits, it's just that most insurers don't want to work for their money and try to discourage trading. That is why it is wise to consult with a professional money manager before investing in a variable life insurance policy.

Why Don't Brokers Want to Sell Variable Life?

Q. Why haven't I heard about this program before?

A. For several reasons;

1. Variable annuities are easier for brokers to sell.

2. If you are an active mutual fund investor, chances are that you invest in no-load funds and just don't encounter insurance salesmen.

3. The late 1980s prohibition of tax-free withdrawals from single premium variable life (SPVLs) policies (which I wrote about in my last book) eliminated the "easy" one-time sales, and few brokers are willing to wait up to seven years to get their full commission.

Should I "Play It Safe" with Their Money?

Q. Are variable annuities always a bad deal?

A. No, the real trick to getting a good value out of a variable annuity is to monitor your investment actively. If you invest in money funds or other low-yielding investments, it will take you much longer to ever improve over investing in the "same" fund outside of an annuity.

The best choices in variable annuities are always the choices that entail risks: small cap stock funds, international stock funds, gold funds, junk bond funds, and the like. However, when you sell one of these and take your profits and, instead of paying taxes currently, reinvest the money to your own benefit (using simple tax-deferral), the benefits of variable annuities are evident. This applies only for long-term investors who can leave the money in long enough to get enough added "lift" out of the compounding to overcome the fees and the fact that withdrawals are always ordinary income (except for the principal, which comes out last).

Where Are the Hidden Costs?

Q. Is there any expense to which I should be particularly sensitive?

A. Yes. In addition to the costs associated with the variable life plan is the cost of insurance, which is determined based on your health, age, smoking status, and the cost schedule set by the insurance company. This may be the biggest expense to compare.

When Does a Variable Annuity Pay Me?

Q. Should I ever "annuitize" (shift from the accumulation period, where I am investing money in the annuity and/or allowing the cash value to build up, to the distribution period, where I start taking regular taxable payments, that is, an annuity) my variable annuity?

A. That's up to you. Life insurance is insurance against dying; annuities are insurance against living too long. The risk is if you convert to a guaranteed lifetime annuity, you give up control over the investments and additional benefits of compounding in exchange for a lifetime of payments. If you live a long time, you could do all right. If you die the next day, your hard-earned savings go back to the insurance company.

Of course, you could create an annuity for the lifetime of you or your spouse (or child or other person), you *and* your spouse (or child or other person), or for period certain (a fixed amount of time).

How Do I Get Money Out of a Variable Life Policy?

Q. Can I annuitize a life insurance policy?

A. No, its not that kind of policy, but what you can do is borrow out each month the amount you need (loans are paid from the cash value when you die), pay NO taxes on the loans and still have the control over the investments. That's why I like variable life insurance much better than annuities. You get more spendable cash, and you don't put yourself at a risk of having to deal with the creditors of a life insurance company.

What about Risk of Insurance Company Failures?

Q. Oh, yes! Are variable life insurance contracts riskier than regular life insurance contracts?

A. From the viewpoint of having to live through the failure of an insurance company, variable insurance is much safer.

Instead of placing the cash value of the insurance policy in the general account of the life insurance company, as most standard policies do, with a variable insurance policy, your money is invested in mutual fund-like separate accounts regulated both by state insurance commissioners and by the Federal Securities & Exchange Commission.

Cash values of variable insurance policies are not available to the creditors of a failed insurance company. The law says that the money is in separate accounts and not commingled with the insurance company's general account. In reality, in one single case, the money was frozen (unable to be traded within the policy as new sales, including trades, were forbidden) for a few months, but no one has ever been denied access to their cash value in a variable life insurance contract.

Approximately two million policyholders' accounts of standard insurance companies are currently frozen due to insurance company failures. So the advantages of variable life insurance are significant.

Q. **How can I check out the safety of a variable life insurance company?**

A. The most reliable answer is to call Weiss Research at 1-800-928-9222, and for $15 Weiss will give you a rating of any life insurance company. Weiss ratings have stood the test of time, at least in the past five years, and earned the respect of professionals. Of the billion dollar insurance companies rated "D" or below by Weiss in 1990, 60 percent failed in 1991, often with high ratings from A. M. Best, who I call "I. R. Worst."

I should alert you to make sure you have the correct name of the variable insurance company that issues the policy as its name may be quite similar to the parent company, which will likely have a different Weiss safety rating.

I should also tell you that Weiss is harder on variable life insurance companies than regular life insurance companies because they have lower capital adequacy. On the other hand, from your viewpoint, they don't need as much since your cash value is not available to the insurance company's creditor as is regular life insurance cash value. Your variable insurance cash values is in a series of mutual fund-like separate accounts and regular insurance cash values lie in the general account of the life insurer.

Loans and Social Security Too?

Q. **How do these loans affect my social security payments or the penalties on large withdrawals from IRAs?**

A. With variable life insurance loans, you can avoid both Form 1099s, which can reduce social security payments, reduce investment income, and trigger more deductions for amounts tied to adjusted gross income, and provide an investment that circumvents the 15 percent excise tax on annual IRA withdrawals over $150,000.

Is Congress Watching?

Q. **Can Congress or the IRS change the rules on variable life insurance?**

A. Of course they can and probably will if too many people take advantage of "the last exciting tax loophole." However, in such cases, the government has normally grandfathered existing policyholders. Besides, Congress revisited variable life in 1988 and installed the seven-year payment process, which has effectively eliminated all but the most patient investors. Are you willing to be patient if it means never paying taxes again on your investment income?

SOME GOOD IDEAS

Let's sum up the variable life insurance story:

1. If you establish your account carefully and "withdraw" only by using the policy loans, you can build a nearly perfect and liquid tax shelter for the rest of your life.

2. You can invest significant amounts of your after-tax liquid wealth reserves, in addition to other retirement programs.

3. You can create a tax shelter that can outlive you if, for example, you insure the lives of your children.

4. In the 1990s, state and federal taxes are the greatest threat to your wealth. "You cannot earn high enough safe returns to stay ahead of taxes." This plan is an effective way to fight that threat.

5. You can trade freely without tax consequences.

6. Your asset management fees (if you choose to use a manager like WEDCO) can be deducted outside of the tax shelter where they may be tax-deductible (to the extent that they, along with other miscellaneous expenses, amount to over 2 percent of adjusted gross income, an increasingly likely event if less of your investment income is not taxable).

7. There are *no* hidden fees or undisclosed payments between the agent and the insurance company. This is a totally "above board" deal.

8. Very importantly, you can avoid both Form 1099s that can reduce social security payments, reduce investment income, and trigger more deductions for amounts tied to adjusted gross income, and provide and investment that circumvents the 15 percent excise tax on annual IRA withdrawals over $150,000.

9. This program could be your *only* savings program as it has the liquidity to support savings for any and all savings needs, such as college education, second or primary home, boat, retirement, emergency uninsured medical expenses, and so on.

A Final Note

The potential of variable insurance as a retirement savings vehicle (the ability to borrow could as much as double your after-tax spendable cash in retirement compared to other after-tax retirement plans, like variable annuities) and a wealth building plan is so significant that I am actively researching a new version of the variable insurance, The Donoghue Plan[SM], which I feel could revolutionize retirement savings. In fact considering the low level of retirement savings and the rising taxes, my plan, if it works, could allow a generation to "retire with dignity."

But that, hopefully, is the subject of a future book. Until then, Happy Investing!

APPENDIX

Donoghue's Load
"Supper-Stars"

Donoghue's Load "Supper-Stars"

4-Dozen Worst Performing $50 MM Load Funds—YTD 12/31/93 (All Bottom 10% in Objective)

Rank	Fund Name	YTD Total Return (%)	Maximum Sales Charge	Net Assets ($ MM)	Investment Objective	800 #
1	Dean Witter Capital Growth	−9.01	5.00	660.00	Growth	869-3863
2	Pasadena Growth	−5.87	5.50	542.20	Growth	882-2855
3	Flag Inv. Quality Growth	−5.61	4.50	51.80	Growth	767-3524
4	Dean Witter Equity-Income	−3.51	5.00	167.70	Equity-Inc	869-3863
5	Franklin Rising Dividends	−3.50	4.00	345.90	Growth-Inc	342-5236
6	PaineWebber Dividend Grth B	−3.31	5.00	405.50	Growth-Inc	647-1568
7	PaineWebber Dividend Grth A	−2.58	4.50	311.70	Growth-Inc	647-1568
8	Eaton Vance Growth	−2.51	4.75	139.00	Growth	225-6265
9	Fountain Square Quality Grth	−1.05	4.50	70.90	Growth	334-0483
10	Pasadena Nifty Fifty	−0.52	5.50	141.00	Growth	882-2855
11	Hyperion Short Duration II	−0.51	3.00	88.50	Adj. Rate Mtg.	497-3746
12	Putnam Adj. Rate U.S. Govt A	0.45	3.25	183.40	Adj. Rate Mtg.	225-1581
13	Dean Witter Premier Income	0.62	3.00	82.50	Income	212-392-2550
14	Eaton Vance Special Equities	1.14	4.75	85.90	Growth	225-6265
15	AIM Weingarten	1.53	5.50	4788.50	Growth	347-1919
16	SunAmerica Federal Secs. B	1.58	4.00	95.90	Gvt Mortgage	858-8850
17	Compass Cap. Growth	1.60	3.75	152.90	Growth	451-8371
18	Kidder, Peabody Equity-Inc.A	1.73	5.75	109.80	Equity-Inc	854-2505
19	Fountain Square Balnced	1.75	4.50	82.40	Balanced	334-0483
20	Heritage Inc. Ltd. Maturity	1.77	2.00	88.60	Gvt General	421-4184
21	Pasadena Balanced Return	2.44	5.50	86.00	Balanced	882-2855
22	Overland Express S/T Govt.	3.10	3.00	58.80	Gvt General	552-9612

23	Retirement Planning Bond	3.69	5.00	51.10	Gvt Mortgage	279-0279
24	Boulevard Managed Income	3.81	3.00	73.80	Corp General	285-3863
25	Merrill Lynch Muni. Ltd. B	3.86	1.00	135.50	Muni Nat'l	637-3863
26	Oppenheimer Target	3.93	5.75	370.10	Aggr Growth	525-7048
27	SunAmerica U.S. Govt Secs B	3.97	4.00	1114.70	Gvt General	858-8850
28	First Investors Government	3.99	6.25	290.80	Gvt General	423-4026
29	Smith Barney Income Return A	4.01	1.50	52.80	Corp Hi Qlty	544-7835
30	Calvert T/F Res. Ltd.-Term	4.02	2.00	643.00	Muni Nat'l	368-2748
31	Investors Pref. Fund Income	4.13	1.50	50.20	Gvt Mortgage	543-8072
32	First American Ltd-Term Inc	4.14	3.00	108.90	Corp General	637-2548
33	Prudential GNMA B	4.25	5.00	323.70	Gvt Mortgage	225-1852
34	Cardinal Govt Obligations	4.37	4.50	203.60	Gvt Mortgage	848-7734
35	Merrill Lynch Muni. Ltd. A	4.39	0.75	887.00	Muni Nat'l	637-3863
36	Keystone Amer. Hartwl EmGr A	4.44	5.75	175.00	Small Company	343-2898
37	Pilgrim GNMA	4.67	3.00	79.90	Gvt Mortgage	334-3444
38	Advisors A	4.73	5.00	126.20	Aggr Growth	451-2010
39	Van Eck World Income	4.90	4.75	255.00	Worldwide Bond	221-2220
40	MIMLIC Asset Allocation	4.91	5.00	56.40	Asset Alloc	443-3677
41	Seligman Capital A	4.98	4.75	200.40	Aggr Growth	221-2783
42	UST Master S/T T/E Sec NonPl	5.51	4.50	55.70	Muni Nat'l	233-1136
43	Enterprise Capital Apprec.	5.71	4.75	100.80	Aggr Growth	432-4320
44	Smith Barney Shear LtMatMuni	7.24	1.25	96.40	Muni Nat'l	451-2010
45	Mackenzie L/T Municipal	7.62	3.00	126.30	Muni Nat'l	456-5111
46	SunAmerica T/E Insured A	7.77	4.75	187.20	Muni Nat'l	858-8850
47	Voyageur MN Interm. Tax-Free	7.85	2.75	72.60	Muni State	553-2143
48	MFS Municipal Limited Mat A	7.99	2.50	92.40	Muni Nat'l	225-2606

APPENDIX

Donoghue's No-Load "Supper-Stars"

Donoghue's No-Load "Supper-Stars"

4-Dozen Worst Performing $50 MM No-Load Funds—YTD 12/31/93 (All Bottom 10% in Objective)

Rank	Fund Name	YTD Total Return (%)	Net Net Assets ($ MM)	Investment Objective	800 #
1	Invesco Strat. Health Scienc	-8.38	563.40	Sp. Health	525-8085
2	Yacktman	-6.58	145.60	Growth	525-8258
3	PaineWebber Dividend Grth D	-3.29	54.80	Growth-Inc	647-1568
4	One Group Blue Chip Fid	-2.17	112.10	Growth	338-4345
5	Vanguard U.S. Growth	-1.45	1825.20	Growth	662-7447
6.	Pax World	-1.05	477.10	Balanced	767-1729
7	Century Shares	-0.36	248.50	Sp. Financ	321-1928
8	Smith Barney Shear W/W Pr A	-0.25	81.90	ST World Inc.	451-2010
9	Scudder Quality Growth	-0.01	121.30	Growth	225-2470
10	State Farm Growth	0.56	725.10	Growth	309-766-2029
11	Dreyfus Appreciation	0.71	238.30	Growth	242-8671
12	Wright Quality Core Equities	1.00	85.60	Growth-Inc	232-0013
13	Signet Sel. Val. Eqty. Trust	1.27	64.30	Growth-Inc	804-771-7131
14	Wright Selected Blue Chip Eq	2.06	173.80	Growth-Inc	232-0013
15	Permanent Port Treas Bill	2.27	161.70	Gvt Treasury	531-5142
16	Janus Intermediate Govt Secs	2.42	61.40	Gvt General	525-8983
17	First Priority Equity Trust	2.45	154.20	Growth-Inc	433-2829
18	SEI Instl Value A	2.47	196.10	Growth-Inc	342-5734
19	Seven Seas Yield Plus	2.72	1259.20	Corp Hi Qlty	617-654-6089
20	Thomson Short-Interm. Govt B	2.78	120.50	Gvt General	227-7337
21	Neuberger&Berman Ultra Short	3.21	103.80	Corp Hi Qlty	877-9700
22	State Farm Balanced	3.31	327.80	Balanced	309-766-2029

23	Marshall Stock	3.35	Growth-Inc	236-8560
24	IAI Reserve	3.37	Corp Hi Qlty	945-3863
25	Marshall Short-Term Income	3.70	Corp Hi Qlty	236-8560
26	Vanguard Muni. Short-Term	3.78	Muni Nat'l	662-7447
27	Managers Short Government	3.87	Gvt General	835-3879
28	Short-Term Municipal Instl	4.04	Muni Nat'l	245-5000
29	Cambridge Government Inc. B	4.12	Gvt General	382-0016
30	Scudder Balanced	4.12	Balanced	225-2470
31	20th Century U.S. Govts.	4.20	Gvt General	345-2021
32	Federated S/I Govt Instl	4.21	Gvt Treasury	245-5000
33	Bernstein Govt Short Dur	4.50	Gvt General	212-756-4097
34	Vista Short-Term Bond	4.54	Corp General	348-4782
35	Shawmut Ltd-Term Inc. Trust	4.61	Corp General	742-9688
36	SEI Cash + Short-Term Govt. A	4.67	Gvt General	342-5734
37	IAI Balanced	4.99	Balanced	945-3863
38	20th Century Vista Investors	5.45	Small Company	345-2021
39	Galaxy Interm. Bond Retail	5.48	Corp General	628-0414
40	USAA Tax-Exempt Short-Term	5.59	Muni Nat'l	382-8722
41	Benham CA T/F Short-Term	5.77	Muni CA	472-3389
42	Dupree KY T/F Short-Medium	5.77	Muni State	866-0614
43	Janus Short-Term Bond	6.08	Corp General	525-8983
44	Vanguard Muni. Limited-Term	6.26	Muni Nat'l	662-7447
45	Evergreen	6.27	Small Company	235-0064
46	T. Rowe Price T/F Short-Int.	6.29	Muni Nat'l	638-5660
47	Nicholas II	6.40	Small Company	414-272-6133
48	Portico Growth & Income	6.50	Equity-Inc	228-1024

APPENDIX C

The Donoghue Signal

THE DONOGHUE SIGNAL—THE LAZY INVESTOR'S LONG-TERM STRATEGY

All strategies, whether investment strategies or lifestyle strategies, evolve over time. The Donoghue Signal Strategy is the latest in a series of strategies that I have followed since 1969, when I first studied the relationship between interest rates and the stock market. (For a fuller explanation of this strategy I recommend you visit your library or bookstore and pick up a copy of *The Donoghue Strategies: Ten Minutes A Week to Investment Success*, Bantam Books, 1989 and 1990. A copy of *Donoghue's Signal SuperStars*, the classic 1991 Donoghue Signal Study is available for $10 at 1-800-982-2455.)

THE SIGNAL THAT WAS

The Donoghue Signal is a market-timing strategy that focuses on the inverse relationship between stock prices, specifically growth stock fund share prices, and interest rates. Very simply put, when interest rates are rising, you should be invested 100 percent in safe, money market mutual funds, and when interest rates are falling, you should be invested 100 percent in growth stock funds. It is that simple.

Okay, It's not that simple. You have to decide on just how you're going to measure interest rate trends. My research indicates that a 25-week, exponentially weighted, moving average of Donoghue's Taxable Money Fund Average™ is a great measure of short- to intermediate-term interest rate trends and their impact on growth stock funds.

So, when the current Donoghue's Taxable Money Fund Average™ is below the trend line (known as the Donoghue Signal™ trend), you stay invested in growth stock mutual funds. When the current average is above the line, when you shift all your assets to ultra-safe money funds.

How does this strategy work in real life? Well, I decided, as a test case, to assemble a list of the 40 top-performing "switch funds" (no-load or low-load funds in existence since 1981 that offered telephone exchange to a money fund). These were the standards against which I would measure the success of the Donoghue Signal Strategy.

During the period from 5/29/81 to 5/31/91, the Donoghue Signal generated eight *BUY* signals and seven *SELL* signals, the last *BUY* being on July 14, 1989. (The Signal remained in a *BUY* mode for over four and one-half years until December 6, 1993. As I was finishing writing this book, rising short-term interest rates generated a *SELL* signal).

For the ten years ended 5/31/91, the Donoghue Signal Strategy beat a *buy, hold, and pray* strategy (where you bought on 5/29/81 and held for the next decade, praying that your investment would rise, sweated through the 1987 crash, and held on for dear life) by an average of 101.9 percent. While those performance figures are in the past, you will have to admit I have found a pretty strong profit-making formula.

This has been a very powerful investment strategy, and while it has missed a number of short-term opportunities, it has earned more money for investors than any other strategy I have introduced over the years. In the long-term the Signal works (in many years, however and in the foreseeable future, asset allocation strategies have done and will probably do better).

DOUBLE THE PROFITS AT 60 PERCENT OF THE RISK

Without considering tax consequences, the Donoghue Signal, had it been used to manage money in your IRA, would have slightly more than doubled your assets by investing in the stock market only 60 percent of the time. The rest of the time your assets would have been invested peacefully and safely in a money market mutual fund.

For those of you who are skeptics and stand ready to say, "What about the taxes?" let me answer that question indirectly. In 15 of the 40 funds tested (including all the top performers), the improvement in total return was over 100 percent. In six cases, it was over 200 percent. That is more than taxes could ever wipe out.

WHERE IS "THE SIGNAL" RIGHT NOW?

Once again, on December 6, 1993, just as I was completing this book, The Donoghue Signal generated a *SELL* signal after four and one-half years. For that period, by investing 100 percent in growth mutual funds our Signal portfolio had a total return of 74 percent, or 20 percent more than the S&P 500 (including reinvested dividends). The trigger was, of course, rising interest rates.

What's next? Frankly, I like investing in a stock market when interest rates *are* falling and have a long way to fall. While that could still happen in the U.S., I am impressed that interest rates are falling from high levels in Europe. Although the Signal was not designed to time international stock funds, the principle holds true. In the absence of negative currency movement (the dollar strengthening against foreign currencies, which could happen if interest rates do indeed continue to rise rapidly in the U.S.), the European stock market does look attractive as did the U.S. stock market in mid-1982 when it took off.

Consequently, I have recommended that Signal investors consider switching, not to money funds, as a literal interpretation of the strategy would suggest, but in part to international stock funds, reducing domestic stock holdings to 55 percent of the portfolio from the 100 percent they had been or 0 percent as the Signal would recommend. However, that is not because the Donoghue Signal so indicated but because "The Donoghue," in his best judgment, so recommended.

My reason is not that the domestic stock market boom is over; rather, it is no longer wise to invest 100 percent in domestic stocks. Besides, opportunities in the international stock markets are much more attractive.

Interest rates in the U.S. may well fall further, and the U.S. stock market may well have another strong upward leg. In that case, the Signal would, no doubt, recommend that Signal investors shift back into the U.S. stock market. For now, I like the odds on the international stock market.

The Donoghue Signal is a powerful long-term strategy. Over a ten-year back-tested period, it did twice as well as the buy and hold returns on average, and all the investor had to do was make 15 toll-free phone calls in a decade to do so. Sounds like a good deal to me.

The Donoghue Signal has been a rewarding long-term investment strategy for the patient investor. At my money management firm, for example, we discourage investors from opening a Donoghue Signal account unless they are comfortable with agreeing to leave the money at least three years. (Today, most choose an asset allocation portfolio).

THE DONOGHUE SIGNAL MAKES GOOD TAX SENSE

If you have the patience and confidence to use the Donoghue Signal, you will often enjoy the compounding of your returns for years before you have to realize your gains and pay taxes. The *SELL* signals help you protect those profits during periods of rising interest rates and significant principal risk. The 4/14/87 *SELL* Signal, had the Signal been active at the time, would have successfully avoided the 1987 crash. It is also fair to say that it also "avoided" the rapid recovery from the crash, as well as the decline.

The overall track record of the Signal is excellent, in spite of its missing several attractive periods of attractive market opportunity. Patience was rewarded. Making the most of a situation is about as good as you might have a right to expect to do.

AS THE BEST PART OF THE SIGNAL STRATEGY IS ON HOLD, WHAT NOW?

Coming off a good investment experience in the Donoghue Signal Strategy, we turn our attention to what will most likely make the most money in the next year or so. I feel your best prospects are in a carefully designed asset allocation strategy.

Index